Where the Action Is
The Foundations of Embodied Interaction

Paul Dourish

A Bradford Book
The MIT Press
Cambridge, Massachusetts
London, England

First MIT Press paperback edition, 2004

©2001 Massachusetts Institute of Technology

This book was set in Sabon by Interactive Composition Corporation.
Printed and bound in the United States of America.

Library of Congress Cataloging-in-Publication Data

Dourish, Paul.
    Where the action is: the foundations of embodied interaction / Paul Dourish.
        p.   cm.
    Includes bibliographical references and index.
    ISBN 0-262-04196-0 (hc.: alk. paper), 0-262-54178-5(pb)
    1. Human-computer interaction.   I. Title.
QA76.9.H85 D68   2001
004.01′ 9—dc21   2001030443

10 9 8 7 6 5 4 3 2

Wl

Contents

Preface

At a workshop I attended not long ago, my colleague Matthew Chalmers made the observation that computer science is based entirely on philosophy of the pre-1930s. Computer science in practice involves reducing high-level behaviors to low-level, mechanical explanations, formalizing them through pure scientific rationality; in this, computer science reveals its history as part of a positivist, reductionist tradition. Similarly, much of contemporary cognitive science is based on a rigorous Cartesian separation between mind and matter, cognition and action. These are philosophical positions of long standing, dating from the nineteenth century or earlier. However, they have been under continual assault since around the 1930s, when philosophers such as Martin Heidegger and Ludwig Wittgenstein began to articulate radically new positions on cognition, language, and meaning. This new approach abandoned the idea of disembodied rationality and replaced it with a model of situated agents, at large in the world, and acting and interacting within it. Practical action and everyday experience replaced abstract reasoning and objective meaning as the foundations of a philosophical psychology.

Why should any of this matter? Surely computer science has nothing to do with philosophy? It is an engineering discipline, and the testaments to its success are all around us, including the laptop I am using to write this preface. Arguments between philosophers scarcely seem to have held back the course of technological progress, have they?

This is all true, of course, but it hides a deeper truth. The development and application of computational technologies is an engineering discipline, and one that has been spectacularly successful over the past fifty or sixty years.

However, it is most certainly also a philosophical enterprise. It is philosophical in the way it represents the world, in the way it creates and manipulates models of reality, of people, and of action. Every piece of software reflects an uncountable number of philosophical commitments and perspectives without which it could never be created. Software depends inevitably on our ideas about representation and reality. Phil Agre comments, "Technology at present is covert philosophy; the point is to make it openly philosophical" (Agre 1997:240). Agre's primary focus was the area of Artificial Intelligence (AI), but the philosophical underpinnings of computer science are every bit as significant in the area of Human-Computer Interaction (HCI) that I will be addressing here. While any software system introduces some kind of formalization of the world, HCI (like AI) deals with formalizations of human cognition and activity. These are the issues that have lain at the heart of philosophical debate for centuries. In some ways, it would be hard to imagine a *more* philosophical enterprise.

Philosophy tends to get short shrift in technical circles. The word itself is often used to denote fuzzy, muddled, and fundamentally irrelevant reasoning. Debates over philosophical foundations seem irrelevant. However, if our technical practice is built on those foundations, then the arguments are deeply relevant, because they determine the limits of what can be done and the chances for success of our efforts to have people and computers work effectively together. This argues that we need to uncover the philosophical assumptions that run throughout both the theory and practice of computer system design, and understand what kind of intellectual commitments are being made.

My goal here, though, is more modest. Reexamining the philosophical foundations of computer science is a task for another person or another time. Instead, I will focus on one particular way in which these philosophical questions have lately arisen in the area of HCI. Recent research activities, focusing on what I call "embodied interaction," reflect the situated, embodied perspective of Heidegger, Wittgenstein, and other post-1930s philosophers.[1] In the pages that follow, I will explore this perspective and show how it applies to these new research programs, and how, by looking at the philosophical background, we can begin to understand the foundational underpinnings of these new approaches. The goal is to develop an understanding that explains the relationship between the various elements of the embodied interaction approach, and that begins to suggest how, when, and why embodied interaction works.

So, this book is about "where the action is," in two ways. First, it is about a perspective that places the action of embodied agents center stage. Rather than take action to be generated from or subservient to abstract reasoning, the perspective I will explore here sees embodied practical action in the world as the foundation for our conscious experience. Second, this approach is "where the action is" in the sense that it provides a way to understand the contributions and opportunities emerging from dynamic new forms of technological practice.

Acknowledgments

No book is ever the work of one person alone, whatever the cover says. That is especially true of one that, as this does, tries to draw together material from many different places. I owe a great deal to the various people who helped me see connections, guided me as I ventured into new areas, and supported the whole process.

This book was written while I was a member of the research staff in the Computer Science Lab at Xerox's Palo Alto Research Center (PARC). My area manager, Karin Petersen, and lab manager, Richard Bruce, were endlessly supportive of my efforts, and the time I spent working on the manuscript, despite the fact that it took much longer than I think any of us had anticipated. PARC is a wonderfully interdisciplinary environment, and while working both there and at its European sister laboratory, I had the opportunity to work with and learn from many people whose insights, one way or another, are reflected here (although perhaps not in ways that they would support). These include Annette Adler, Bob Anderson, Victoria Bellotti, Graham Button, Gregor Kiczales, Steve Harrison, Austin Henderson, John Lamping, Wendy Mackay, Brian Cantwell Smith, and Lucy Suchman.

Without Mark Weiser's initial encouragement as I first attempted to articulate these ideas, the book would probably never have been written. He was an endless source of insight and optimism; his enthusiasm, energy, and irreverence made him an inspiring colleague. Sadly, Mark passed away while this book was being written. He is hugely missed.

The work reported here also has its roots in research conducted in the Discourse Architecture Laboratory at Apple Computer during 1996 and 1997, and the many useful and insightful interactions I had with my colleagues there, including David Curbow, Allen Cypher, Nicholas Damiris, Tom Erickson, Jed Harris, Austin Henderson (again), and Don Norman.

Beyond these, a network of sustaining friends and colleagues have provided both intellectual and emotional sustenance and valuable feedback on earlier presentations of this material. I am particularly indebted to Matthew Chalmers, Judith Donath, Geraldine Fitzpatrick, Beki Grinter, Kristina Höök, Hiroshi Ishii, Natalie Jeremijenko, and Beth Mynatt for discussions about the material here and comments on earlier drafts. Bob Prior at MIT Press was also a great supporter and deftly helped steer this book through the whole process. Deborah Cantor-Adams smoothly managed the production of the book itself, while Danyel Fisher, Wayne Lutters, Jack Muramatsu, Madhu Reddy, and Suzanne Schaefer provided last-minute assistance reading and correcting proofs.

Most of all, my thanks to Melinda Stelzer, my love and inspiration, who has endured my being absent and preoccupied for much longer than either of us anticipated. And also to Elwood, of course, for his own special contributions.

Where the Action Is

1

A History of Interaction

It is a truism that computers are becoming faster and more powerful all the time. They play an ever larger role in our lives, giving us access to more and more information, being incorporated into more and more of our devices, and creating whole new forms of interaction and activity that we would never otherwise have imagined. From desktop computers to laptops to personal digital assistants, not to mention bank teller machines, microwave ovens, cellular telephones, and ticket machines, we encounter computers in all aspects of everyday life. The ever-expanding province of computation is a commonplace, the topic of a million coffee-shop conversations, television reports, and newspaper headlines. We talk about how fast it is changing, but we talk much less about the ways in which it is not. Many things about computers are not changing at all. Our basic ideas about what a computer is, what it does, and how it does it, for instance, have hardly changed for decades. Nor have the difficulties we encounter actually using computers.

Our experience using computers reflects a trade-off that was made fifty years ago or more. When computers were first being developed commercially, they were extremely expensive devices. Computer time was much more expensive than your time or mine. In that context, efficiency dictated that we minimize the amount of computer time any job or activity needed, even if that meant burdening the people who wanted to submit the job. If a rigid, formalized input language was easier for the system to process, for example, then the cost in people's time to format their data in that language was more than offset by the savings in processing time that would result. Because most uses of computers were military and commercial rather than personal, it was hard to disagree with this sort of economic argument. It gave rise to a model that favors performance over convenience, and places a premium on the computer's time rather than people's time. This model is still with us today.

However, in light of those commonly observed transformations in computer power, we are now in a position to reconsider the trade-off. Arguably, we *must*. Computers are now so much faster and more powerful, giving us access to so much more information that we are simply no longer able to manage and assimilate it. At the same time, those powerful computers spend 95 percent of their time doing absolutely nothing. Modern personal computers perform very few tasks that use their full capacity for longer than a second or two. Outside these brief bursts of activity, most of the time they do nothing at all, generally while we try to figure out what to make of what just happened or what we want to do next.

At the same time, we increasingly see computers incorporated into devices other than the traditional PC sitting on the desk. Computation is part of your cellular telephone, your microwave oven, your car, and a host of other technologies. The rise of so-called embedded computing reflects the fact that computation can be usefully harnessed for more than just traditional desktop computing. It can also help us as we get up and move about in the world, which we generally do more of than sitting at desks (or would, if the computers didn't shackle us to them). However, this new form of computation exacerbates the effects of the trade-off between the work that the user and the system do. As I sit at my desktop computer, it occupies the whole of my attention; but that would be a terrible idea in a computer I'm using while driving, or crossing the street, or trying to enjoy a conversation with friends.

These two trends—the massive increase in computational power and the expanding context in which we put that power to use—both suggest that we need new ways of interacting with computers, ways that are better tuned to our needs and abilities. Over the last few years, research into Human-Computer Interaction (HCI) has begun to explore ways to control and interact with a new breed of computer systems. Prototype systems have been developed; new forms of interaction explored; new research groups established; new designs developed and tested.

This book is a contribution to the emerging literature on this new approach to interacting with computers, one that I call "Embodied Interaction." Embodied Interaction is interaction with computer systems that occupy our world, a world of physical and social reality, and that exploit this fact in how they interact with us.

There are two ways in which the material I want to present in this book differs from other explorations in HCI. The first difference concerns the set of entities that will appear here. In particular, although computer interfaces are the general topic, interfaces themselves will not appear too often. Here, I am more concerned with interaction than I am with interfaces, and more concerned with computation than I am with computers. When I say that I am more concerned with interaction than with interfaces, I mean that I will be dealing with the ways in which interactive systems are manifest in our environment and are incorporated into our everyday activities, rather than with the specific design of one user interface or another. Similarly, when I say that I am more concerned with computation than with computers, I mean that I want to address the idea of computation per se—of active representations embodied in hardware and software systems—rather than the specific capabilities of systems available at the start of the new millennium. So, gigabytes and megahertz will not be at issue, but representational power will be.

The second difference is in the way that those topics will be addressed. In particular, as you might guess on the basis of my concern with interaction and computation, I want to address a set of topics that are more foundational than technical. This is not a source book of design solutions, or a how-to manual for interface developers—although these practical matters will certainly arise, and I hope that designers will find something useful here. In fact, the very reason for exploring foundations is to support the design and evaluation of new systems, tools, and interaction modalities. The goal of this foundational exploration is to provide resources to designers and system developers, by giving them tools they can use to understand and analyze their designs.

Traditionally, the central component of any account of computation has been algorithms or procedures—step-by-step models that specify the sequential behavior of a computer system. In turn, because they are based on an analogy between mental phenomena and computation, cognitive science and AI have also predominantly espoused a step-by-step model of procedural execution. In the last few years, though, this procedural approach has been challenged by a new conceptualization of computational phenomena that places the emphasis not on *procedures* but on *interaction* (Wegner 1997). Interactional approaches conceptualize computation as the interplay between different components, rather than the fixed and prespecified paths that a single, monolithic computational engine might follow. These models of computation have more in common with ecosystems than with the vast mechanisms we used to imagine. They emphasize diversity and specialization rather than unity and generality. Perhaps there is, in this, something of the spirit of the times; perhaps, too, the rise of new computational paradigms such as parallel systems, object-oriented programming, and Internet-style software design is implicated in this change. The change, though, has occurred across a wide range of areas of computational investigation. It has affected how we think about computation from a mathematical perspective, leading to new theoretical accounts of systems such as Hoare's CSP (Hoare 1985) or Milner's work on CCS and the Pi Calculus (Milner 1995, 2000); it has affected how we think about computational models of mind, as reflected by Minsky's "Society of Mind" (Minsky 1988), Agre's critique of computational reasoning (Agre 1997), or Brooks's approach to robotics (Brooks 1999); and it has led to new accounts of the practice of programming (Stein 1998).

You might think that studies of how people use computers must always have been built around a model of the world that gives pride of place to interaction, but in fact HCI has traditionally been built on a procedural foundation. HCI, from its very beginning, took on the trappings of the traditional computational model and set out its account of the world in terms of plans, procedures, tasks, and goals. In contrast, the model of HCI I set out here is one that places interaction at the center of the picture. By this I mean that it considers interaction not only as *what* is being done, but also as *how* it is being done. Interaction is the means by which work is accomplished, dynamically and in context.

Some background will help to clarify what this means and to set the stage for the argument this book will develop. The context is the historical evolution of the idea of interaction and the technology of HCI.

A Historical Model of Interaction

Just as computers have evolved considerably in their short history, so have styles of human-computer interaction. There are many ways to conceptualize the history of interaction with computer systems. The purely technological view, for example, would recount the history of the input and output devices that have characterized different stages of interface development, and would describe their computational demands. A political view would consider the movement of ideas from one laboratory to another as researchers respond to the demands and interests of funding agencies and so forth, while an economic view would consider how user interface development has influenced, and been influenced by, the growth of the high-tech industry and PC economy. Grudin (1990) describes the history of interaction as the story of the "computer reaching out," in which interaction moves from being directly focused on the physical machine to incorporating more and more of the user's world and the social setting in which the user is embedded. Although Grudin's analysis is now a decade old, it is interesting to see the ways in which later trends in HCI design—including some that are of particular interest in this book—have followed quite closely the directions that he laid out.

I want to explore a slightly different view here, in order to set some context for the discussion that will follow. In particular, I want to present the stages in the historical development of user interfaces in terms of the different sets of human skills they are designed to exploit. This is not a different history of HCI, of course, but merely a different telling of the history, with the emphasis in a slightly different place. As is perhaps appropriate for a discipline that concerns itself as much with human abilities as with technological opportunities, it draws attention to the human experience of computation. The are four separate phases of development to discuss. I characterize them as electrical, symbolic, textual, and graphical forms of interaction.

Electrical

Today, when we talk of "computers," we invariably mean digital devices. The computer as we know it is inescapably bound up with the ones and zeros of digital logic. It was not always this way. Originally, the word "computers" referred to human beings—people whose daily work was the figuring of calculations, such as for producing engineering tables. However, even when "computers" became electronic devices, they were not necessarily digital ones. Before digital computers came analog computers. Analog computers did not rely on the discrete logic that characterizes modern computing devices; instead, they relied on the use of standard components such as resistors and capacitors to create electronic models of continuous natural phenomena (such as wave motion, the interaction of electronic forces, or the movements of objects under gravity). Essentially, the analog computer was the apparatus for laboratory simulations that took place not in the physical world, but in an analogous electronic reality. To set up a new experiment, the machine would have to be reconfigured, possibly quite radically, through the incorporation of new circuits. This task-specificity was shared by the early digital computers, too. Even after we had made the move from analog electronics to digital logic, the earliest digital computers were special purpose devices, designed as automatic calculators to solve specific problems—often, inevitably, in military domains (such as calculating missile trajectories or exploring patterns in coded messages).

Although there is some debate about precisely who was the first to make the move—perhaps Eckert and Mauchley with EDVAC in Philadelphia, or Williams and Kilburn building the Small-Scale Experimental Machine, known as "Baby," at Manchester, or one of the other contenders—what *is* generally accepted is that the critical development in digital computing was that of the *stored program computer*. In contrast to earlier designs, a stored program computer is a machine whose operation is not directly encoded in its circuits, but rather is determined by a sequence of instructions held in its memory—instructions that can, clearly, be changed or replaced much more easily than the electrical circuits could be reconfigured. Nonetheless, the first age of computing, around the time that this transition took place, relied heavily on an understanding of the electronics that made up any given machine. Every machine was a prototype; every program, uniquely designed for a specific computer (and perhaps even a specific version or configuration of that computer). What we currently refer to as "instruction sets"—the set of low-level operations that processors such as the Pentium or PowerPC can understand—were, at that stage in the history of computation, intimately tied to the individual details of the circuitry of any particular computer. So, even as we made the transition from hardware configuration to digitally stored programs, the dominant paradigm for interaction with the computer was electronic. Entering a new program, even if that program was to be stored digitally in the memory of the computer, could still bear a remarkable resemblance to electronic reconfiguration, involving plugboards and patch cables. Indeed, such programming activity was often accompanied with the development of new circuits that could extend the operation of the system. The boundary that we now take for granted between hardware and software was much fuzzier then; interacting with the system, and developing new programs, relied on a thorough understanding of the electronic design.

Symbolic

The next stage of development is characterized by the emergence of symbolic forms of interaction. The movement from one stage to another is not a sudden and clear transition; instead, it is a general trend that emerges in a number of different ways. We can see it in the basic models offered for programming systems, which was the primary form of interaction between human and computer at a time when "users" as we now know them did not yet exist.

As the transition from electrical to symbolic approaches gradually took hold, programming computers came to require less understanding of the detailed construction of each particular machine, and relied increasingly on regularized and well-understood capacities that would be available across a wide range of machines—register files, index registers, accumulators, and so forth. At the same time, the primary form of programs moved from a numeric form (that is, the "machine language" of raw instructions that a machine would understand) to other symbolic forms that were more readily understandable to human beings. So-called assembly languages are essentially symbolic forms of machine language, using mnemonic codes that stand in one-to-one correspondence with the machine level instructions, so that a sequence of instruction codes such as "a9 62 82 2c" is rendered as a symbolic expression such as "movl (r1+), r2."[1]

Since assembly languages are simply a different rendering of machine languages—symbolic forms that describe sets of specific instructions—they are just as tied as machine languages to particular systems, although, by this stage, computer systems were being produced industrially rather than developed as one-off prototypes in laboratories. But they are in no way portable between machines of different sorts, even today—assembly programs for an Intel processor yield machine instructions that will run only on Intel processors, and not on other processors made by Motorola. A further progression along the symbolic path, though, came with the development of the early programming languages such as LISP and FORTRAN. Essentially, these lay down two sets of rules. The first set describes what structural properties a set of instructions will have to be valid programs—what rules must be followed when creating something that is a FORTRAN program rather than simply gibberish. The second describe how programs can be turned into a set of (machine language) instructions for the computer to execute. The important point is that, whereas programs would previously be specified with relation to a specific machine language (perhaps encoded as assembly instructions, but still tied to a particular sort of computer), the programmer's activity was now lifted to a more abstract level that was simultaneously a more natural form of expression and independent of the precise details of any specific computer, its implementation and configuration.

The introduction of programming systems such as assemblers and programming languages moved computer interaction, then, from an electronic level to a symbolic one. It introduced a set of symbolic representations of computer system operation as the primary modality by which interaction was conducted. Interestingly, this was also reflected in the physical interaction with systems. Punched cards, for example, can be regarded as a primitive form of symbolic interaction, especially because punched card systems quickly came to incorporate both *data* cards (that is, cards that carried information for programs to process) and *control* cards (instructing the system to begin and end jobs, etc.) The control cards, then, provide a symbolic language for controlling the behavior of the system.

The reason I want to cast the history of interactive computing in terms of these different sorts of interaction modalities is that it draws our attention to the fact that they exploit quite different sets of skills. We are all highly skilled at various forms of symbolic interaction; language and communication, for us, are largely symbolic in nature, whether these symbols take the forms of icons, traffic signs, flags, maps, or marks on paper. Symbolic interaction is a much more natural and intuitive form of interaction for us than the electronic form that had previously been necessary; and it allows us to bring to bear a much more powerful set of intuitions and abilities to the interactive task. So, finding errors in assembly language programs is much less error-prone than trying to do the same in machine language; and debugging programs written in so-called high level languages is easier still (although, as any programmer will tell you, it is still the most time-consuming and intricate part of the process of developing software). We are generally able to exploit a greater range of skills—visual, cognitive, and so on—as we move from electrical to symbolic forms of interaction.

Textual

The best-developed form of symbolic interaction with which we are familiar is, of course, written language and textual interaction. So it is only natural that symbolic interaction with computers should gradually extend into the textual domain.

Of course, most of the examples I provided for symbolic interaction were textual in nature, one way or another. For my purposes, a distinction can be made between symbolic and textual interaction by looking at the *actual interaction* with the computer. So, although programs written in assembly language are clearly textual, the form in which they arrive at the computer might not be textual at all, but might be encoded on punched cards or other symbolic media. However, the modes of interaction with technology are continually shifting as technology develops and new opportunities present themselves, and before long the primary form of direct interaction with computers was, indeed, textual interaction, at teletype machines and video terminals.

When this transition took place, textual interaction was no longer simply a means to describe computer operations, but became the primary form of interaction. Arguably, this is the origin of "interactive" computing, because textual interfaces also meant the appearance of the "interactive loop," in which interaction became an endless back-and-forth of instruction and response between user and system. Even in these days of graphical and virtual reality interfaces, this model is still often the only recourse for some operations.

One reason that textual interaction remains so powerful is that it draws not only on the use of textual characters but on how those characters can be combined into words and sets of words. In other words, along with textual interaction came a "grammar" of interaction, one that broke input text into commands, parameters, arguments, and options. So, just as the move from electrical to symbolic interaction meant that interface designers could draw upon a new set of human skills and abilities, so too did textual interaction. Textual interaction can draw on our linguistic skills, not by letting us simply "talk" to computers (at least, outside of science fiction films), but rather by drawing on our abilities to create meaningful sentences by combining elements each of which contributes to the sense of the whole.

The compositional character of textual interaction has proven hard to replace as interfaces have developed. The value, as we will see, of later interaction modalities such as graphical user interfaces is that they make the abstract entities of computation into "real," individuable objects supporting direct interaction. However, because our programs are still constructed in terms of abstract entities, textual interaction still proves its value by giving us the ability to create instructions that operate in terms of generalities—loops, conditions, patterns, and more.

The other significant feature of the textual interface paradigm is that it brought the idea of "interaction" to the fore. Textual interaction drew upon language much more explicitly than before, and at the same time it was accompanied by a transition to a new model of computing, in which a user would actually sit in front of a computer terminal, entering commands and reading responses. With this combination of language use and direct interaction, it was natural to look on the result as a "conversation" or "dialogue." These days, this idea of dialogue is central to our notion of "interaction" with the computer, replacing configuration, programming, or the other ideas that had largely characterized the interplay between users and systems in the past. So, although the notion of "interaction" with computers had important predecessors before this period—such as Ivan Sutherland's hugely influential work on Sketchpad (Sutherland 1963)—it was arguably from the paradigm of text-based dialogue that people drew the idea of "interacting with the machine." And interacting was something that we already knew how to do.

Graphical

Probably the most significant transition, in terms of the development of the user interface models that are familiar to us today, was the transition from textual to graphical interaction. Graphical interaction developed from the work of many people, including Sketchpad on the TX-2 (Sutherland 1963), and the work of Alan Kay and his colleagues at PARC, based in turn on the developmental psychology of Piaget, Bruner, and others (Kay 1993).

Just as the move from symbolic to textual interaction did more than simply replace one symbolic language with another, the move from textual to graphical interaction did not simply replace words with icons, but instead opened up whole new dimensions for interaction—quite literally, in fact, by turning interaction into something that happened in a two-dimensional space rather than a one-dimensional stream of characters. Traditional textual interaction took place at teletype machines or serial terminals, where information appeared at the bottom of the screen and scrolled up to disappear off the top. The user's input and the system's output together formed a single stream of information, arranged linearly, character by character. In contrast, graphical interaction is characterized by its use of space; information is spread out over a larger screen area, so that the locus of action and attention can move around the screen from place to place or can even be in multiple places simultaneously (e.g., in different windows). The task of managing information becomes one of managing space.

Moving from one-dimensional to two-dimensional interaction made it possible, again, to exploit further areas of human ability as part of the interactive experience. These included:

Peripheral Attention   Distributing information around a two-dimensional space allows us to arrange it so that it can be selectively attended to.

For example, many applications divide the screen (or window) into two areas—a large area taking up most of the space in which the primary interaction takes place, and a smaller area, at one edge or off to the side, in which messages are displayed about the current progress of other tasks, or other ancillary information. My word processor uses this approach. It has a status bar at the bottom of the screen that shows when the document is being updated, saved, printed, and so forth and provides various pieces of information that might be helpful in managing my activity but are not central to it. By placing them in the periphery, the application exploits my ability to focus on one area while passively attending to other activity in the edge of my visual field.

Pattern Recognition and Spatial Reasoning   Laying out information in two dimensions lets us apply the skills we use managing visual information in the everyday environment. Actions as simple as walking across the room or picking up a cup involve spatial reasoning skills, and these can be exploited in two-dimensional interfaces. In particular, our ability to recognize patterns in the spatial organization of information provides new ways to convey information, and opportunities to arrange data elements so that they convey information as a whole. The same techniques that allow graphs, charts, and other visual information designs to provide insight into collections of information can also be exploited when we move computational information and interaction into a two-dimensional space.

Information Density   Pattern recognition draws upon the way in which certain arrangements of data can draw attention to patterns and other items of "meta-information." In turn, this raises a question of "information density." Some information can be conveyed more succinctly in graphical form than in lists of numbers or other textual representations. A picture really can be worth a thousand words; it can often be displayed more compactly and apprehended more rapidly than can its thousand-word equivalent. Of course, there are also forms of information for which a textual presentation is either desirable or required, but graphical interaction has never been *purely* graphical; instead, it extends the vocabulary of interaction to incorporate graphical as well as textual presentation forms and allows textual information to be presented within a framework that incorporates graphical elements and two-dimensional layout.

Visual Metaphors   As well as giving new ways to depict data, the graphical approach can also add value by providing new ways to represent actions and the context in which actions take place. This leads to the development of visual metaphors for information management. The most widespread is the office or desktop metaphor, in which information management tasks are based around a metaphorical model incorporating filing cabinets and trashcans, graphically displayed on the screen along with the basic data elements, and so conveying a sense of the activities that can be performed over the data. In more recent systems, this has been extended. General Magic's "Magic Cap" interface, used a metaphorical depiction of an office featuring a desk (along with various desktop tools), a telephone, and a door open to a world outside; note-taking applications often feature graphical depictions of notebooks or index cards; and so on.

The development of graphical interaction techniques led to a model of interface design known as *direct manipulation,* in which these elements are combined and extended. The fundamental principle in direct manipulation interfaces is to represent explicitly the objects that users will deal with and to allow users to operate on these objects directly. Uploading a file to a server by naming it, or even by selecting it from an "open file" dialog, is not a direct manipulation approach; direct manipulation would advocate selecting the file icon, dragging it and dropping it onto a representation of the server. The direct manipulation style of interface extends the idea of the visual metaphor to a richer model in which the abstract objects that make up the system's conceptual model—be they records, files, connections, servers, transactions, or whatever—are realized in a metaphorical world that also defines how they interact with each other. From these separate elements, the designer builds an inhabited world in which users act. Direct manipulation interfaces exploit and extend the benefits of graphical interaction. Because the system can be controlled entirely through the manipulation of on-screen objects, all opportunities for action are "out in the open." This eliminates (or, at least, reduces) the need for long sequences of action, paths that might be difficult to recognize or hard to follow.

Progress

It has been a long transition from interacting with computers using a soldering iron to interacting using a mouse. It has been neither smooth nor planned. Instead, the evolution of interaction models has gone hand in hand with the evolution of technologies, models of computation, and perceptions of the roles that computers will play in our lives.

Despite the rather chaotic evolution of interaction, it is still possible to draw out some general trends. The trend I have emphasized here is the gradual incorporation of a wider range of human skills and abilities. This allows computation to be made ever more widely accessible to people without requiring extensive training, and to be more easily integrated into our daily lives by reducing the complexity of those interactions. The "skills and abilities" perspective also offers a model for what sorts of opportunities new research directions might offer.

New Models for Interactive System Design

Graphical interaction remains the dominant paradigm for interaction with computers. In 1981 Xerox's Star was the first personal computer to ship with the features of a graphical user interface as we recognize them today—windows, menus, and a mouse—and the Macintosh, three years later, was the first to ship in volume at an affordable price. Perhaps more significantly, the release of Macintosh signaled a sea change in the way in which we interacted with computers. It simply became clear that this new paradigm was how we would interact with computers from then on.[2] Other manufacturers started shipping their machines with mice and with displays capable of supporting windowed interfaces, and the graphical user interface became the familiar face of computing.

Twenty years later, this is still true. As I write this, there are four computers here in my office, running three different operating systems; but they all display similar graphical user interfaces comprising windows, menus, and widgets such as buttons and scroll bars, controlled by a mouse sitting next to the keyboard. Although the Macintosh is arguably the only one that was designed that way from Day 1, the style that it introduced has remained largely unchallenged. In fact, the graphical interface predominates even in those areas where its application is more questionable, from wall-sized electronic whiteboards to small handheld computers.

However, recent research programs have begun to explore new paradigms for interaction and interactive system design. Some of these will be the topics of the next few chapters, but a quick sketch is in order here.

Tangible and Social Approaches to Computing

This chapter opened by discussing how we are increasingly encountering computation that moves beyond the traditional confines of the desk and attempts to incorporate itself more richly into our daily experience of the physical and social world. Each of these areas—physical and social—has been a focus of research attention.

Work on physical interaction has been a particularly active topic in the last few years. A variety of terms have been used to encompass the different activities being carried out and concerns being addressed. I use "tangible computing" here as an umbrella term.[3]

Tangible computing encompasses a number of different activities. One general trend is to distribute computation across a variety of devices, which are spread throughout the physical environment and are sensitive to their location and their proximity to other devices. In these sorts of environments, printers and fax machines might advertise their presence to handheld computers, which can then reconfigure themselves around the set of services available in the local environment; or tags identifying individuals might signal their presence to each other so that their wearers can find out which people in a meeting room share their interests, or even just who the people are. A second trend is to augment the everyday world with computational power, so that pieces of paper, cups, pens, ornaments, and toys can be made active entities that respond to their environment and people's activities. A toy might know when it has been picked up and change the computer display to reflect the fact that its owner is clearly feeling more playful rather than concentrating on work. Or picking up a piece of paper might cause my computer to show me related documents or remind me about other things I was working on when I last worked on it. A third topic of investigation in tangible computing is how these sorts of approaches can be harnessed to create environments for computational activity in which we interact directly through physical artifacts rather than traditional graphical interfaces and interface devices such as mice. Mice provide only simple information about movement in two dimensions, while in the everyday world we can manipulate many objects at once, using both hands and three dimensions to arrange the environment for our purposes and the activities at hand. A child playing with blocks engages with them in quite different ways than we could provide in a screen-based virtual equivalent; so tangible computing is exploring how to get the computer "out of the way" and provide people with a much more direct—tangible—interaction experience.

Although perhaps less focused as a research activity than tangible computing, the last decade or so has also seen increasing attempts to incorporate understandings of the social world into interactive systems. By analogy with tangible computing, I refer to this as "social computing."

Again, it encompasses a range of different activities that are more or less aligned. One set of activities involves incorporating social understandings into the design of interaction itself. That is, it attempts to understand how the "dialogue" between users and computers can be seen as similar and dissimilar to the way in which we interact with each other. Social science offers models of social action and the establishment of social meaning, which provide insight into the design of interaction with software systems. At the same time, anthropological and sociological approaches have been applied to uncovering the mechanisms through which people organize their activity, and the role that social and organizational settings play in this process. These investigations have yielded both prototype systems and generalized understandings of the influence that social and organizational settings can have on the organization of activities around computer systems. Finally, here, a third set of investigations has explored how what we normally consider to be "single-user" interaction—one person sitting in front of one computer—can be enhanced by incorporating information about others and the activity of others. This information can, in turn, assist individuals in exploring the electronic world of a computer application in the same way that the real world reveals to us signs and indications of the activities of others that can help us find our way around and carry on our actions—whether by "following the crowd" to find an event, sizing up the clientele when deciding on a restaurant, or knowing that a hotel is a good place to catch a taxi.

These are brief sketches of research areas, to be explored in more detail later on. However, even these overviews show that Human-Computer Interaction research is responding to the challenges of computation that inhabits our world, rather than forcing us to inhabit its own.

From Tangible and Social Computing to Embodied Interaction

My reason for viewing the history of interaction as a gradual expansion of the range of human skills and abilities that can be incorporated into interaction with computers is that I believe that it provides a valuable perspective on activities such as tangible and social computing. In particular, it shows that these two areas draw on *the same* sets of skills and abilities. Tangible and social computing are arguably aspects of one and the same research program.

This is the hypothesis that this book sets out to explore. The rest of the book will discuss the hypothesis and its implications in more detail, but I will set the argument out briefly here. It has four parts.

First, I want to argue that social and tangible interaction are based on the same underlying principles. This is not to deny their obvious differences, both in the approaches they adopt and the ways in which they apply to the design of interactive systems. Nonetheless, they share some important elements in common. In particular, they both exploit our familiarity and facility with the everyday world—whether it is a world of social interaction or physical artifacts. This role of the everyday world here is more than simply the metaphorical approach used in traditional graphical interface design. It's not simply a new way of using ideas like desktops, windows, and buttons to make computation accessible. Instead of drawing on artifacts in the everyday world, it draws on *the way the everyday world works* or, perhaps more accurately, *the ways we experience the everyday world*. Both approaches draw on the fact that the ways in which we experience the world are through directly interacting with it, and that we act in the world by exploring the opportunities for action that it provides to us—whether through its physical configuration, or through socially constructed meanings. In other words, they share an understanding that you cannot separate the individual from the world in which that individual lives and acts.

This comes about in contrast to a narrowly cognitive perspective that, for some time, dominated the thinking of computer system designers and still persists to a considerable degree. The positivist, Cartesian "naive cognitivism" approach makes a strong separation between, on the one hand, the mind as the seat of consciousness and rational decision making, with an abstract model of the world that can be operated upon to form plans of action; and, on the other, the objective, external world as a largely stable collection of objects and events to be observed and manipulated according to the internal mental states of the individual. From this perspective, a disembodied brain could think about the world just as we do, although it might lack the ability to affect it by acting in it. In contrast, the new perspective on which tangible and social computing rest argues that a disembodied brain could not experience the world in the same ways that we do, because our experience of the world is intimately tied to the ways in which we act in it. Physically, our experiences cannot be separated from the reality of our bodily presence in the world; and socially, too, the same relationship holds because our nature as social beings is based on the ways in which we act and interact, in real time, all the time. So, just as this perspective argues that we act in the world by exploring its physical affordances, it also argues that our social actions are ones that we jointly construct as we go along. A conversation between two people is shaped in response to the moment rather than abstractly planned, in much the same way as a juggler has to respond dynamically to the way in which each ball falls.

This leads to the second part of my argument, which is that the central element of this alternative perspective is the idea of *embodiment*. By embodiment, I do not mean simply physical reality, although that is often one way in which it appears. Embodiment, instead, denotes a form of participative status. Embodiment is about the fact that things are embedded in the world, and the ways in which their reality depends on being embedded. So it applies to spoken conversations just as much as to apples or bookshelves; but it's also the dividing line between an apple and the *idea* of an apple.

Why is embodiment relevant to these sorts of interactions with computers? It is relevant in at least three ways.

First, the designers of interactive systems have increasingly come to understand that interaction is intimately connected with the settings in which it occurs. In adopting anthropological techniques as ways to uncover the details of work and develop requirements for interactive systems to support that work, we have begun to realize just how important a role is played by the environment in which the work takes place.[4] This is true of both physical environments and social or organizational ones. Physical environments are arranged so as to make certain kinds of activities easier (or more difficult), and in turn, those activities are tailored to the details of the environment in which they take place. The same thing happens at an organizational level; the nature of the organization in which the work takes place will affect the work itself and the ways it is done. The increasing sensitivity to settings leads naturally to a concern with how work and interaction are embodied within those settings, because that embodiment determines how it is that computation and the setting will fit together.

Second, this focus on settings reflects a more general turn to consider work activities and artifacts in concrete terms rather than abstract ones. Instead of developing abstract accounts of mythical users, HCI increasingly employs field studies and observational techniques to stage "encounters" with real users, in real settings, doing real work. These encounters are often very revealing, as they show that the ways the work gets done are not the ways that are listed in procedural manuals, or even in the accounts that the people themselves would tell you if you asked. Attention to detail, to specifics, and to actual cases, leads in turn to thinking about computation in similar terms. In particular, it leads to a concern with how interaction is manifest in the interface. Tangible computing reflects this concern by exploring the opportunities for us to manifest computation and interaction in radically new forms, while social computing seeks ways for interaction to manifest more than simply the programmer's abstract model of the task, but also the specifics of how the work comes to be done. In the real world, where the artifacts through which interaction is conducted are directly embodied in the everyday environment, these are all manifested alongside each other, inseparably. Tangible and social computing are trying to stitch them back together after traditional interactive system design approaches ripped them apart.

Third, there is a recognition that, through their direct embodiment in the world we occupy, the artifacts of daily interaction can play many different roles. As an example, consider the revealing studies of the role of medical record cards in hospitals (Nygren, Johnson, and Henriksson 1992). From a technical perspective, patient record cards are simply carriers of well-defined information concerning the patient's diagnosis and treatment, and, as embodied on paper, present various problems: they can be lost, they can be hard to read, and they can only be in one place at a time. From this perspective, it seems both straightforward and beneficial to replace the paper records with electronic versions. However, in practice, such straightforward replacements are rarely successful. Studies of the failure of such systems show that the paper records are more than simply carriers of information about patients. They carry other important information as a result of the way that they are used in the work of the hospital. For example, handwriting on the forms reveals who performed different parts of the treatment; wear and tear on the form indicates heavy use; and the use of pencil marks rather than pen informally indicates tentative information. To trained eyes, a card conveys information not just about the patient, but also about the history of activities over the card and around the patient. It can do this because it not only represents the world of the patient, but it also participates in that world—it is an embodied artifact, and it participates in the embodied activities of those administering medical care. So, one relevance of embodiment for interaction with computational systems is that, for many tasks, it is relevant to consider how computation participates in the world it represents. Computation is fundamentally a representational medium, but as we attempt to expand the ways in which we interact with computation, we need to pay attention to the duality of representation and participation.

The third element of this book's argument is that the idea of embodiment as a common foundation points us to other schools of thought. Embodiment is not a new phenomenon, or a new area for intellectual endeavor. In fact, it is a common theme running through much twentieth century thought. The notion of embodiment plays a special role in one particular school of philosophical thought, phenomenology.

Phenomenology is primarily concerned with how we perceive, experience, and act in the world around us. What differentiates it from other approaches is its central emphasis on the actual phenomena of experience, where other approaches might be concerned with abstract world models. Traditional approaches would suggest that we each have an understanding of the elements of which our world is constructed, and an abstract mental model of how these concepts are related. We understand that there are entities we can drink from, and that cups, glasses, and mugs are examples; we understand that we can sit on things like sofas and stools, and that people might keep cats and rabbits as house-pets, but rarely elephants or seals. This information, abstractly encoded in our heads, guides our actions in the world. Armed with a model of appropriate concepts and relations—an ontology—we can look around us and recognize what we see. So, the traditional model supposes that when I encounter a glass of wine, even though I have never seen this particular one before, I can still recognize it as being a glass of wine because of the way in which it fits into my model as an instance of the abstract class of glasses and other drinking vessels.

In contrast, the phenomenologists argue that the separation between mind and matter, or between what Descartes called the *res cogitans* and the *res extensa*, has no basis in reality. Thinking does not occur separately from being and acting. Certainly, there is nothing in our experience to support such a separation. In every case, we encounter them together, as aspects of the same existence. Consequently, phenomenology has attempted to reconstruct the relationship between experience and action without this separation. Rather than the Cartesians' theory- or model-driven approach to perception, the phenomenological approach argues for what we might call a *preontological* apprehension of the world. Perception begins with what is experienced, rather than beginning with what is expected; the model is to "see and understand" rather than "understand and see."

To say that phenomenology is all about perception is to limit it unfairly. In addition to perception, it is also concerned with action, with understanding, and with how these are all related to each other, as part and parcel of our daily experience as participants in the world. In the hands of some, such as Alfred Schutz, phenomenology has also been a tool to understand social action and practice; others such as Wittgenstein, while not phenomenologists, have developed allied approaches to topics such as language and meaning. As we will see, these approaches provide an extensive set of investigations of the questions of presence, embodiment, and action.

In turn, the fourth element of the book's argument is that we can build on the phenomenological understandings to create a foundational approach to embodied interaction. Such a foundation should do two things. First, it should account for the ways in which social and tangible computing— and, perhaps, further areas to be defined—are related to each other, showing how they can be draw upon each other's work and provide a unified model for Human-Computer Interaction. Second, it should inform and support the design, analysis and evaluation of interactive systems, providing us with ways of understanding how they work, from the perspective of embodiment.[5]

This, then, is the four-part hypothesis that this book sets out to explore: that tangible and social computing have a common basis; that embodiment is the core element they have in common; that embodiment is not a new idea, but has been a primary topic for phenomenology; and that phenomenology and related investigations of embodiment can provide material for developing a foundation for embodied interaction.

This has all been presented so far in very broad strokes. The chapters to come will explore the issues in more depth and provide much more background. The two chapters that follow describe the recent trends in HCI research that are the starting point for this work. Chapter 2 deals with tangible computing, while chapter 3 explores social computing. Each presents both the research and the context in which it emerged. However, they present tangible and social computing as self-contained; in chapter 4, we begin to examine how they might be brought together, and how ideas from phenomenology and other philosophies of presence and experience can be brought to bear to understand the relationships between them. Just as chapters 2 and 3 try to introduce the set of ideas from tangible and social computing that will inform the later discussion, so chapter 4 provides an introduction to the phenomenological work that we will draw upon later. With this background, chapter 5 explores the notion of embodiment in more depth, drawing out a number of constituent elements whose relationships can be used to analyse interaction case studies. Chapter 6 builds on this and presents a framework that arranges these foundational elements to be able to draw on them for design, and chapter 7 points to some future directions.

2

Getting in Touch

For a device whose fundamental properties have changed so radically over the past thirty years, the personal computer itself—the familiar beige box sitting by the desk—has changed remarkably little.

The personal computer (PC) as we currently know it has its origins in work carried out at Xerox's Palo Alto Research Center in the early 1970s. The forerunner of the modern PC was, arguably, the Alto workstation developed by researchers there; it pioneered such now-common features as bitmapped displays with overlapping windows, graphical interfaces with multiple fonts and pop-up menus, and computers linked together over local-area networks. Although underpowered by today's standards (it was clocked at 6 MHz rather than the many hundreds of today's PCs), it nonetheless set the stage for what was to come, and its basic feature set, built around "the three 'M's"—millions of pixels, a megabyte of memory, and a million instructions per second—is still with us today.

On the other hand, an Alto in those days cost around $16,000 to build, scarcely affordable enough to put "a computer on every desk," as Microsoft would later set out to do. A more affordable option in 1977 (by which time the PARC researchers were working on the Dorado, a considerably faster and more powerful machine) was the Apple II, the device which, arguably, kick-started the personal computer industry. The Apple II was powered by a 6502 8-bit processor running at 1.5 MHz. It had 8 kilobytes of semiconductor memory and stored programs on cassette tape; optional floppy disk drives stored around 150 kilobytes each. Compare that to the modern personal computer. The laptop computer on which I'm writing this is certainly not top-of-the-line; it wasn't even top-of-the-line when I bought it a year ago. It has a 166 MHz 32-bit processor, 64 megabytes of memory, and a 13-inch color display and can store up to 6 Gb on an internal hard disk; and it cost under \$4,000.[1]

Imagine what it would be like if any other technology had undergone such rapid advances in price/performance. A car would cost a few dollars; airplanes would travel at hundreds of times the speed of sound; televisions would weigh a few ounces. More to the point, if cars, airplanes, and televisions had been so radically transformed, they would not be cars, airplanes, and televisions any more. They would have transformed themselves into something else altogether.

Computers, though, remain computers. As we enter the twenty-first century, today's PC still looks remarkably similar to that of the late 1970s (and perhaps even more like the Alto of the earlier part of that decade; see figure 2.1). This is not simply a matter of packaging and

Figure 2.1
Xerox's Alto (1974). This early personal computer is somewhat bulkier than today's, but is otherwise very recognizable in form. Reprinted by permission of Xerox Palo Alto Research Center.

industrial design, although it is certainly the case that with a few notable exceptions, we seem to be firmly stuck in an age of beige boxes. My concern is not so much about the boxes themselves as about the relationship of the user to the box. Despite the fact that computers are so radically different from the computers of twenty years ago, and that their capabilities are so vastly different, we interact with them in just the same way; we sit at a desk, watching the screen and typing on the keyboard. If you were to look at a photograph of people using computers some time over the last twenty years, their clothes and hairstyle might give you a clue to the date when the picture was taken, but the style of interaction with the computer certainly would not.

Similarly, the style of interaction concerns not simply the set of physical devices (keyboards, screens, and mice) or the set of virtual devices (dialog boxes, scroll bars, and menus) through which we interact, but also the ways in which the computer fits into our environments and our lives. Interaction with screen and keyboard, for instance, tends to demand our direct attention; we have to look at the screen to see what we're doing, which involves looking away from whatever other elements are in our environment, including other people. Interaction with the keyboard requires both of our hands. The computer sits by the desk and ties us to the desk, too. So, it is not simply the form of the computer that has changed remarkably little over the last thirty years; it is also the forms of computer-based activity and the roles that we imagine computers playing in our everyday lives.

Although this model of everyday computing might be conventional, it is not inevitable. The rise of the personal computer—and, more broadly, of personal computing—was an attempt to break away from the then-dominant paradigm of mainframe computing. Similarly, while personal computing may now be established as the dominant model, a variety of alternatives have been explored in the research community; departures from the world of the conventional PC as radical as the PC was from the world of the mainframe. In this chapter, I will take a brief tour through some of the research laboratories where these alternatives are being explored. In particular, I will focus on an approach that looks at the relationship between computers on the desktop and the world in which they (and we) operate. This is a model of interaction that I refer to as "tangible computing." Although it is only lately that the tangible computing paradigm has become broadly established, its has emerged from a research program that stretches back over a decade.

Ubiquitous Computing

We begin the tour, ironically enough, in the Computer Science Lab at Xerox PARC—the same place that gave us the desktop PC. In the 1970s, Xerox had set up PARC to explore "the architecture of information," and the Computer Science Lab, under the guidance of former ARPA manager Bob Taylor, had delivered what was to become the basic elements of office information technology in the decades to follow—powerful personal workstations, laser printers, and shared servers, linked together on local area networks. Xerox, famously, had failed to recognize its own future in PARC's vision, so today's office technology generally doesn't carry a Xerox label (Smith and Alexander 1988).

By the start of the 1990s, the situation was different. PARC's vision of the architecture of information had, largely, come to pass; and, in the opinion of the new manager of the Computer Science Lab, Mark Weiser, it was time for a new and equally radical vision of the future of technology.

What Weiser proposed was a research program that he dubbed "Ubiquitous Computing." Weiser saw that the development and diffusion of general-purpose computers, and in particular PC's, had resulted in a focus on the computer rather than on the tasks that the computer was used to accomplish. He argued that ongoing technological developments, particularly in mobile and low-power devices, would transform the nature of computers and the way we interact with them. Why deal with a single, large, expensive computer when you could harness many tiny, low-cost devices spread throughout the environment? Instead of always taking work to the computer, why not put computation wherever it might be needed? Through the technical developments that supported this new model, he saw an opportunity to turn attention away from the dominating focus on the computer sitting on the desktop and back to the applications, and to the artifacts around which those applications were structured. Weiser's vision of "ubiquitous computing" was one of computationally enhanced walls, floors, pens, and desks, in which the power of computation could be seamlessly integrated into the objects and activities of everyday life.

One analogy that Weiser proposed as a way of understanding his vision for the new role of computation was that of solenoids, the electronically actuated switches that are part of the fabric of many everyday technologies. For example, he observed, a modern car has a vast number of solenoids, invisibly controlling everything from the air conditioning to the fuel intake. Solenoids are a critical component of modern technological design and are used in all sorts of settings. And yet, we don't deal directly with solenoids in the way we do with computers. We don't have to think about the design of the "human-solenoid interface"; we don't have programs on "solenoid literacy" in schools; you can't take a degree in "solenoid science," and nobody had to upgrade to "Solenoids 2000."

Why have computers and solenoids followed different paths? Various possibilities present themselves. Perhaps it is because of the nature of computers as multipurpose devices; or perhaps it is a historical accident, a feature of how computer technology was introduced into the home and work environments. And to be sure, there are all sorts of computer technologies surrounding us that are far more like solenoids than they are like PCs, such as the computer processors inside my television set, microwave oven, and car. The difference between my PC and those other devices is that those other devices are organized around human needs and functions.

Weiser's model of ubiquitous computing was also, paradoxically, one of invisible computers. He argued for a vision of computers in which the computer had become so ubiquitous that it had, essentially, disappeared. He proposed that the computer of the twenty-first century would have proceeded further along the path from the mainframe to the processor in my microwave oven, and that the intermediate step—the desktop PC— would be all but gone. However, in this world, although there might be no more computers as we understand them today, there would certainly be computation. In fact, there might be a great deal more computation than there is now. Computational devices would be embedded in all sorts of technologies, Weiser argued, creating a variety of specialized devices augmented with computational power. Computers would disappear into the woodwork; computers would be nowhere to be seen, but computation would be everywhere.

Computation by the Inch, Foot, and Yard

In the Computer Science Lab at Xerox PARC, Weiser initiated a wide-ranging research program around his vision of Ubiquitous Computing, fostering the development of new computational technologies, the infrastructure necessary to support them, and new application models. PARC's ubiquitous computing strategy followed three tracks: they were known as computation by the inch, the foot and the yard (see figure 2.2).

"Computation by the inch" focused on the development of small devices, like electronic tags or computational "Post-It" notes. One focus of attention was the use of devices called "Active badges," originally developed at the Olivetti Research Centre in Cambridge, England (Want et al. 1992). Active badges are devices measuring roughly 1.5 inches square that are intended to be worn like normal identity badges. However, they house some simple electronics and emit a fixed, coded infrared signal every thirty seconds or so (or whenever a button on the badge is pressed). These signals are detected by a network of infrared receivers located in the environment, and which are connected to a computational server process. Because each badge emits an individual code, and because its signal will generally only be received by the closest detector, the server can maintain a map of the location of each badge within the sensor network, which in turn can locate the badge's wearer within the environment.

When people wear active badges, then applications can help make the environment responsive to their movements. The system can route telephone calls to the current location of the person being called, display relevant information on nearby monitors as they pass by, or customize the behavior of a computer system to the needs of the person sitting at it. In Weiser's model, badges or similar tags could also be attached to books and other artifacts, so that their location and mutual proximity could become a resource to computer-based applications.

If computation "by the inch" sought a model of computationally enhanced Post-It Notes, the computation "by the foot" was concerned with computationally enhanced pads of paper. The primary focus of this

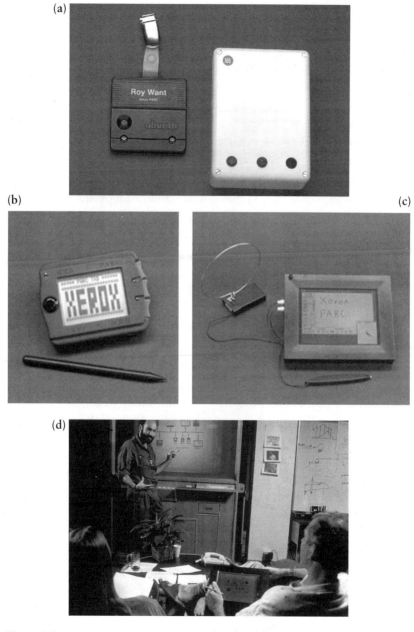

Figure 2.2
Computing by the inch, the foot, and the yard: (*a*) an active badge, (*b*) the PARC Tab, (*c*) the PARC Pad, and (*d*) a meeting at the Liveboard. Reprinted by permission of Xerox Palo Alto Research Center.

area of work was the development and use of computational devices of about the size and power of recent laptop computers. Laptop computers were, of course, already widely available at this point, but they tended (as they still do) to function simply as scaled-down versions of their desktop cousins. In contrast, the goal of ubiquitous computing research was not simply on the size and packaging of the devices, but of how they would fit into a world of everyday activities and interaction. As a result, research concentrated on other concerns. Examples included stylus-based interaction, which could eliminate keyboards as the primary source of interaction, and which could support note-taking and sketching, and mobile operation, so that devices could be moved from place to place without interfering with their operation.

Finally, investigations into computation "by the yard" introduced the opportunity to consider much larger devices. In particular, attention focussed on wall-sized devices such as the LiveBoard. LiveBoard was a large-scale display (approximately five feet by three feet) supporting multiple pens, a sort of computationally enhanced whiteboard. Researchers observed how the very physical form of this device was an important component in structuring interactions with it. On the one hand, the use of pen input meant that collaborative activities (such as brainstorming in a meeting) would be implicitly structured by the fact that the board was large enough for everyone to see at once, but that two people could not stand in front of the same part of the board or write in the same area at the same time. On the other hand, the board's large size also meant that new interaction techniques would have to be developed; using a scroll bar or pull-down menu on a board a board five feet wide could be, quite literally, a pain in the neck.

Discussing each of these components of PARC's ubiquitous computing strategy independently can mask the critical integration of the various facets of the program. None of these devices was intended to operate on its own. The focus, after all, was on a form of computation more deeply integrated with the everyday environment, and the everyday environment is filled with a variety of objects and devices. So it was with the ubiquitous computing vision. A single user might have, at his or her disposal, tens or more of the inch-sized devices, just as we might have many Post-It notes dotted around, stuck to computer screens, walls, books, and sheets of paper; at the same time, they might also have three or four foot-sized devices, just as I might have a number of notebooks for different topics or projects; but just as I probably only have one or maybe two whiteboards in my office, there will be fewer of the devices at the larger scale. What is more, information is expected to be able to move around between the different devices. Notes that I have prepared on an electronic pad might be beamed onto the board for group consideration in a meeting; while action items might be migrated off into a hand-held device that stores my calendar and to-do list. In the everyday environment, information continually undergoes transformations and translations, and we should expect the same in a computationally enhanced version of that environment such as might be delivered to us by ubiquitous computing.

The Digital Desk

At much the same time as Weiser and his PARC colleagues were developing the ubiquitous computing program, related activity was going on in another Xerox lab, in Cambridge, England. EuroPARC had been set up as a European satellite laboratory of PARC. It was a much smaller lab (with a research complement of around twenty) with a focus on interdisciplinary research into Human-Computer Interaction and Computer-Supported Cooperative Work.

EuroPARC was home to a variety of technological developments, but the particular technology that concerns us here is the Digital Desk, designed and developed by Pierre Wellner (Wellner 1991; Newman and Wellner 1992). In common with many people, Wellner had observed that the "paperless office" envisioned by many in the 1970s and early 1980s had manifestly failed to develop. However, that was not to say that the development of personal computers, and increasingly networked personal computers, had not caused an massive increase in the number of digital or online documents that we all have to deal with everyday. Wellner was concerned with how we could work with both paper and electronic documents in a much more fluid and seamless way than is normally the case. The traditional approach to these problems was either to scan in the paper documents to bring them into the electronic realm, or to print out the electronic documents to bring them into the physical realm. By moving across the boundary from online documents to paper documents and back again, users could take exploit the advantages of each; the digital malleability and computational power of electronic documents with the portability, readability, and informal interaction of paper ones. As many studies have attested, paper has many properties that are hard to reproduce in the electronic world (Sellen and Harper 1997; Henderson 1998), while, at the same time, electronic documents increasingly exploit features (such as animation, hyperlinks, or interactive elements) that paper documents cannot capture. So, the move back and forth between electronic and paper forms is not only inconvenient but also impoverished, since some features always remain behind. Taking his cue from Weiser's ubiquitous computing work, Wellner wondered if there wasn't a way to combine the two worlds more effectively by augmenting the physical world with computational properties.

Wellner's Digital Desk (figure 2.3) combines elements of each. The Digital Desk was a physical desktop, much like any other, holding papers, pens, coffee cups, and other traditional office accoutrements. However, it was also augmented with some distinctly nontraditional components. Above the desk were placed a video projector and a video camera. Both of these were pointed down toward the desktop; the projector would project images onto the desk, over whatever objects were lying there, and the camera could watch what happened on the desktop. These devices were connected to a nearby computer. Image processing software running on the computer could analyze the signal from the video camera to read documents on the desk and watch the user's activity. At the same time, the computer could also make images appear on the desk by displaying them via the video projector.

The result was a computationally enhanced desktop supporting interaction with both paper and electronic documents (Wellner 1993). Electronic documents could be projected onto the desktop by the video projector, but then could be moved around the (physical) desktop by hand (using the video camera to track the user's hand movements and then "moving" the displayed document in coordination). Similarly, physical documents could be given computational abilities on the same

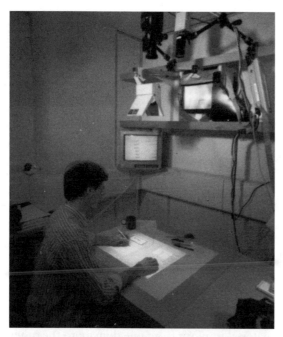

Figure 2.3
Wellner's Digital Desk allowed interaction with paper and electronic documents on the same desktop. Reprinted by permission of Xerox Research Centre Europe.

desktop. For example, a paper document containing a list of numbers could be used as input to a virtual calculator; the computer could use the camera to "read" the numbers off the printed page, and then project the result of a calculation over those figures.

Two features of the Digital Desk were critical to its design. The first was its support for manipulation. In Wellner's first prototype, one moved objects around on the desk with one's fingers; in contrast with the prevailing approach to interface design, this was *really* direct manipulation. What's more, of course, while our computer systems typically have only one mouse, we have *two* hands and *ten* fingers. By tracking the position and movements of both hands or of multiple fingers, the Digital Desk could naturally support other behaviors that were more complicated in traditional systems, such as using both hands at once to express scaling or rotation of objects. The second critical design feature was the way in which electronic and physical worlds were integrated. A document on the digital desk could consist of both physical content (printed on a page) and electronic content (projected onto it), and printers and cameras allowed material to move from one domain to the other fluidly so that objects created on paper could be manipulated electronically. The Digital Desk offered developers and researchers an opportunity to think about the boundary between the physical and virtual worlds as a permeable one.

While the work on ubiquitous computing had shown how computation could be brought out of the "box on the desk" and into the everyday world, Wellner's work on the digital desk expanded on this by considering how, once the real world was a site of computational activity, the real and electronic worlds could actually work together.

Virtual Reality and Augmented Reality

Weiser and Wellner shared the goal of creating computationally augmented reality. They both attempted to take computation and embed it in the everyday world. This follows in the trend, outlined earlier, to expand the range of human skills and abilities on which interaction can draw. In this case, the abilities to be exploited are those familiar ways in which we interact with the everyday world; drawing on whiteboards, moving around our environments, shuffling pieces of paper, and so on. One of the interesting feature of these approaches, at the time, was the way in which they developed in opposition to another major trend—immersive virtual reality.

Virtual reality (VR) is, at least in the popular consciousness, a technology of recent times; it became particularly prominent in the 1990s. Immersive VR as we know it today came about through the increase in computer power, and particularly graphics processing, that became available in the late 1980s, as well as some radical sensor developments that gave us data gloves and body suits. The technical developments supporting immersive VR became widespread at around the same time as William Gibson's notion of "cyberspace"—a technically mediated consensual hallucination in which people and technology interacted—also entered the popular consciousness. Virtual reality has been around a good deal longer than that, however. Ivan Sutherland, the father of interactive computer graphics, went on to investigate what we now recognize as virtual reality technology back in the 1960s, and the use of digital technology to create environments such as flight training simulators is well-known. Howard Rheingold's book *Virtual Reality* (1992) documents some of the early history of this seemingly recent technology.

Virtual reality immerses the user in a computationally generated reality. Users don head-mounted displays, which present slightly different computer-generated·images to each eye, giving the illusion of a three-dimensional space. By monitoring the user's head movements and adjusting the image appropriately, this three-dimensional space can be extended beyond the immediate field of view; the user can move his head around, and the image moves to match. With appropriating sensing technologies, the user can enter the virtual space and act within it. A "dataglove" is a glove augmented with sensors that report the position and orientation of the hand and fingers to a computer; the hand of the user wearing the glove is projected as a virtual hand into the same computer-generated three dimensional space that the virtual reality system generates, so that the user can pick up virtual objects, examine them, move them around, and act in the space.

The ubiquitous computing program was getting under way at about the point when virtual reality technology began to make its way out of research laboratories and into newspaper articles. Both approaches to the future of computing are based on similarly science-fiction notions; immersion in a computer-generated reality, on the one hand, and computers in doorknobs and pens on the other. They embody, however, fundamentally different approaches to the relationship between computers, people and the world. In the virtual reality approach, interaction takes place in a fictional, computer-generated world; the user moves into that world, either through immersion or, more commonly these days, through a window onto the world on a computer screen. The world of interaction is the world of the computer. The ubiquitous computing approach to interaction—what Weiser dubbed "physical virtuality" and would become known as augmented reality—does just the opposite. It moves the computer into the real world. The site of interaction is the world of the user, not that of the system. That world, in the augmented reality vision, may be imbued with computation, but the computer itself takes a back seat.

The Reactive Room

The ubiquitous computing model distributes computation throughout the environment. All sorts of objects, from walls to pens, might have computational power embedded in them. For someone concerned with interaction, this raises one enormous question—how can all this computation be controlled?

At the University of Toronto, Jeremy Cooperstock and colleagues explored this question in an environment they called the Reactive Room (Cooperstock et al. 1995). The Reactive Room was a meeting room supporting a variety of physical and virtual encounters. It grew out of both the ubiquitous computing perspective and the "media space" tradition, an approach to supporting collaboration and interaction through a combination of audio, video, and computational technology (Bly, Harrison, and Irwin 1993). The room was designed to support not only normal, face-to-face meetings, but also meetings distributed in space (where some participants are in remote locations) and time (recording meeting activity to be viewed later by someone else). To that end, it also featured a shared computer display, for electronic presentations and application-based work; a variety of video and audio recorders; and audio and video units connected to a distributed analog A/V network that could be connected to similar "nodes" in people's offices, so they could remotely "attend" meetings.

However, such a complex and highly configurable environment presented considerable challenges for control and management. To configure the room for any given situation (such as a presentation to be attended by remote participants), each device in the room would have to be configured independently, and adjusting the configuration to support the dynamics of the meeting was even more challenging. The design of the Reactive Room sought to use ubiquitous computing technology as a means to manage this problem. The critical move here was to see ubiquitous computing as a technology of *context;* where traditional interactive systems focus on what the user does, ubiquitous computing technologies allow the system to explore *who* the user is, *when* and *where* they are acting, and so on.

In the case of the reactive room, contextual information could be used to disambiguate the potential forms of action in which a user might engage. For example, by using an active badge or similar system, the room's control software can be informed of who is in the room and can configure itself appropriately to them. Similarly, if the room "knows" that there is a meeting in progress, then it can take that information into account to generate an appropriate configuration. If a user presses the "meeting record" button on a VCR, to record a meeting in progress, the Reactive Room can determine whether or not there are any remote participants connected to the audio/video nodes and, if so, ensure that it adds those signals to the recording. When someone in the room makes use of the document camera or the projected computer display, the room software can detect these activities and automatically make the document camera view or the computer display available to those people attending the presentation, either locally or remotely.

In other words, the design of the Reactive Room attempts to exploit the fact that the people's activities happen in a context, which can be made available to the software in order to disambiguate action. Clearly, of course, the sort of context that can be gathered with current technology is limited; the Reactive Room would make use of motion in particular parts of the room, presence and activity as detected using active badges or pressure sensors, and so on. The other, perhaps most important, piece of context it made use of was *the fact that it was the Reactive Room.* That is, the room was designed for meetings and presentations, and so much activity in the room could be interpreted as being appropriate to meetings and presentations. The same sorts of inferences would probably be inappropriate in other settings, such as a private office, or a home. The "meeting" context, then, also serves to disambiguate the user's goals.

The Reactive Room demonstrated the way that ubiquitous computing did not simply move out of the box on the desk and into the environment but, at the same time, also got involved in the relationship between the environment and the activities that took place there. The topic of "setting-ed" behavior will come back into focus in the next chapter; for the moment, however, we will continue to explore the development of tangible computing.

Design Trends

The systems that have been described—the vision of Ubiquitous Computing, and the Digital Desk and Reactive Room prototypes—have been firmly located in the domain of Computer Science research. However, "academic science" has by no means been the only contributor to the development of Tangible Computing. In fact, one striking aspect of the development of this line of investigation has been the contributions from the perspectives of art and design. Two pieces that have proved to be particularly inspirational to a number of researchers in this area were Durrell Bishop's Marble Answering Machine, and Natalie Jeremijenko's Live Wire.

The Marble Answering Machine was a design exercise undertaken by Bishop in the Computer-Related Design department at the Royal College of Art in London (Crampton-Smith 1995). It explored possible approaches to physical interaction for a telephone answering machine. Rather than the traditional array of lights and buttons, Bishop's answering machine has a stock of marbles. Whenever a caller leaves a message on the answering machine, it associates that message with a marble from the stock, and the marble rolls down a track to the bottom, where it sits along with the marbles representing previous messages. When the owner of the machine comes home, a glance at the track shows, easily and distinctly, how many messages are waiting—the number of marbles arrayed at the bottom of the track. To play a message, the owner picks up one of the marbles and drops it in a depression at the top of the answering machine; because each marble is associated with a particular message, it knows which message to play. Once the message has been played, the owner can decide what to do; either return the marble to the common stock for reuse (so deleting the message), or returning it to the track (saving it to play again later).

The Marble Answering Machine uses physical reality to model the virtual or electronic world. In Bishop's design, marbles act as physical proxies for digital audio messages. By introducing this equivalence, it also enriches the opportunities for interacting with the device. The problem of interacting with the virtual has been translated into interacting with the physical, and so we can rely on the natural structure of the everyday world and our casual familiarity with it. So, counting the number of messages is easy, because we can rapidly assess the visual scene; and operations such as playing messages out of order, deleting messages selectively, or storing them in a different sequence, all of which would require any number of buttons, dials, and controls on a normal digital answering machine, all become simple and straightforward because we can rely on the affordances of the everyday world.

Natalie Jeremijenko's piece "Live Wire," also sometimes known as "the Dangling String" and described by Weiser and Brown (1996), was developed and installed at Xerox PARC in 1994 and explored similar questions of the boundary between the virtual and physical worlds. Physically, Live Wire was a length of plastic "string" around eight feet long, hanging from the ceiling at the end of a corridor. Above the ceiling tiles, the wire was connected to a small stepper motor, which in turn was connected to a device on the local ethernet. Every time a data "packet" passed by on the ethernet, the stepper motor would move, and its movements would be passed on to the string. Ethernet, in its classic form, is a "shared medium" technology—all the traffic, no matter which machine sends it or which machine is to receive it, travels along the same cable.

The busier the network, the more data packets would pass by, and the more the stepper motor would move. The ethernet can carry thousands of packets per second, and so when the network was busy the motor would whir and the string would spin around at high speed, its loose end whipping against the wall nearby.

Others have followed in the footsteps of Bishop and Jeremijenko and continued to explore the design "space" around these issues of the borders between physical and virtual worlds. Feather, Scent, and Shaker (Strong and Gaver 1996) are devices for "simple intimacy." "Feather" features a feather that is gently lifted on a column of air, to indicate to its owner that, perhaps, a photograph of them has been picked up somewhere else; it is designed to convey a sense of fondness across distance. Scent, similarly, releases a pleasant, sweet smell in similar circumstances providing an awareness of distant action.

The topic of "awareness" is one that has concerned the developers of technologies for group working, who want their systems to be able to support the casual and passive awareness of group activity that coworkers achieve in a shared physical space. Strong and Gaver turn this around, though, and give us technologies for supporting shared intimacy rather than shared work. Their pieces are designed to be evocative and emotive rather than "efficient." What is particularly interesting about this group of devices is that they originate not from a technical or scientific perspective, but from a design perspective. The result of this shift in perspective is that they a reflect a very different set of concerns. It is not simply that they reflect an aesthetic component where the scientific developments are marked more by engineering concerns. That is certainly one part of it, of course; the design examples certainly do reflect a different set of principles at work. However, there is more than this.

First, the design examples discussed here reflect a concern with *communication*. What is important is not simply what they *do*, but what they *convey*, and how they convey it; and the communicative function that they carry is very much on the surface. There is an "at-a-glance readability" to these artifacts that stands in marked contrast to the "invisibility" of ubiquitous computing. Second, they reflect a holistic approach that takes full account of their physicality. The physical nature of these pieces is not simply a consequence of their design; it is fundamental to it. While it was a tenet of ubiquitous computing, for example, that the technology would move out into the world, the design pieces reflect a recognition that the technology *is* the world, and so its physicality and its presence is a deeply important part of its nature. Third, they reflect a different perspective on the role of computation, in which computation is integrated much more directly with the artifacts themselves. In the other examples, while they have aimed to distribute computation throughout the environment, there has always been a distinct "seam" between the computational and the physical worlds at the points where they meet. In these examples, however, the computational and physical worlds are much more directly connected.

The result is an approach to tangible computing that sees computation within a wider context. Ubiquitous Computing pioneers saw that, in order to support human activity, computation needs to move into the environment in which that activity unfolds. These design explorations take the next step of considering how computation is to be manifest when it moves into the physical environment, and recognizing that this move makes the physicality of computation central.

Tangible Bits

Most recently, perhaps the most prominent site for development of these ideas has been the Tangible Media group at the MIT Media Lab. A group of researchers led by Hiroshi Ishii has been exploring what they call "Tangible Bits," a program of research that incorporates aspects of both the Ubiquitous Computing program and the design perspective explored by people like Jeremijenko.

The term "Tangible Bits" reveals a direct focus on the interface between the physical and virtual worlds. The rhetoric of the computer revolution has, pretty consistently, focused on a transition from physical (the world of atoms) to the virtual (the world of bits). We talk of the future in terms of "electronic cash" to replace the paper bills and coins we carry about with us, or we speak of the "paperless office" in which paper documents have disappeared in favor of electronic documents stored on servers and displayed on screens. We envision a world in which we communicate by electronic mail and video conferencing, in which we read from "e-books," telecommute over great distances via digital communication lines, and play in virtual worlds. What these visions have in common is the triumph of the virtual over the physical. They suggest that we will overcome the inherent limitations of the everyday world (such as the need to be in the same place to see each other, or that a thousand books actually take up real shelf space) by separating the "information content" from the physical form, distilling the digital essence and decanting it into a virtual world.

The MIT Media Lab, where Ishii and his colleagues are based, is one of the most prominent proponents of this vision, especially, perhaps, in the writings of its founding director, Nicholas Negroponte. His collection of essays *Being Digital* (Negroponte 1995), explores the relationship between atoms and bits and how the development and deployment of Internet technologies is changing that relationship.

The work on Tangible Bits provides some balance to the idea that a transition from atoms to bits is inevitable and uniformally positive. It is certainly not defined in opposition to the gradual and ongoing movement of traditionally physical forms into digital media. However, it observes that while digital and physical media might be *informationally* equivalent, they are not *interactionally* equivalent. By building information artifacts based on physical manipulation, the Tangible Bits programme attempts to reinvest these distilled digital essences with some of the physical features that support natural interaction in the real world.

metaDESK, Phicons, and Tangible Geospace

Let's take an example from the work of the Tangible Bits group. The metaDESK (Ullmer and Ishii 1997) is a platform for tangible interaction. It consists of a horizontal back-projected surface that serves as the top of the physical desk itself; an "active lens," which is a small flat-panel display mounted on an arm; a "passive lens," which is transparent, also digitally instrumented; and a variety of physical objects called *phicons* (for "physical icons"). The metaDESK is shown in figure 2.4.

The functions of the various components of the metaDESK platform are best seen in terms of an application running on the desk. Tangible Geospace is a geographical information system augmented with tangible UI features and running on the metaDESK. It allows users to explore a

Figure 2.4
Interactions with geographical information on the metaDESK, using phicons, the passive lens, and the active lens. Reprinted by permission of The MIT Media Lab.

visualization of a geographical space, such as the area of Cambridge, Massachusetts, around MIT.

The geographical information, in the form of a two-dimensional map, is back-projected onto the desk, so that the user seated at the desk can see it. The user can move and orient the map using phicons. One of the phicons represents MIT's Great Dome, and when it is placed on the desk, the map is adjusted so that the position of the Great Dome corresponds to that of the phicon. As the user moves the phicon, the system adjusts the map to ensure that the phicon is always aligned with the point on the map that it represents. By moving the phicon around on the desk, the user can cause the map to move too, "scrolling" around in the geographical space. By rotating the phicon on the desk, the user can cause the map to rotate.

If a second phicon is added to the desk, say one representing the Media Lab building itself, then another degree of freedom can be constrained. The two icons, together, can be used to control the scale of the map display. If the metaDESK always ensures that the virtual Great Dome always co-occurs with the Great Dome phicon, and the virtual Media Lab always co-occurs with the Media Lab phicon, then the user can control the scale of the map by moving these two phicons closer together or further apart.

The active and passive lenses can be used to provide access to other sorts of information. In the Tangible Geospace example, the active lens is used to view a three dimensional model of the MIT Campus. The active lens is a computer display mounted on an arm over the desk. It is instrumented so that the metaDESK computer system can determine the position and orientation of the display. When this information is coordinated with the current position, scaling, and orientation of the map being displayed on the desk, the result is that the active lens can be used to control a "virtual camera" moving through the geographical space being displayed on the metaDESK. When this is combined with a three dimensional model of the campus, then the active lens can be used to give a three-dimensional viewport onto the two-dimensional map. The illusion is of "looking through" the lens and seeing a transformed view of the map underneath.

The passive lens works in a similar way, although it rests on the desk surface. The passive lens is simply a piece of transparent plastic. As it is moved around the desk, the computer system can track its current location. On the desk area directly underneath the lens, the metaDESK replaces the map with a view onto a photographic aerial record of the campus. As before, this is correlated with the current position, scaling, and orientation of the basic map, as well as the position of the lens. The effect is that it seems to the user that the lens reveals the photographic model underneath as it moves across the desk. This is similar to a user interface technique known as "magic lenses" (Bier et al. 1993), user interface components that selectively transform the content of interfaces as they are moved across the screen, although, of course, in the case of the metaDESK the lens has a physical manifestation.

The Ambient Room
Tangible interfaces such as the metaDESK explore interaction that is situated in the environment, rather than on a screen. This is even more

clearly demonstrated by another of the MIT prototypes, called the Ambient Room (Wisneski et al. 1998).

The Ambient Room is a small office cubicle that has been augmented with a variety of "ambient displays," designed to provide peripheral, background information to the occupant of the room without being overwhelming or distracting. Examples of ambient displays include projected light patterns, non-speech sounds, and objects that respond to changes in air flow.

The information that the Ambient Room conveys is typically information about activities in either physical or virtual space, such as the presence or activity of others, e-mail arriving, people logging in and out, and so forth. These can be mapped onto the displays available in the room. For instance, light patterns projected on the wall can respond to the activities of a networked computer system, conveying information about network traffic and hence activity in the virtual space; or movements in a shared project room can be mapped onto subtle sounds in the Ambient Room so that the occupant can be aware of comings and goings in the project space. Reminiscent of the Feather, Scent, and Shaker work of Strong and Gaver, these ambient displays can be used to project the actions in one space (either physical or virtual) into another; like the technologies of the Reactive Room, they can also respond to the activity of the room's occupant, providing a display that is appropriate to the context in which they are working.

It is tempting to think of the metaDESK as exploring the potential for tangible media as input technologies, and the Ambient Room as exploring their potential for output. To do so, though, would be to miss an important point, which is that, in the everyday environment, "input" and "output" are fundamentally interconnected. This is a critical feature of the tangible media explorations. They should be characterized not in terms of "input" and "output," but in terms of the coordination between phenomena; between activity in a space and the pattern of light on a wall, or between the movement of objects on the desk and the information presented there. This sort of coordination, or coupling, is fundamental to the explorations presented here; they depend upon it for the causal illusion they want to maintain.

Illuminating Light and Urp

Two other applications developed in the MIT group echo the Digital Desk in their creation of mixed physical/virtual environments for task-focused work. These are Illuminating Light and Urp, both developed principally by John Underkoffler (and illustrated in figure 2.5).

Illuminating Light (Underkoffler and Ishii 1998) is a simulation of an optics workbench, aimed particularly at students of laser holography. The interface is based on a combination of phicons and a camera/projector arrangement (which Underkoffler dubs the "I/O Bulb") similar to that of the Digital Desk. The application allows users to experiment with and explore configurations of equipment for laser holography. Real laser holography is a complex business, conducted using delicate and expensive instruments. Setting up and fine-tuning an experimental configuration can be extremely time-consuming, especially for novices. Illuminating Light allows holographers to simulate the effects of particular configurations and to explore them so as to develop a better intuitive sense for the interaction of their elements. Phicons represent physical elements such as lasers, lenses, mirrors, and beam-splitters, while the system provides a simulation of light paths through the experimental equipment, showing light emitted by the laser, redirected by mirrors, and so on. As the phicons are moved around a physical surface, the system continually updates its projection of the simulated light paths to reflect the moment-by-moment physical configuration. In addition to the simulated light beams, the system can also provide numerical descriptions of the configuration; incidence angles, distances, and so forth. In this way, users can rapidly explore a variety of configurations and develop an understanding of the consequences of different changes on the set-up.

Urp (Underkoffler and Ishii 1999) is an urban planning workbench in which physical models of buildings are combined with electronic simulations of features such as air flow, cast shadows, reflectance, and so forth. The underlying technology is similar to that of Illuminating Light but applied to a different domain. There are two sorts of phicons used in Urp. The first represent building structures. By placing these on the surface, the user can obtain a visualization of the shadows that the buildings will cast, or the wind patterns around them. Combining multiple structures allows urban planners and architects to explore the

(a)

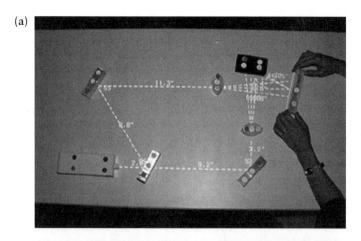

(b)

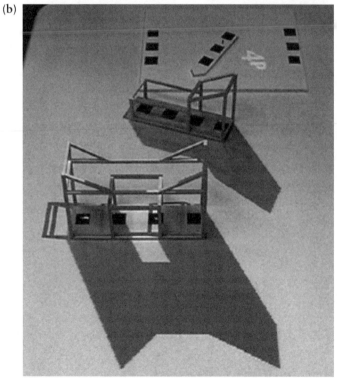

Figure 2.5
Illuminating Light (*a*) and Urp (*b*) apply tangible interaction techniques to the
domains of optics and urban planning. Reprinted by permission of The MIT
Media Lab.

interactions of wind, reflection, and shadow effects in an urban land-
scape. As with Illuminating Light, real-time tracking of the position and
orientation of these phicons allows the system to update the display con-
tinuously, so that users can move the buildings around or rotate them
until they find a satisfactory arrangement. The second set of phicons act
as controls for the simulation. For example, a "wand" can be used to
change the material of the buildings, so that the computed reflectance
patterns will simulate buildings clad in brick or glass, another controls
the direction of the simulated wind, while a "clock" has hands that can
be moved to specify the time of day and hence the position of the sun for
the shadow simulation. In this way, the simulator's controls are introduced into the same space that is the focus of the system's primary input
and output.

Interacting with Tangible Computing

Tangible computing takes a wide range of forms. It might be used to
address problems in highly focused and task-specific work, or in more
passive awareness of activities in the real world or the electronic. It
might attempt to take familiar objects and invest them with computation, or it might present us with entirely new artifacts that disclose something of the hidden world inside the software system. The bulk of this
chapter has explored a range of tangible computing systems, but the sur-
vey has been far from comprehensive; indeed, I have said nothing about
whole areas, such as wearable computing and context-based computing,
that are clearly strongly related. My goal, however, was not to provide a
catalogue of tangible computing technologies, but rather to introduce a
sample of the systems that have been developed, and to begin to look for
some common features of their design.

The first of these general issues that we see across a range of cases is
that, in tangible computing, there is no single point of control or interaction. Traditional interactive systems have a single center of interaction,
or at least a small number. Only one window has the "focus" at any
given moment; the cursor is always in exactly one place, and that place
defines where my actions will be carried out. Cursors and window focus
insure that the system always maintains a distinguished component

within the interface, which is the current locus of interaction. To do something else, one must move the focus elsewhere. When computation moves out into the environment, as in the tangible computing approach, this is lost. Not only is there not a single point of interaction, there is not even a single device that is the object of interaction. The same action might be distributed across multiple devices, or, more accurately, achieved through the coordinated use of those artifacts. Imagine sitting at your desk to write a note. The writing comes about through the coordinated use of pen, paper, and ink, not to mention the desk itself and the chair you sit in; you might write on the page with your dominant hand while your nondominant hand is used to orient the page appropriately. These are all brought together to achieve a task; you act at multiple points at once. In the same way, ubiquitous computing distributes computation through the environment, and, at one and the same time, distributes activity across many different computational devices, which have to be coordinated in order to achieve a unified effect.

A related issue is how tangible interaction transforms the sequential nature of interaction at the interface. The single point of control that traditional interfaces adopt leads naturally to a sequential organization for interaction—one thing at a time, with each step leading inevitably to the next. This ordering is used both to manage the interface and to simplify system development. For instance, "modal" dialog boxes—ones that will stubbornly refuse to let you do anything else until you click "okay," "cancel," or whatever they need—both structure your interaction with the computer, and save the programmer from the need to handle the complexity of worrying about other actions that might transform the system's state while the dialog box is displayed. When we move from traditional models to tangible computing, sequential ordering does not hold. It is not simply that interaction with the physical world is "parallel" (a poor mapping of a computational metaphor onto real life), but that there is no way to tell quite what I might do next, because there are many different ways in which I might map my task onto the features of the environment.

These two issues are particularly challenging from a technical perspective, because they address the programming models we use to develop systems, embedded in software toolkits and applications. The third feature of tangible interaction may, however, provide some relief. This is the fact that, in tangible design, we use the physical properties of the interface to suggest its use. This is nothing new; arguably, it is what product design or other forms of physical design are all about. Kettles are designed so that we can tell how to safely pick them up; remote controls are designed to sit comfortably in the hand when oriented for correct use (at least when we're lucky). What is more, this sort of design that recognizes the interaction between the physical configuration of the environment and the activities that take place within it can also be a way to manage the sequential issues raised earlier. For instance, Gaver (1991), in his discussion of "sequential affordances" (which will be presented in more detail in chapter 4), gives the example of a door handle, which, in its normal position, lends itself naturally to turning and then, in its turned position, lends itself naturally to pulling; the whole arrangement helps "guide" one through the sequential process of opening the door through careful management of the physical configuration of the artifact. Taking this approach, designers can create artifacts that lead users through the process of using them, with each stage leading naturally to the next through the ways in which the physical configuration at each moment suggests the appropriate action to take. The relationship between physical form and possible action can give designers some purchase on the problems of unbounded parallel action.

Interacting with tangible computing opens up a new set of challenges and a new set of design problems. Our understanding of the nature of these problems is, so far, quite limited, certainly in comparison to the more traditional interactional style that characterizes most interactive systems today. The theories that govern traditional interaction have only limited applicability to this new domain. At the same time, tangible computing has been explored, largely, as a practical exercise. Most prototypes have been developed opportunistically, driven as much by the availability of sensor technology and the emergence of new control devices as by a reasoned understanding of the role of physicality in interaction. We have various clues and pointers, but there is no theory of tangible interaction. Why does tangible interaction work? Which features are important, which are merely convenient and which are simply wrong? How does tangible computing mediate between the environment and the activity that unfolds in it?

This book is about developing answers to these questions. The interpretation that it will offer is one that is concerned not just with what kind of technology we use, or with what sorts of interactions we can engage in with that technology, but about what makes those interactions meaningful to us. From this perspective, the essence of tangible computing lies in the way in which it allows computation to be manifest for us in the everyday world; a world that is available for our interpretation, and one which is meaningful for us in the ways in which we can understand and act in it. That might seem to be quite far removed from looking at application prototypes, reactive rooms, and digital desks. The path from practice to theory will be easier to see after looking at the second aspect of embodied interaction—social computing.

3

Social Computing

Embodied Interaction draws together ideas from two areas of recent research in Human-Computer Interaction. The previous chapter dealt with the first, the tangible computing perspective that blends computation and physical design to extend interaction "beyond the desktop." This chapter will deal with the second, social computing.

Broadly speaking, social computing refers to the application of sociological understanding to the design of interactive systems. *Sociology*, though, is a very broad term. As a discipline, it encompasses a diverse set of interests, topics, objectives, concerns, and methodological approaches. Similarly, many different methods and topics from sociology have been applied to the design and deployment of interactive computer systems, from questions of the economic and social consequences of the information economy to studies of how the conversational paradigm for software compares with our own conversational behavior. Not all of these will be of concern here. In particular, nothing will be said here about the broad range of work on the social and economic consequences of computerization and automation, or other investigations that we might characterize as "social consequences" or "social policy" concerns. Although those are critically important and often neglected as aspects of the design process, they are not immediately relevant to the issue of embodied interaction.[1] Instead, this chapter will explore the way in which sociological methods and reasoning have increasingly been adopted as a part of the design, development, and evaluation of interactive systems. In other words, the relationship in "social computing" between sociological and technical issues is not just that of a sociologist talking about technology, but of sociologists and technologists working together in the design process.

At first blush, it might seem strange to look at interactive system design from a sociological perspective. Sociology is concerned with the structure and function of society, while interactive systems are tools that people use; we might as well study the sociology of screwdrivers.[2] However, although that position seems immediately appealing, the significance of a sociological approach becomes clear when we look at the *context* in which computation is put to work. Context can mean many things; it might be the tasks that the system is being used to perform, the reasons for which the tasks are being carried out, the settings within which the work is conducted, or other factors that surround the user and the system. The context, though, is as much social as technical. When we think in these terms, we can see that the work that computation does, and the uses to which we put it, are very much the sort of thing that a sociological perspective might help us to understand. Computation is part of a richer fabric of relationships between people, institutions, and practices that sociology can help us explore.

Another critical aspect of context that is often overlooked is the interaction between the designer and the user *through* the system. Human-computer interaction can be thought of as a form of mediated communication between the end user and the system designer, who must structure the system so that it can be understood by the user, and so that the user can be led through a sequence of actions to achieve some end result. This implies that even the most isolated and individual interaction with a computer system is still fundamentally a social activity. The communication between designer and user takes place against a backdrop of commonly held social understandings. Even the metaphors around which user interfaces are constructed ("private" files versus "public" ones, "dialog" boxes, electronic "mail," documents, wizards, and "publishing" a web page) rely on a set of social expectations for their interpretation and use.

However, sociology is not a unified discipline, but something of an umbrella term for a variety of theoretical and methodological approaches. Unsurprisingly, widely different sociological perspectives have been applied to different aspects of human-computer interaction and system design. In the discussion that follows, I am not going to attempt to describe them all, but instead will focus on a few particular approaches. They share three common characteristics. First, they are concerned with the details of the organization of social conduct rather than broad social trends. Second, they are primarily oriented toward real activities and experiences rather than abstractions or models. Third, they all adopt an anthropological perspective on collecting, interpreting, and using field materials. Although this is only a fraction of the possible range of concerns that could be addressed, two features recommend these approaches in particular. The first is their relevance to issues of embodiment, and so the sort of argument that I will develop from them; the second is their prominence, perhaps even dominance, in current HCI research.

As an introduction, I will begin by setting out some of the historical background and characteristics of the perspectives that we will encounter. That background will set the stage for a discussion of the adoption of sociological approaches in HCI.

Sociology, Ethnography, and Anthropology

One common feature of the set of sociological approaches that will be discussed here is their reliance on field materials, or observational studies of behavior. A fieldwork orientation contrasts with other possible approaches in sociology, including the use of laboratory studies, surveys, statistical techniques, or primarily theoretical analysis. In basing their investigations on fieldwork, the different approaches reveal a common tradition that originates not in sociology but in anthropology.

Sociology and anthropology are closely related, and in some places almost overlap; it can be hard to see where one ends and the other begins. Clifford Geertz (1973) suggests that whereas sociology examines the emergence and maintenance of social structures and patterns of social interaction, anthropology studies the cultural webs of signification that give those structures and interactions meaning. This distinction is perhaps unavoidably approximate, but it nonetheless sets out a rough and ready basis for distinguishing between the disciplines.

Anthropology, as a distinct body of enquiry, emerged in the mid-nineteenth century. In Europe, this was a period of colonial occupation, and it was the colonial experience that served as the basis for European anthropological research, drawing, in the first instance, on the reports and experiences of explorers, travelers, traders, and colonial officers.[3] At around the same time, American interest in anthropology grew out of the encounter with the Native American cultures, as represented particularly by the work of Franz Boas in the Pacific Northwest (Boas 1921).

One distinction between European and American approaches to anthropology at that stage was in their use of fieldwork and observational methods. By fieldwork, here, I mean extensive, detailed observations of the daily life and practices of other peoples. With the immediate and local availability of the native society, American anthropology was based in fieldwork from its inception. In Europe, however, the peoples who constituted the objects of anthropological interest were generally at some considerable distance from the anthropologists themselves. The result of this was that a good deal of European anthropology of the time was conducted from the safety and comfort of libraries, and compiled second-hand from field reports. The separation between experience and theorizing was largely taken as read, as illustrated by this snippet from a travel handbook:

It is the duty of every civilised traveller in countries newly opened up to research to collect facts, pure unvarnished facts, for the information of those leading minds of the age, who by dint of great experience, can ably generalize from the details contributed from diverse sources. (Johnson 1889:398)

So, perhaps the most radical change in European anthropology was to arise in the role of field work investigations, and in particular in the development of ethnographic methods.

The Emergence of Ethnography

Arguably, the dominant figure in developing the role of ethnography in anthropology is that of Bronislaw Malinowski. Malinowski was a Pole working in the United Kingdom in the early part of the twentieth century. In 1914, he joined a field trip to Australia and New Guinea under the leadership of C. G. Seligman. Unfortunately, war between Britain and Germany was declared while Seligman's party was en route from the United Kingdom to Australia; and Malinowski, as a subject of the Austro-Hungarian empire, was subject to internment on reaching the destination. However, he persuaded the authorities that, if their concern was merely to have him in a safe place where he could do no harm, there was no need to lock him up in an internment camp; they could, instead, let him spend the time ensconced in some remote place, safely out of the way.

The result was that Malinowski spent most of the following few years on the Trobriand Islands, an archipelago to the east of New Guinea. He spent this time in the detailed study of the culture and practices of the native population. His explication of the "Kula Ring," a hitherto mysterious practice involving arduous and dangerous sea journeys undertaken to engage in the ritual exchange of seemingly worthless gifts, is perhaps the best known of a landmark series of writings (Malinowski 1922, 1930, 1935) that emerged from this period of intensive observation of daily life among the Trobrianders, and in which he set out the principles that helped establish him as one of the preeminent anthropologists of his day.

Malinowski's work in the Trobriand Islands, however, is also a landmark in a different sense, not simply for what it revealed, but for how it was conducted. It is not least from Malinowski's long-term, in-depth engagement with the Trobriand Islanders, his analytic approach and form of reportage, that modern ethnographic fieldwork has been developed. In many ways, Malinowski established ethnographic fieldwork as the dominant paradigm for anthropological research.[4]

Ethnography places an emphasis on the detailed understanding of culture, through intensive, long-term involvement and what anthropologist Clifford Geertz (following Gilbert Ryle) calls "thick description." It is often based upon participant-observation, in which the ethnographer immerses himself or herself in the culture in question. The central element is to explore the member's own view of his or her life and culture. That implies the need to be able to describe not just what the members of that culture *do* but *what they experience* in doing it; why it is done and how it fits into the fabric of their daily lives. Of course, the idea that the member's perspective is primary does not mean that the ethnographer's job is simply to ask people what they're doing, write it down, and bring it home. The member's own report is clearly a major element in the story, but it cannot be accepted blindly. Rather, in attempting to represent the culture from the member's point of view, the ethnographer attempts to avoid preconceptions or analytic orientations from outside the specific setting of the investigation. In this way, the development of ethnographic fieldwork was a radical departure from approaches, such as survey-based work, that preceded it, at least in the European tradition.

Although ethnography developed as an approach to the anthropological investigation of "exotic" cultures, it has come to occupy an important place as a basis for fieldwork not just in anthropology but in sociology too. The cross-fertilization between two disciplines as closely related as anthropology and sociology is, of course, a continuous process; but for our purposes here, trying to trace the particular strands of development that have led to the role of ethnography in interactive system design, the work of the Chicago School of sociology is particularly relevant.

Ethnography and Sociology: The Chicago School   The Chicago School emerged from research conducted at the Department of Sociology at the University of Chicago. Particularly in the period from the 1930s until the 1960s, under the direction Robert Park and, later, Everett Hughes, Chicago sociologists engaged in a wide-ranging program of investigations focused particularly on urban and working life in contemporary America. In addition to a distinctive analytic perspective that they brought to these investigations, the Chicago School sociologists also adopted ethnographic, participant-observer approaches to the collection of field materials. The anthropological aspect to their writings is heightened by the fact that their topics are frequently subcultures on the fringes of ordinary society, such as those of tramps and hoboes, alcoholics, recreational drug users, and jazz musicians.

One particularly relevant feature of the work of the Chicago School was its detailed exploration of particular modes of work. Examples include Becker, Geer, Hughes, and Strauss's (1961) classic study of the "career" of medical students, as well as investigations of the working lives of nurses (Davis 1968), funeral directors (Hebenstein 1954), airline pilots (Wager 1959), janitors (Gold 1964) and schoolteachers (Becker 1952). The critical role that these played was to introduce a concern with the detail of how work gets done, and the use of ethnographic methods in studying working practice. This perspective, and the understandings that emerged about how work was conducted, subsequently came to play an important role in the adoption of sociological approaches in Computer-Supported Cooperative Work, such as in Gerson and Star's (1986) seminal paper on office procedures.[5]

By that time, though, sociology was already being adopted as an approach to understanding Human-Computer Interaction in other ways.

Sociology in HCI

HCI's "origin myth" traces its emergence to the development of a relationship between psychology and computer science. In particular, it originates (for many) in, first, the application of techniques and models from cognitive psychology to the problem of understanding what goes on when people work with computers and, at the same time, how those understandings can be reflected back into the design of those systems. Given the psychological background, then, it is perhaps not surprising that the first appearance of "the social" in HCI was not sociology but social psychology.

Social psychology is concerned with how an individual's thoughts and emotions are affected by interactions with others. With the advent of digital communication systems and computer networks, social psychologists became interested in how these interpersonal relations could be manifested in communication mediated by computer systems (e.g., Kiesler, Siegel, and McGuire 1984). For example, phenomena such as "flaming"—indulging in abusive and heated electronic mail exchanges—are extreme examples of social interactions whose existence seems to suggest some particular characteristic of electronic communication. More generally, computer-mediated communication provided a novel environment in which to study issues such as self-presentation, attribution of personality traits, and other features of everyday communication, and in turn to refine our understandings of how these take place in other communicative media.

So, in the same way that psychologists could help inform the design of interactive systems by understanding the cognitive implications of particular forms of design, sociologists could lend an understanding of the settings in which these computer systems would be deployed, and the ways in which they would both affect and be affected by those settings. At the same time, sociologists also introduced a set of techniques by which the workings of those settings could be examined and uncovered; methods, like ethnography, that could be used to gain detailed understandings of how work was conducted.[6] The effect of the introduction of these techniques was to broaden the scope of inquiry and show how the use of computer systems involved more than simply the user and the computer, but also the context of the activity that the user was engaged in—a turn, as one writer characterized it, from "Human Factors" to "Human Actors" (Bannon 1991).[7]

Currently, social science research features most prominently in HCI as part of the processes of requirements gathering and system evaluation. The use of ethnographic materials is most common here. Advocates for socially based studies of work have found that ethnographic approaches can be used to uncover requirements for a system design through the detailed observation of the working setting. In contrast, more traditional approaches—based perhaps on functional specifications or on laboratory-based usability studies—tend to be disconnected from the lived detail of the work. Usability evaluations are generally concerned with the detail of interactional features of software systems, are carried out in laboratories in controlled conditions, and measure performance on artificial tasks across a range of subjects; they are designed to answer questions such as, "Does our new visualization improve the speed with which people can find information?" From an ethnographic perspective, these sorts of questions are meaningless when decontextualized and examined in the sterile confines of a laboratory. Ethnographers look for a more direct engagement. The ritual gift exchange of the Kula Ring can only be understood within the context of the life of the Trobriand Islanders; by the same token, the only way to come to a good understanding of the effectiveness of a software system is to understand how it features as part and parcel of a set of working practices, as embodied by a group of people actually using the system to do real work in real working settings. Ethnographic studies, then, tend to take a broader view of the relationship between technology and work.

On a more analytic level, the use of ethnographic methods for this sort of work is also rooted in a distinction between *work processes* and *work practice*. Work processes are the formalized or regularized procedures by which work is conducted; procedures for authorizing payments, for ordering supplies, for repairing machines, or whatever. Work processes are captured and codified in rulebooks, manuals, recipes, and similar artifacts. In contrast, ethnographers in HCI have frequently drawn attention to work practice—the informal but nonetheless routine mechanisms by which these processes are put into practice and managed in the face of everyday contingencies. Work practice is frequently informal and seemingly innocuous, but often provides the lubrication that prevents formalized processes from seizing up. Filling out a form in pencil so that work can proceed before the numbers are finalized, proceeding without a rubber-stamp authorization when relevant managers are not available, routinely "calling ahead" to inform other people of work that might be coming their way, or responding to such a call by beginning to schedule time for jobs that have not yet arrived—these are all examples of the practices that people develop to make processes work. What the "working practice" researchers observe is that the actual, practical business of making processes work involves a considerable amount of approximation, invention, improvisation, and ad hoc-ery. "Getting things done" means being able to step outside the rules, being able to interpret and anticipate them, and so achieve a smooth organization of work despite everyday problems like lost receipts, broken fax machines, unreadable notations, missing ingredients, and absent colleagues.

It is important to recognize that the duality of practice and process is inevitable. No matter how clearly or carefully framed, a process description can never eliminate the need to interpret it for specific occasions. Similarly, the ways in which people may deviate from formalized procedures tend to reflect a better or more fruitful adaptation of the process to the specific circumstances in which the activity is carried out. So, in understanding and uncovering the everyday practices through which people manage and accomplish their work, the goal is not to eliminate them, nor is it to turn those practices into processes by rigidly appropriating them. Attempting to eliminate or stabilize practice would result in effects similar to the labor practice of the "work-to-rule": a rigorous adherence to process and procedure in which effective work grinds to a halt. Practice is always dynamic, arising as a way to mediate between processes and the circumstances in which they are enacted. The reason to study practice is to understand how this dynamic mediation takes place.

This is particularly relevant for the development of information systems where, all too often, designers presume that the formalized work processes set down in the organizational handbook constitute a perfectly adequate description of what actually goes on. They are encoded into software systems without accounting for the flexibility with which they will be put into practice. Work practice studies emphasize that the handbook's description is, inevitably, only a part of the story. Their view of the relationship between people and technology emphasizes the critical creative involvement of the people doing the work even in cases of what seems like rote procedure, ripe for automation. The emergence of Computer-Supported Cooperative Work from the "office automation" community was partly a result of different perspectives on this process/practice dichotomy.

The most common form of this sort of research, then, is the ethnographic investigation of a particular domain of work, with an eye toward the technological opportunities it offers or design constraints that it imposes. I will give two examples here, from the domains of air traffic control and factory production printing.

Ethnography of an Air Traffic Control Center

One of the best-known ethnographic field investigations of work carried out in the domain of CSCW is that into air traffic control conducted by a multi-disciplinary team of sociologists and computer scientists based at Lancaster University in England (Hughes et al. 1995).[8] In fact, commercial Air Traffic Control (ATC)—the real-time management of the air space occupied by commercial flights—has become something of a canonical workplace example in CSCW; in addition to the pioneering Lancaster work, ATC has been explored by a number of other researchers (e.g., Rognin, Salembier, and Zouinar 1998; Berndtsson and Normark 1999; Mackay and Fayard 1999). Although certain common features arise across these different studies, the Lancaster work will be the main focus here.

As an ethnographic study, the topic for this investigation was not the rules and procedures of air traffic control as they might be laid down in an organizational manual. Instead, it looked at the actual practice of air traffic control as it occurs and unfolds, moment by moment, day to day, and as it is executed and experienced by the air traffic controllers themselves.

One seemingly obvious thing to say about air traffic control, as it is done by air traffic controllers, is that it happens in air traffic control centers. Location is important. The fact that these sorts of studies are often referred to as "workplace studies" is significant; the work happens in a place, and the actual practical activity that is the object of investigation cannot be divorced from the environment or setting in which it unfolds. So the first place to look to understand air traffic control is the center itself.

At the air traffic control center, the focus of the controller's activity is one of a number of stations or "suites." Each suite is generally responsible for one "sector" of airspace and is manned by two air traffic controllers, two assistants, and one sector chief. Each suite provides staff with various resources to manage the air traffic, including radar displays and communications equipment.

In exploring the conduct of the work in situ, the Lancaster group began to uncover the particular importance of one of the resources by which the work is managed—the "flight strip." A flight strip is a strip of card approximately eight inches long and one inch tall that is used to represent a particular airplane en route through the sector. The various items on the strip show relevant information such as the call signal of the airplane, its heading and altitude, airspeed, and so forth. Flight strips are arranged in racks, arrayed in the working space of the air traffic controllers (see figure 3.1).

Although relevant flight information is maintained in a database and shown on the radar displays, it is not the electronic representations but rather the physical flight strips that are the primary focus of the air traffic controllers' activity and their primary resource in managing the air space. Indeed, the ethnographers observe, "It is possible, and on occasion necessary, to perform ATC with the strips but without radar. To do so with radar but not flight strips, however, would pose extreme difficulties" (Hughes et al. 1992:115).

Essentially, the controllers *manage the airspace by managing the strips*. For example, when a flight is instructed to move to a different level, the controller will write the new level on the strip underneath the current level indication; and when the pilot acknowledges the instruction, then the old flight level will be crossed out. During the transition, the flight strip represents not

(a)

(b)

Figure 3.1
Air traffic controllers use flight strips (*a*), arrayed in a bay by their console (*b*), to represent the work of managing air space. Photographs courtesy of Wendy Mackay and the Centre d'Etudes de la Navigation Aerienne.

just the plane, but also the plane's movement and the controller's work in managing the airspace. Strips can convey information not just through their contents, but also through their physical configuration. The arrangement of strips in the different racks available to the controller indicates the status of the various flights, and the controllers are observed to "cock out" strips (pulling them out of alignment) to draw attention to them and indicate that there is some pending work to be done.

So, by the ways in which they employ flight strips, the air traffic controllers transform some of the work of managing airspace into a physical process of monitoring and managing the set of strips corresponding to current traffic. This is more than simply using the strips to represent the state of the airspace. The work of managing the space becomes the embodied performance of physical activity, arising around the specific details of the work site itself.

Although strips are manipulated by individual controllers working at their suites, their role goes beyond individual controllers. Recall that the controllers work in teams, with two controllers working together with assistants and a coordinator. So, in addition to the work of managing the airspace, controllers also have to deal with the work of coordination between members of the team. Strips are used to tackle these problems too; the work of the team and the coordination of distributed activities are also intricately bound up with the physicality that the flight strips lend to the task. Flight strips arrayed around the workspace are not only a way of coordinating the work, but also a way of making it publicly accessible to others who understand how to read and interpret the physical configurations. Critically, the flight strips do not just represent the state of the airspace, but also represent the *activity of the controller* managing that space. The strips provide an easy, at-a-glance summary of the state of the work, manifested as part of the immediate environment, and this provides a resource to others who have to coordinate their work in that environment. So, for example, controllers coming on shift were observed to stand for a while behind the working controller, watching their activity to become familiar with the current state of the airspace. Watching the activities within the physical setting allows them to learn about the state of the work.

The Lancaster study looked at the management of air traffic not as an abstract, clinical affair, but as the practical and practiced everyday work of air traffic controllers. What it uncovered was the way in which this work is in every way organized around the features of the setting in which it takes place. The flight strips, for example, do not just record information, but are part of the very way in which the work is done, both for an individual controller and for the others whose activity must be coordinated with that of the controllers. For the system designers, partners in the investigation, this turned the design away from the management of decontextualized information toward the ways in which information resources could not only represent the work but also themselves be the medium through which the work was conducted.

Ethnography of a Print Shop

The second example I want to present here explores a different workplace. In this case, the setting is a production print facility. This is an industrial print shop handling small-scale print runs (that is, brochures, forms, manuals, and similar materials, rather than commercial books) for a variety of clients. The print shop is capable of handling all aspects of the printing process, including design, prepress, reproduction of various sorts, binding, and finishing. It handles large and small jobs, both regular and one-off. Bowers, Button, and Sharrock (1995) present an ethnographic investigation of this setting. In particular, they are interested in the relationship between, on one hand, the set of practices through which the print workers organize and arrange their daily activity, and, on the other, their use of a computer system that embodies a formalized model of the production printing process—in other words, the two sides of the process/practice coin.

One of the issues they investigate is how the print shop operators achieve what they call a "smooth flow of work" through the print shop. By a "smooth flow," they mean a balanced work load that keeps the print machines busy, avoids bottlenecks and backlogs, and ensures that all the print jobs are completed in a timely manner. These are all important concerns—expensive print machines are only producing income when they are running, bottlenecks put an undue load on people and resources, and timely completion is important if the print shop is to satisfy its customers. On the other hand, these goals may conflict, especially because the print shop has, at best, limited control over the jobs it will be asked to handle and the order in which they might arrive.

So, as Bowers and his colleagues observe, ensuring a smooth flow of work is not a straightforward process. It involves making skilled judgments about the requirements of each print job, anticipating likely future load, interleaving or concurrently carrying out different jobs, and so forth. It is a continual juggling of resources, demands, and expectations. Knowing that a regular job is about to arrive, for instance, the operators can anticipate the demands that will have to be met and organize their current workload more effectively in anticipation (perhaps clearing a machine that will soon be needed for another job). Similarly, the mix of jobs that are waiting to be performed at any given moment can affect the decisions about which jobs, or which *parts* of which jobs, should be performed next. Bowers, Button, and Sharrock detail a range of these practices and show how they feature as part of a system of practical reasoning about the work of the shop. Through these practices, the print-shop workers manage the practical problems of achieving a smooth flow of work.

However, the particular occasion for this investigation was the introduction of digital reprographic technologies and an associated system that offers the opportunity to manage and regulate the work of the shop. Digital reprographic machines offer a variety of features that traditional machines cannot, such as separating scanning from printing, storing digital files for printing later, offloading jobs from one machine to another, and so forth. In addition, because these new print machines are essentially computers, they can also communicate across a network with a management system designed to handle scheduling and job management. It could achieve this through an internal representation of the process of handling a print job—a "workflow" representation—that it could use to coordinate and account for print-shop activity. Although this offers a number of advantages and opportunities to both the management and the clients of the print shop, the fieldwork shows the negative impact that the system's introduction had on the ways in which the print workers organized their work.

Of course, the workflow system also set out to achieve a smooth flow of work. However, the formalized procedures around which it was built did not account for the ways in which the practical work of the print shop would often involve stepping *outside* the regularized and formal procedures. For instance, where the print-shop operators could, themselves, preallocate machine time to regular jobs whose arrival could be anticipated, the computer-based system could not begin to process a job that had not yet arrived in the shop. Similarly, while the print-shop workers could divide their time between two jobs, or complete a short job on one machine while a long job ran unattended on another, the computer system maintained a rigorous one-to-one relationship between jobs and operators that could not account for the standard practices by which the operators would actually manage their activities.

The outcome of the ethnographic work is to see the management of activity on the print-shop floor as a "setting-ed," "occasioned," or "situated" activity. In other words, the actual moment-to-moment organization of the work is contingent on the setting in which it emerges; the physical environment, the time of day, the stack of jobs awaiting completion, the materials available at hand, the understanding of the context of the work, and so forth. This is in contrast to the decontextualized view that the workflow system took, a view that focused on *this* job or *that* job but not on *the whole work of managing the print shop*. It failed to account for the real work of the print shop by divorcing that work from the setting in which it was carried out.

Both of these studies, then—in the print shop and at the air traffic control center—use detailed observation of the conduct of working activities to draw attention to the ways that people accomplish their work. The work doesn't just "happen"; it has to be *made* to happen by the people who do it. In turn, this "making" is not an abstract process, but one that is firmly tied to the setting in which the work takes place and the specific circumstances in which it emerges.

One of the reasons that both of these studies focus on the occasioned nature of the practical accomplishment of work features is that they are both drawn from a particular analytic position. Both of these investigations are ethnographies, of course, but in addition they both draw on a sociological perspective called ethnomethodology. Ethnomethodology is a sufficiently common perspective in the HCI literature that we should explore it a little more deeply.

An Analytic Perspective

Although, as I have shown, there had long been a general sociological interest in interactive technology, a decisive turning point for the role of sociology in HCI was the publication of Lucy Suchman's book *Plans and Situated Actions* (Suchman 1987). What Suchman set out in this book was a detailed analytic critique of the then-dominant paradigm for modeling human behavior in Artificial Intelligence; but, in focusing on "the problem of human-machine communication," she also provided the basis for a radical reorientation of the role that sociology could play in the development and analysis of interactive systems.

The primary focus of Suchman's critique is the notion of a "plan" as it then featured, both technically and conceptually, in the domain of Artificial Intelligence. The "planning" paradigm in AI is as old as the discipline itself (which, of course, is not so old). It models human activity in terms of the formulation and execution of plans. According to this paradigm, plans are scripts for sequences of actions. Plans are formulated through a set of procedures beginning with a goal, which is then decomposed into a sequence of subgoals. The subgoals may themselves be similarly and repeatedly decomposed, until the resultant subgoals are primitive enough that they can be achieved through simple actions. These simple actions can be pieced together in sequence to form a plan for achieving the main goal. As the plan is executed, the results of each action are monitored to make sure that the system is still on track; in case of failure, a new plan may be formulated. So, if I want to drink some coffee, I can reduce this to a sequence of subgoals (fetching the beans, grinding them, mixing them with water, and so on) that must be achieved in order to attain my primary goal. These subgoals have an ordering; to grind the beans, I will first have to fetch them from the jar where I keep my coffee; the water has to be boiling before I can use it, which means I'll have to fill the kettle, and so forth. If there's no coffee in the jar, I may have to make a new plan to go to the store. By a continual process of this sort, a plan is formulated, and then the process of actually making myself some coffee involves simply progressing through the plan and carrying out the actions it describes, monitoring and replanning as necessary (see figure 3.2).

The "planning" model was, at the time Suchman was writing, the dominant paradigm for the development of intelligent applications. It could be used to guide robot motion (goal: reach the door) or to create systems that derive mathematical proofs (goal: show that $x^2 > 2x$ for $x > 2$). It could be applied across a range of domains because of its seemingly natural occurrence as a feature of human problem-solving. What Suchman did, however, was to show how this model failed to take into consideration a range of ways in which social sciences had radically revised our

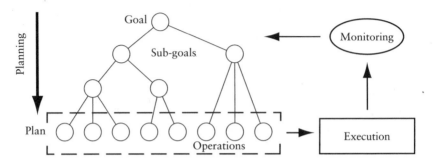

Figure 3.2
The planning model, in outline.

notion of how people act in the world. Drawing on a range of analytic perspectives, especially ethnomethodology, Suchman showed how the basic elements of the planning model had been under a sustained attack that questioned the cognitivist position. The planning model sees features of the world (and of our interaction with it) as stable, objective phenomena; this enables the relatively unproblematic execution of a plan formed around these objective phenomena. In contrast, Suchman presented a model of interaction with the world in which the apparently objective phenomena of the cognitivist model were, instead, active interpretations of the world formed in response to specific settings and circumstances. In this model, a "plan" might provide a resource that guides an individual's action, but the plan is not "executed." Instead, it is one of the features that shapes active individuals' moment-by-moment responses to the situations in which they find themselves. The sequential organization of behavior, in Suchman's model, is an ongoing, improvised activity. Our actions are organized in response to the features of the setting in which they arise; action is "situated."

Suchman used this perspective to explore the problem of human-machine communication. Her observation is that the planning model that so dominated cognitive science was also the basis of the design of interactive devices. Interaction models assumed that users engaged in actions according to preformulated plans, and used the same techniques in order to build up representations of users' skills and intentions. In terms of the planning model, intentions, requirements, steps, problems, and outcomes are all stable features of interaction to be used to build models of what the user needs and how to achieve it. Suchman provided detailed analyses of the interactional problems arising from the mismatch between, on one hand, the clean-cut, abstract, and stable models that a system might have of interaction and, on the other hand, the much more messy, immediate, and fluid circumstances in which the system's users find themselves.

One of the particularly important features of Suchman's work for the account I am developing here is that her investigation was an analytic one. Her goal was not to investigate the use of computer technology in some particular working setting, but rather to tackle the ways in which the account of cognitive action that the planning perspective represents is incommensurate with the analytic account of situated social action she presents. In doing so, Suchman turned sociological discourse in HCI away from the purely empirical, and introduced an analytic perspective to the discussion. In fact, as it turned out, she brought into particular focus the specific analytic position from which her argument was developed, that of ethnomethodology. Through the influence of Suchman's work, ethnomethodology came to be a prominent sociological position within HCI.

Ethnomethodology

Although ethnomethodology is a far from dominant or even widely understood position within sociology, it has nonetheless come to occupy a position of some significance within HCI, and particularly within CSCW. Suchman's early work is certainly one reason for this, but since that time a number of other ethnomethodologists have also turned their attention to technological issues. In fact, the ethnographies described earlier in this chapter—of air traffic control and of print-shop operation—both form part of a program of ethnomethodological investigations in CSCW.

Ethnomethodology originated in the work of Harold Garfinkel in the 1960s, first brought together in his book *Studies in Ethnomethodology* (Garfinkel 1967). Ethnomethodology is not simply another theory of social action, sitting comfortably alongside the others that have been put forward. Ethnomethodology rejects the very notion of abstract theorizing on which most analytic accounts are based, and practiced by "the worldwide social science movement and its armies of social analysts."[9] Ethnomethodology's program is a *respecification* of the issues, methods, and very terms of reference of sociology.

It arises from Garfinkel's reconsideration of one of the fundamental problems of sociology, the "problem of social order." This problem, essentially, deals with the question of how stable and orderly social facts and relations can arise out of the independent action of individuals. How is it that each of us acting on our own nonetheless reproduces a stable social world? This is arguably *the* central sociological problem, and it had been taken as such by Talcott Parsons, whose landmark book *The Structure of Social Action* (1937) sets out the theoretical model that dominated American sociology for decades.

Garfinkel was not simply attempting to work out some small but knotty theoretical problem that Parsons had left unaddressed. Instead, he wanted to question the very foundations on which Parsons's work, and all of conventional sociology, was built.

Emile Durkheim, one of the founding fathers of sociology, had observed that "the objective reality of social facts is sociology's fundamental principle" (Durkheim 1938). This principle motivated the scientific investigation of that objective social world, which, in turn, spawned the development of a variety of theories cast in terms of grand themes such as class, capital, and gender. For Garfinkel, however, the problem of social order undermined the whole edifice of sociological theorizing. For him, Durkheim's "objective reality of social facts" was not a principle at all, but a phenomenon. It was not to be assumed, formulated, and refined, but to be studied; it was the *topic* of sociology rather than the starting point. In Garfinkel's view, the objective of sociology was not to develop abstract theories of social reality, but rather, to understand how social reality was achieved; how people *made it work*. This study of the commonsense methods by which people manage and organize their everyday behavior, he called "ethnomethodology" (for the study, *logos,* of native, or *ethno-*, methods).

One way to understand Garfinkel's position on traditional sociological theorizing is to think about what sorts of things the theories are, and, even more importantly, who knows and applies them. These are, after all, theories of social action, governing the everyday action of members of society. However, in conventional sociology, these facts and rules are not available to us as members of society, but rather, remain to be uncovered by sociologists. Garfinkel uses the term "cultural dope" to describe the actor as theorized by conventional sociology, blindly acting in accordance with a set of social rules of which he remains unaware. Critically, though, ethnomethodology observes that people *do* have reasons for acting the way they do. They continually operate according to explicable mechanisms by which they regulate and organize their action and understand the action of others. These commonsense understandings ("common" in the sense that they are shared—"what everyone knows that everyone knows") are the object of ethnomethodology's investigation. Garfinkel denies the right of the professional sociologist to any privileged insight into the rules that govern everyday, orderly social action; to ethnomethodology, "lay and professional sociological theorising are epistemologically equivalent." In other words, in the course of everyday life, everyone, always, is engaged in "practical sociological reasoning," when, as part and parcel of what they do, they have to figure out what other people mean and in turn figure out how to act themselves in order to get things done. The knowledge that people bring to bear in carrying out this practical sociological reasoning is no less valid than the theoretical models that professional sociologists might offer when *they* try to figure out what "society does."

Ethnomethodology, then, turned its attention to the detailed analysis of actual practice, often drawing on ethnographic materials, and attempted to find, within them, evidence for the ways in which people achieved orderly social conduct. One particularly good example of this is the subfield of Conversation Analysis, pioneered by Harvey Sacks (1992). Sacks used recordings of real conversations as the basis for highly detailed analyses that attempted to uncover the mechanisms by which conversational interaction was structured. In these studies, again, we can see reiterated the theme of ethnomethodology, to look for the emergence of social order out of the details of what people do rather than from abstract theory. So, for example, Conversation Analysis claims that the word "hello" is not defined as a greeting in some vast social dictionary, but rather that specific *uses* of the word "hello" can *constitute* a greeting when interactionally organized in such-and-such a way or at such-and-such a time. It acts as a greeting when people use it as a greeting (at the opening of a conversation, or when someone arrives) and, as a corollary, it can also be used as, and be heard to be, something other than a greeting—an exclamation, an inquiry, a solicitation, an exclamation of surprise, and so forth when used in other ways or at other times.

The two ethnographic studies discussed earlier both reflect an ethnomethodological orientation. They used ethnographic methods to collect and arrange the field materials, but relied on ethnomethodology to inform the analysis. It provides a particular stance toward the organization of action that is reflected in the analysis of what the materials demonstrate and the conclusions that can be drawn from them. This pairing of ethnographic fieldwork and ethnomethodological analysis has often been a source of confusion in HCI. It has sometimes led people to believe that ethnography and ethnomethodology are the same thing, or that one necessarily implies the other. Certainly neither is the case. However, these two studies follow in a tradition of ethnomethodological studies of work, in which the ethnomethodologists' attention is directed toward the practical logic not of conversation or generic action, but of specific domains of activity. Examples include the work of the police (Bittner 1967), mathematicians (Livingston 1982), 911 call operators (Whalen 1995), and a range of studies of scientists (Garfinkel, Lynch, and Livingston 1981; Lynch 1982; Lynch, Livingston, and Garfinkel 1983).

Across these specific domains of inquiry, ethnomethodology takes the same approach. On the basis of specific observations of activity, it attempts to uncover the commonsense methods by which people achieve the orderliness of action. People invoke these methods as practical solutions to practical problems. While the concern with practical rationality and commonsense methods is a hallmark of the ethnomethodological approach, it does not entirely originate with ethnomethodology. In focusing sociology's attention on the experiences of everyday life rather than on abstract theorizing, Garfinkel was quite consciously following in a philosophical tradition called phenomenology. Phenomenology had originated with Husserl, but Garfinkel drew primarily from the work of Alfred Schutz, who had explored the consequences of Husserl's thought for theories of social action. Like ethnomethodology, phenomenology places primary emphasis on the experience of the everyday world rather than disconnected or abstract reasoning.[10]

The phenomenological character of ethnomethodology is an important element in the story of embodied interaction, and it will be explored at length in later chapters. First, though, I want to return to the issue of the relationship between social science and interactive system design.

"Technomethodology"

The two case studies presented earlier are examples of the most common way to use sociology in interactive system design. Sociological approaches can been harnessed to help us understand how work is conducted in real settings, and so, how interactive technologies can be designed to assist it (or at least, to hinder it less than they often do already). Although this approach can often result in better designs that are a much better fit for the ways in which people work, they do not go very far in addressing the kinds of critique that Suchman was making. Her target was not a specific design, but rather, the way in which a conceptual model was used to support a whole range of technologies. This is a much deeper issue. So a number of people have called for a deeper connection between sociological understandings and the design of interactive technologies. This would be an approach that deals not so much with *this* technology or *that* form of work, but rather more generally with interactive technology per se and the generally operative social processes that underpin any sociological account of behavior.

Graham Button and I coined the term *technomethodology* to describe a deeper relationship between technological design and ethnomethodology (Dourish and Button 1998). The word itself is a little flippant, but the model it proposes is not. By a "deeper" relationship, we mean one that satisfies two criteria. The first is that it attempts to draw not simply on a set of observations of a specific working setting, but rather on ethnomethodology's fundamental insights about the organization of action as being a moment-to-moment, naturally occurring, improvisational response to practical problems. The second is that it attempts to relate these understandings not simply to the design of a *specific* interactive system aimed at a *specific* setting, but rather, at the basic, fundamental principles around which software systems are developed—ideas such as abstraction, function, substitution, identity, and representation.

There are a number of reasons to look for connections at this more foundational level. One is that we believe that there are a number of *systematic* ways in which conventional system design undermines or removes the resources upon which human interactional behavior is based. (This is the sort of critique that Suchman made of the planning model.) If that is so, then we need to address the problems in an equally systematic way, considering not just this design or that design but the basic models around which those designs are built. A second reason is that we want to do this in a way that preserves the distinctive character of ethnomethodological reasoning, rather than simply the ethnographic observations of particular working settings.

Developing such a foundational relationship is a long-term objective. We have, so far, been approaching it by exploring particular areas of both technical and ethnomethodological interest, trying to find overlaps and mutual orientations to common issues. One that we have explored is the relationship between ethnomethodology's conception of "accountability" and the role that "abstraction" plays in the analysis and development of software systems. These two ideas are conceptually complementary, but in the differences between them lie some interesting problems for interaction.

Accountability   The notion of "accountability" is a fundamental feature of the ethnomethodological perspective. As we have seen, ethnomethodology's concern is with the commonsense understandings by which people find the world rational, and so available for their own practical actions and activities. Again, "commonsense" here means "commonly held," even if the domain is high-energy physics rather than more mundane matters. This is important because it highlights ethnomethodology's contention that what it means to be a member of a language community (or, perhaps, an "action-community") is to share a set of understandings of how to act, and how to understand action, within that community. In other words, "acting rationally" and "perceiving action to be rational" are reciprocal aspects of the same set of understandings. This is the basis of ethnomethodology's notion of accountability:

[The] central recommendation [of ethnomethodological studies] is that the activities whereby members produce and manage settings of organized everyday affairs are identical with members' procedures for making those settings "account-able." [. . .] When I speak of accountable, my interests are directed to such matters as the following. I mean observable-and-reportable, i.e. available to members as situated practices of looking-and-telling. I mean, too, that such practices consist of an endless, ongoing, contingent accomplishment: that they are carried on under the auspices of, and are made to happen as events in, the same ordinary affairs that in organizing they describe; that the practices are done by parties to those settings whose skill with, knowledge of, and entitlement to the detailed work of that accomplishment—whose competence—they obstinately depend upon, recognize, use and take for granted; and *that* they take their competence for granted furnishes parties with a setting's distinguishing and particular features, and of course it furnishes them as well as resources, troubles, projects and the rest. (Garfinkel 1967: 1–2).

This characteristically dense passage deserves close reading. There are two aspects of it that are especially relevant here: first, the explanation of what accountability is from an ethnomethodological perspective, and second, an exploration of how accountability arises as a feature of conduct.

Let's start with the first of these, the definition. As a feature of action, accountability, in this sense, does not mean moral or political accountability, as it might in everyday speech, but rather means "observable and reportable." Other members can observe and report, that is, make sense of, the action in the context in which it arises. These two concepts, membership and context, are important. Members are those who share the "common sense understandings," and the context in which action arises provides part of the means by which that action can be interpreted as understood as normal, rational action by them. The observable-and-reportable nature of conduct is available *to members* and as *situated* practices.

There is more than this, though. Accountability lies in the *reciprocality* of action and understanding. Garfinkel's argument is not simply that action can be found to be rational by those who understand it, but rather that the methods of understanding and making sense of action and the methods for engaging in it *are the same methods* ("the activities whereby members produce [action] . . . are identical with [their] procedures for making those actions 'account-able'"). In other words, being a competent member of some setting *is* being able to engage in action in ways that are recognizable to other members. So, the accountability of action is not simply the property of being recognizably rational as it emerges in context, but also that it is organized so as to allow this. The organization of action serves to demonstrate what that action is. Recall the example of conversation earlier; I suggested that the world "hello" does not carry "greeting-ness" as an intrinsic feature or property, but rather that it is *used* in such a way that people can understand that it is being used as a greeting, through the way it is said and interactionally organized within a conversation and a sequence of social action (e.g., when directed to a new person arriving in the conversation). This is a feature of conversational practice, that the organization of talk demonstrates features of that talk to members sharing an understanding of language practice. It is an example of the role of accountability.

The second aspect of accountability dealt with in the passage is *how* accountability arises as a feature of social action. Garfinkel details a number of features of the accountable nature of action, and in particular, the relationship between accountability and action. In particular, he emphasizes that action and accountability cannot be separated from each other ("made to happen . . . in . . . the same ordinary affairs that . . . they describe"). The accountable aspect of activity is never a "commentary" on the activity, standing separately from it; rather, it is an intrinsic and inseparable feature of how the activity is woven into the fabric of action and interaction. At the same time, he also emphasizes that the accountability of action is not an absolute matter. It is an "endless, ongoing, contingent accomplishment;" the account that matters is one that is good enough for the needs and purposes at hand, in the circumstances in which it arises and for those who are involved in the activity.

The analytic concept of accountability emphasizes that the organization of action, as it arises in situ, provides others with the means to understand what it is and how to respond in a mutually constructed sequence of action. It turns our attention away from simply the perceived result or outcome of an action, to include how that result is achieved. We pay attention not just to the destination, but also to the route taken to get there. Ethnomethodological investigations, such as those into the organization of conversation, show how this is critically important in providing a basis for rational mutual action.

However, this idea does not mesh very well with the way in which we currently design interactive software systems. In fact, in some ways, it seems that the design of software is carefully arranged to undermine this very principle. The problem lies in the way in which software relies on a notion of abstraction.

Abstraction   Software systems are built from abstractions. The extent to which abstraction is fundamental to software systems can be hard to explain to someone who hasn't built them; while to someone who has, it can be so ubiquitous as to have become invisible. But the very essence of software system design is the manipulation, combination, and creation of abstractions.

User interfaces offer us abstractions in the form of generic user interface components or "widgets" such as menus, buttons, labels, and scroll bars. Widgets are arranged to form an interface by a programmer, who manipulates them in the form of objects with certain definable and controllable characteristics (such as color, size, or font). These objects are abstractions in the traditional software sense—entities whose essence lies in the range of manipulations they allow, and whose inner workings can be ignored as long as the external constraints are maintained. The very notion of "object" in a software system is itself an abstraction, exposing the "essence" of the object (that is, exposing the ways in which it can be examined and manipulated) while hiding a range of details of implementation (such as where the object resides in system memory, or how the details of its internal components will be represented). Object systems are themselves implemented on top of programming languages, which are abstractly manipulated by other programs to yield machine-language representations, sequences of operations in the instruction set of whatever processor will run the program. Here, again, we encounter abstractions. The instruction set is an abstraction that hides a variety of possible implementations (as we see when "clone" processors appear using completely different technology to implement the same instructions, or when a manufacturer produces a new generation of processors that are "backward compatible" with last year's instruction set). Similarly, the notion of a uniform processor abstracts away the specific details of each individual device. Software systems, in other words, constitute a tower of mutually constituted abstractions, right down to the abstractions of binary logic that we use to isolate ourselves from the messy world of continuous voltages and variable current.[11]

Before it sounds as if I somehow disapprove of computational abstractions, I should make it clear that I do not. There are extremely good reasons that abstraction is such a fundamental principle. First, at each point in the chain from binary digits to interface widgets, abstraction makes it possible for us to treat a complex set of computational behaviors as a simple, higher-level object out of which we can build something new and even more useful. Second, it also allows us to use a single abstract object (such as a scroll bar) to capture a range of potential needs and uses. Third, it helps isolate one component from another so that they can be managed and maintained separately. Without these properties, it would be impossible to build a modern software system. Abstraction also offer some very practical, everyday opportunities to the users of computer systems. The flexibility implied by reusable abstractions is one of the reasons for the success of general purpose computing systems today—it allows them to be a word processor one minute, a financial planner the next, and a game once you're done working. At the same time, we rely on the isolation offered by abstractions every time we install a new piece of software on an old PC (or upgrade the machine without having to buy completely new hardware).

The essence of abstraction in software is that it *hides implementation*. The implementation is in some ways the opposite of the abstraction; where the abstraction is the gloss that describes how something can be used and what it will do, the implementation is the part under the covers that describes how it will work. If the gas pedal and the steering wheel are the abstraction, then the engine, power train, and steering assembly are the implementation. Hiding the implementation and dealing with something in terms of its abstraction allows us to *isolate* one piece of a system from all the rest, and so to adopt a modular approach to design that sees the system as an assembly of interoperating components, with all the advantages alluded to earlier.

By enabling a modular, component-based approach to design, the idea of "information hiding" has become critical throughout the design of software systems. However, at the user interface, the situation is more problematic. Within a system, we know that the different components will interact in fixed and predictable ways. Users are less predictable, though, and their actions less fixed. Users may have different goals in mind, different reasons for using the system and different ways in which they want to use it. In just the same way as they approach all other activities, they need to be able to decide what to do in order to get things done. In everyday interaction, as we have seen, ethnomethodology argues that accountability is the key feature that enables them to do this. The way that activities are organized makes their nature available to others; they can be seen and inspected, observed and reported. But this feature—the way that actions are organized—is exactly what is hidden by software abstractions. Not by accident, either, but by design. In the "information hiding" approach, the information that is hidden is information about how the system is doing what it does, how the perceived action is organized.

Here is an example. Most computers store files in a hierarchical arrangement of folders and subfolders. Many, these days, also offer networked file servers, which store files centrally for users connected across a network. Generally, these file servers are arranged so that they appear as part of the local file system. They look like another disk on your PC; or perhaps you have a folder on your desktop that is actually located on the remote system, but which you use just as if it were local. It even looks the same. Dragging a file onto that folder doesn't write it directly to disk, but transfers it across the network to be stored on the file server.

The transfer is "transparent"; it happens automatically as part of the action of moving the file. This transparency is something of an illusion, of course, because there are at least two ways in which transparency breaks down and the network comes into view. The first is performance; copying a file across a network is slower than doing the copy on your own disk, and so the operation will take a good deal longer. The second is "failure modes"; because there are more things that can go wrong (network errors, remote server crashes, and so forth), there are more and different sorts of errors that can result from the networked copy than the local one (which will generally only fail because your disk is full).

The abstraction argument claims that the differences between the local folder and the remote folder do not matter. Both of them implement the "folder" abstraction, which captures all the relevant features of folders; any other differences are simply "a matter of implementation." However, the ways in which the copy is not transparent *do* matter. The differences between the folders *are* consequential. Two folders on my desktop, one for my local disk and one for a file server, may look the same, but I will use them differently. I arrange my work around the ways in which they work; for instance, although it might be acceptable to keep document files on the file server, I need much faster access to the program source files that make up my current project when I try to compile them, and so I will partition my work across these two disks as is appropriate. However, the means to make my decision—that is, the different characteristics of these two folders—are not revealed by the interface. The whole point of the interface, in fact, is to ensure that a single abstraction, the folder containing files and subfolders, is supported uniformly by both the local and remote implementations. The features that matter to me as a user are ones that have been hidden by the interface and by the abstraction that it supports.

Accountability in Interface Abstractions   The question is: Would it be possible to address this problem by introducing a form of "accountability" for the interface, or more generally for the abstractions in terms of which computer system design is organized? Accountability, in this sense, means that the interface is designed so as to present, as a part of its action, an "account" of what is happening. The goal of the account is to make the action of the system concrete *as a part of* an ongoing interaction between the system and the user. So, the account should not simply be an abstract description of the system's behavior, but rather an explication of how the system's current configuration is a response to the sequence of actions that has led up to this moment, and a step on the path toward completing the larger action in which it is engaged.

The design of a user interface that presents such an account is certainly challenging, and elsewhere I explore some specific examples that are suggestive of a general pattern (Dourish and Button 1998). The user interface determines the form of the account, but that is not what I want to focus on here. The important issue here is not the *account,* but *accountability*— that is, how the account is related to the behavior it describes.

The relationship between an account and the behaviour it accounts for is the key feature of accountability in Garfinkel's analysis of social action, and so it is for us here too. It requires a technical approach that provides three primary features. First, we need to find a way to ensure that the account that is offered of the system's behavior—a representation of that behavior—is strongly connected to the behavior that it describes. The goal is not to ensure that they can never disagree, but rather that the programmer can be in control of the ways in which they agree or differ. Second, we need to find a way to allow this representation to be tied to the action in such a way that the account emerges along with the action rather than separately from it. The account is not a commentary on the activity it describes, but is part and parcel of the activity as it is carried out. Third, we need to ensure that the account that is offered is an account of the current specific behavior of the system, in its current configuration and tackling exactly this piece of work, rather than a generic account that says little more than, "Oh, this is how the system generally behaves."

One promising way that we have been exploring to achieve these goals is through the use of a software design technique called "computational reflection" (Smith 1984; des Rivières and Smith 1984). The reflection technique emerged originally in the domain of AI programming, but has found perhaps its most widespread application in the design of programming languages (e.g., Kiczales, des Rivières, and Bobrow 1991). The observation upon which reflection rests is that there are two domains of concern in the execution of any program; the domain about which the program is dealing (e.g. cells and formulas for a spreadsheet, words and paragraph formats for a word processor, or tanks and spaceships for a game) and the domain of the program itself (comprising its internal structures, program encoding, execution state, and so on). Normally, these two worlds of representation are kept separate. However, reflection provides a link between them. The reflective link allows a programming system to change the domain of its operation from one to another; to perform computation using not only the representations that refer to the outside world but also those internal representations that refer to its own operation. This gives a program the ability to describe its own internal state and even to operate upon itself by revising those internal structures. The link between the two domains is called the "causal connection" between the representation of a program and its own behavior. The connection is "causal" because it allows the program not only to view but also to change the way that the internal structures operate. The difference between a computer's representation of a book in a library database and its representation of its own program is that it can effect changes on the program representation, whereas no amount of computation in the database system can move the book from a borrower's desk back to the library shelf. The system's representation of its own behavior is within its effective reach. What is more, the representation of the program not only *describes* the program, but also *gives rise* to it; the program is, in effect, no more than the "performance" of the representation.

So, the "causal connection" is a two-way relation between a program and its reflective representation. As the program executes, the representation is changed; as the representation changes, so the behavior of the program is transformed. Reflection's causal connection is also a route toward accountability in interactive systems. It provides the features required of the relationship between an account (representation) and the actual behavior of a system (program). It ties the two together in a way that can be controlled (because the system itself is managing the representation), that ensures that the account emerges inseparably from the action it describes (because it is not only a description of it but also the source of that action, and therefore cannot be separated from it), and that it describes the specific, ongoing activity of the system rather than an abstract and generic specification of it (because it reflects the here-and-now).

The details of using the reflection approach in interactive system design are not relevant here, and are still a topic of ongoing research. What is important, though, is that it turns on the ability to change the subject matter of a computation, from the representations of external entities to the internal representations by which those other representations are sustained. This ability to redirect and refocus attention and reference will be a significant element of the account of embodied interaction to be developed shortly.

The proposal that reflection can provide a basis for interface accountability is a radical one, but not necessarily in the ways that people sometimes imagine. For example, it is sometimes interpreted as a proposal that interface representations can be "meaningful" in the same sense as human ones, or that by this representational sleight-of-hand we can make computer systems interact in just the same ways as people do. Of course, this is not the case. Reflective interface design does not mean that computers and humans are "conversing" on the same level, or even that the structure of computer-based dialog will now mirror that of human conversation. The accountability of the user interface is not the accountability of human social action. Despite the fact that its implementation turns on a rather esoteric technique, the proposal can actually be thought of as being very straightforward. Put simply, it says that because we know that people don't just take things at face value but attempt to interrogate them for their meaning, we should provide some facilities so that they can do the same thing with interactive systems. Even more straightforwardly, it's a good idea to build systems that tell you what they're doing.

What is radical about the proposal is something quite different. What is radical is the relationship it proposes between technical design and social understandings. It argues that the most fruitful place to forge these relationships is at a foundational level, one that attempts to take sociological insights into the heart of the process and fabric of design.

Technomethodology is, perhaps, the most extreme proposal to bring these two elements together. However, it is by no means the only attempt to take the relationship between sociological reasoning and system design to be a deep one. By contrast with the technomethodological approach, let us consider one of a rather different nature.

Space, Place, and Locales

Our second example is a rather more obvious place for sociological understandings to provide insight, inasmuch as it focuses on collaborative settings in which social action takes place. However, what it has in common with the technomethodology approach is that it attempts to forge deeper connections between the disciplines than simply requirements for the operation of a particular system in a particular working setting, and to provide a more general set of understandings that are applicable across a range of applications and domains. This example concentrates on the development of spatial models and metaphors in interactive and, especially, collaborative systems.

The idea of "space" is a fundamental aspect of how many interactive systems operate. System designers create spaces of all sorts; virtual ones such as "name spaces," and real ones such as the two-dimensional computer "desktop" on which files and icons are arrayed. Across these different sorts of spaces, there are certain common elements. For instance, things generally appear *within* the space. There can generally be only one object at any given point in space. Things tend to stay where they've been put. Spaces define distances; things can be nearby or far apart once they're in the space. And so on.

There is no mystery to the pervasive use of space as an organizing principle in user interface or software design. Space is so fundamental to our everyday experience that it permeates the way we think. In their book *Metaphors We Live By*, George Lakoff and Mark Johnson (1980) explore the role that metaphor plays in human cognition, by looking for key metaphorical ideas around which a host of specific metaphors arise. For instance, the core metaphor "argument is war" leads to such expression as "He went on the offensive," "She destroyed my argument," "His position is indefensible," "They won the point," and so forth. Many of their examples emphasize the importance that spatial concepts play in our thinking and our language; notions of distance (such as when two positions are "far apart"), up and down (up, they observe, is generally good, and down bad), and so forth.

The use of spatial metaphors as a basic organising principle has been adopted particularly within certain areas of Computer-Supported Cooperative Work (CSCW). One feature of the spatiality of the everyday environment, after all, is that we share it in common, and so a number of researchers have argued that spatial models provide a natural metaphor for collaborative systems design. So, "shared workspaces" of one sort or another have become a common feature of many collaborative tools. In particular, the design of Collaborative Virtual Environments (CVEs) such as DIVE (Frecon and Stenius 1998) or MASSIVE (Greenhalgh and Benford, 1995) uses space as a way for people to manage their accessibility, orient toward shared artifacts, and provide a "setting" for particular forms of interaction. The spatial model in a CVE can be used to manage interactions between individuals, by, for example, requiring that they stand close to each other and face each other in order to have a conversation. In turn, this use of the spatial setting means that others will be able to see that two individuals are oriented in that way, and so understand that they are talking to each other. So, the design of CVEs is arranged to exploit the ways in which we understand how to interact with each other in the real world; CVE designers argue that by reproducing the consequences of spatial arrangements in virtual environments, those same interactional patterns can be carried over to the online setting.

However, over the last few years, an alternative view has emerged concerning the role of space in collaborative settings. It argues that "space," although important, is not the constitutive element of the ways that interactions are organized in these settings. Instead, the new view draws a distinction between those interactive phenomena that are derived from the nature of the *space* in which they unfold, and those that are instead predicated on an understanding of the *place* that is occupied (Harrison and Dourish 1996).

The distinction between space and place is, approximately, a distinction between the physical and the social. "Space" is largely concerned with physical properties (or metaphorical physical properties). It concerns how people and artifacts are configured in a setting; how far apart they are, how they interfere with lines of sight, how actions fall off at a distance, and so on. By configuring the space in different ways, different kinds of behaviors can be supported. A raised stage, facing banked rows of seats, supports presentations to large crowds, while clusters of low, comfortable seats are more conducive to intimate or informal conversations. However, space is not enough to account for the different kinds of behaviors that emerge in different settings. Two settings with the same physical configurations and arrangements of artifacts may engender quite different sorts of interactions due to the social meaning with which they are invested. For example, although the stage of an academic conference is physically configured in ways very similar to a concert hall, it is generally not appropriate to get up and sing there. Similarly, meeting rooms and dining rooms can have similar arrangements, but we behave differently in them. Our behavior in these environments is governed by social norms, not by physical constraints. So while "space" refers to the physical organization of the environment, "place" refers to the way that social understandings convey an appropriate behavioral framing for an environment. It's not for nothing that we use the term "out of place," but not "out of space"; the idea of "place" often plays a much more central role in determining behavior.

Our reason for setting up this contrast, of course, is to consider design implications. What are the design implications of taking a view centered on "place" rather than "space"? I'll outline three here.

The first is that it turns our attention away from the structure of the space and toward the activities that take place there. Activities take center stage, and the structure of the space in which they happen falls away except in as much as it features as a part of those activities. So, for example, in collaborative environments, an appeal to "real-world" metaphors—to three-dimensionality, to reciprocity of movement and access, and so forth—is valuable only in as much as it contributes *directly* to the activities that take place there. Of course, the structure of the environment is often a key issue in controlling how interactions develop. Tom Erickson (1999) provides an enlightening example centered on the collaborative production of limericks in a chat room, and he makes a very convincing argument for the way in which the specific design details of the chat software involved play a significant role in engendering the particular sort of word play at work in his example; Lynn Cherny (1999) has some similar examples drawing on interaction in textual multiuser environments. However, in both of these cases, the spatial features themselves are not brought into the foreground as design elements; they emphasize not how to *design the space*, but how to *design for the interaction*. This is an important difference.

The second consequence is that "place" reflects the *emergence of practice*. That is, it is knowledge that is shared by a particular set of people based on their common experiences over time. Practice emerges over time in the space; but at the same time, the space is also turned toward the particular needs of the moment. Take an everyday example. In a meeting room, chairs are moved around to fit the occasion and the group of people. Discussions may work best in a circle where everyone can see everyone else; presentations, on the other hand, require a different configuration of the environment. A meeting room in which the chairs and tables were fixed down and did not support these kinds of fluid rearrangements would not be a popular or a pleasant place. We need to be able to customize the space to our changing needs; we need to be able to *appropriate* it to the purposes at hand. Similarly, in virtual environments, we also need the ability to turn and twist the setting to suit our immediate purposes, which in turn requires that the environment be malleable enough to support this sort of appropriation. The important point to recognize here is that these practices emerge not from the designers of the system, but from the actions of its users. This means two things; first, that true places emerge only when really occupied day-to-day, not in demonstrations or experiments that last a few hours; and second, that place can't be *designed,* only designed *for.*

The third consequence of the place-centric view is that an idea of place is relative to a particular *community* of practice. The practice that constitutes the place is shared by a particular set of people. The community of practice might be defined by a particular set of skills or training; it might be defined according to a particular point in space and/or moment in time. But places will be different for different communities in the same setting. So, for example, a shopping street will be a different sort of place early in the morning, when the delivery trucks arrive; in the afternoon, as children swarm out of school; in the evening, as people come out to meet and dine; and on a lazy weekend afternoon, as people sit in cafes, to chat, see, and be seen. Similarly, we can see these sorts of differences in technological settings, such as the wide range of responses that people might have and practices they might develop around communication technologies. The same sort of regular patterns of people associated with particular times of day can be seen, for example, in MUDs (Curtis 1992); and one of our experiences with media space technologies was the range of different expectations and practices that arose around privacy and connection models even with very similar technologies and overlapping groups (Dourish 1993).

This understanding of the ways in which behavior depends on the social connotations of physical settings has also been a topic for sociological investigation. Perhaps the best-known social scientist to tackle these questions was Erving Goffman. Goffman's book *The Presentation of Self in Everyday Life* (Goffman 1959) drew attention to the ways in which people managed their conduct as a way of managing the impressions that others would form of them, and how, consequently, the ways in which they conduct themselves will vary with the particular "audiences" for their conduct at any given moment. Drawing on a theatrical metaphor, he contrasted "front-stage" and "back-stage" behaviors. So, for example, shop assistants will treat customers deferentially when "on-stage" (that is, on the shop floor) but act differently when among themselves in the back of the store. Front-stage and back-stage are not specific locations, of course, but rather are situations from which particular modes of conduct are drawn; and similarly, there may be multiple degrees of front-stage-ness or back-stage-ness.

The Locales Framework

In addition to Goffman's work, the idea of place as a setting for action has also featured in other sociological writings. In Structuration Theory, Anthony Giddens (1984) uses the concept of "locale" to capture the same idea:

Locales refer to the use of space to provide the settings of interaction. [. . .] It is usually possible to designate locales in terms of their physical properties, either as features of the material world or, more commonly, as combinations of those features and human artifacts. But it is an error to suppose that locales can be described in those terms alone. (Giddens 1984:188)

So, if these examples demonstrate the way in which place has featured in sociological theorizing, then we can look for attempts to relate these understandings to the practice of design, in ways perhaps similar to the technomethodological approach we have already encountered. One is the framework developed by Geraldine Fitzpatrick (1998) as a foundation for the design of collaborative systems.

Fitzpatrick's work on the "Locales Framework" uses locales as the central element of a framework designed to help system designers understand the social organization of activity and to support design activities that take these understandings into account. Although the term *locale* is that used by Giddens, the Locales Framework is in fact built around the theory of action developed by Anselm Strauss (1993). Various elements of Strauss's model of activity are woven into the framework in such a way as to reveal their interconnectedness with respect to particular settings for study and design.

The Locales Framework has five primary components or *aspects,* called Foundations, Civic Structure, Individual Views, Interaction Trajectory, and Mutuality.

Foundations encompasses the social world being addressed, and the sites and means that make up the locale. The idea of a social world is drawn directly from Strauss. A social world is a group of individuals brought together by a common commitment to collective action; both the common action or goal, and the communicative means by which a collective orientation can be established, are central elements of the idea. Social worlds, too, are settings for action, and action is carried out against a backdrop of previous activities (and with an expectation of future ones), so the social worlds perspective attempts to address not merely social groupings, but the *dynamics* of social action. Elements of the social world to which the Locales Framework draws attention include membership, duration, structure, roles, culture, focus, and tasks. The activities of a social world are supported by *sites* (the spaces or domains of activity) and *means* (the "furnishings" of a site). Whether sites are real or virtual, the introduction of sites and means relates the actions of the social world to specific manifestations and objects of action. In Fitzpatrick's framework, a Locale arises from the relationship between a social world and the sites and means by which its activity is carried out.

On top of this foundation, the other aspects of the framework incorporate other elements of social settings. Civic Structure examines how the locale relates to others. In the same way as the meanings of actions are constituted by the other actions that come before and after them, so, too, can locales only be understood in relation to others. Going in the other direction, locales are also made up of individuals who have their own perspectives, concerns, roles, and forms of participation; the Individual Views aspect of the framework addresses this.

Strauss uses the term *Trajectories* to refer to the emergence of a particular course of action as it may be evolved through time and involving multiple actors. In relation to the rest of the framework, this ties together the way in which actions are situated within particular histories, and the notion of the collective action of social worlds. Similarly, social worlds have trajectories, as do individuals. The Interaction Trajectory aspect of the framework introduces Trajectory as a way of understanding how social worlds develop, how people enter and leave, and how the activities in which they engage contribute to the various courses of action in which the social world is engaged. The temporal aspect of Trajectory also provides the means to consider phases, rhythms, and schedules—dynamic aspects of action that are more than simply sequence.

Finally, the Mutuality aspect explores the way in which these elements are made manifest or present in a space as a consequence of the manifestation of entities in a shared environment, made mutually accessible to the other participants:

For interaction to happen in a locale, there are basic requirements for presence and awareness. First, the potential interactants need some form of representation or way of making themselves (or being made) *present* in the locale. Secondly, the potential interactants need some way of being *aware* of the other's presence. Both presence and awareness possibilities for the interactants are facilitated by various *mechanisms* that are part of the locale domain(s). [. . .] For the purpose at hand, the interactants will make selective choices, consciously or unconsciously, about the use of such mechanisms or features according to their *capability* to do so. Hence, mutuality is the interplay of presence and awareness for interaction purposes, mediated by capability and choice. (Fitzpatrick 1998:134; emphasis in original)

So, where the locale foundations explored the sites and means of action—the furnishings of the locale—Mutuality considers the ways in which these sites and means are made manifest to members of the social world, and the ways in which those members and their activities are themselves made manifest to others *through* the sites and means of action, are key elements in the ongoing maintenance of the social world.

In terms of the directions explored in this chapter, the Locales Framework, first, takes the distinction between place and space and uses it to talk about the issues of the setting in which action unfolds; second, relates it to a specific set of theoretical insights into the organization of social action; and third, arranges this in such a way as to support the design of novel systems.

The goal of the Locales Framework is not to present a theory of social action, but rather to package a set of sociological understandings so that they can be used to inform the analysis of working situations and the design of technologies to support cooperative work. It reflects a distinct orientation toward design, and so its effectiveness has to be judged in terms of the ways in which it can be applied in design settings.

The most fully developed application of the Locales Framework to design is in a system called Orbit (Mansfield et al. 1997), an environment for distributed collaborative work. Orbit was the successor to an earlier system called wOrlds (Fitzpatrick, Tolone, and Kaplan 1995), and it is perhaps in the differences between wOrlds and Orbit that we can see most clearly the influence that the Locales Framework had on the system's design. Orbit and wOrlds are both persistent collaborative workspaces, but they embody different approaches to the organization of activity in the workspace. If wOrlds was a system built around "space," then Orbit was one that took "place" as its primary focus. For wOrlds, the simulation of aspects of a shared physical environment was the primary mechanism by which activities could be migrated from the physical to the virtual environment. In Orbit, by contrast, the design is organized around the social action that takes place in the space and the ways in which the space provides a setting for the activities of people engaged in common tasks. Where wOrlds provided rooms that gave participants shared access to artifacts, Orbit provides a more nuanced sense of participation, in response to the ways in which people may occupy many different social worlds at a time, with greater or lesser degrees of intensity, and in different roles. Similarly, in Orbit, mechanisms are provided for maintaining a richer view of activity in the space, both synchronously and asynchronously, as uncovered by the mutuality aspect of the Framework.

The Locales Framework provides a basic set of orientations toward the problems of social action—ways of looking at social settings and systematically uncovering the issues at work—for the purpose of design. When the task is finding a way to make sociological understandings available to computer scientists for their unashamedly practical ends, there is clearly a set of compromises to be made. The same is true for the idea of technomethodology explored earlier. Relating sociological understandings to technical design principles is a different enterprise from either sociology or system design, with different goals and methods. What determines success at the end of the day is the ability to develop systems that resonate with, rather than restrict (or, worse, refute), the social organization of action.

Although the topics addressed by the Locales Framework and the technomethodology approach are radically different, they have some of the same spirit. In different ways, they attempt to draw out relationships between aspects of technological design and aspects of sociological analysis. They provide frameworks that help system designers invest interactive systems with sociological understandings. In their attempt to develop a model of "social computing," they look for deeper connections than the ethnographic requirements capture approach. Although this is a riskier approach, it is one that offers considerable payoff.

Summary

This chapter has introduced a wide range of approaches to understanding social action and its relationship to the use of technology. These different approaches are not all compatible, and they reflect different sets of assumptions and commitments. Rather than focus on these differences, though, I want to try to draw out some common features.

First, a common theme through this chapter has been that social action is *embedded*. By this I mean that it is firmly rooted in the setting in which it arises, where that setting is not just material circumstances, but social, cultural, and historical ones as well. When talking about social action, we need to talk about the specifics of the action, when and how it arose, where and for whom it was conducted, and so forth. This concern with specifics often means, at the same time, a concern with the *mundane* aspects of social life, the taken-for-granted background of everyday action. This is a distinctive element of the sociological positions we have looked at here, even though they may themselves take different perspectives.

However, the observation that social action is inseparable from the uncountable minutiae of everyday life does not mean that it is completely chaotic. Social action is clearly organized. The focus of our attention, though, changes when we see social order as emerging from practice. The focus of attention becomes *how* orderly social conduct emerges from the detail of each setting in which it is undertaken, and how orderliness is *achieved* in the face of the endless contingencies to which it is subject.

When interactive technology enters the picture, it does so in a variety of ways. First, it is itself part of the setting; the specific features of each technology and how they are deployed and used introduce transformations to the conduct of everyday action. So, for example, the ways in which electronic communication systems have tended to increase our connectedness to each other and access to information have, in turn, changed our expectations about the availability of other people or information sources; being "out of touch" for a week seems strangely quaint (and ever harder to achieve). Second, technology is increasingly the medium within which activity takes place. We are used to the ways in which the physical world mediates our actions, and how it forms a shared environment whose characteristics are thoroughly predictable; when we converse face to face, I understand how my gestures will appear to you (and in fact, if I didn't, there would be little point in making them). Technological systems as a medium for social conduct are very different inasmuch as the inherently disconnected, representational nature of computer systems means that actions can be transformed in unpredictable ways. Finally, technological systems are themselves embedded in a set of social and cultural practices that give them meaning at the same time as being constrained and transformed by them.

Putting these together yields the conclusion that, just as the embedded approach to social action turned attention to how the orderliness of social conduct was achieved (rather than simply assuming it), so too, given the role that technology places in social settings, the key question is to understand *how* the relationship between technology and social action comes to be worked out in different situations, and from these to understand how the features of technological design and the features of everyday social settings are related.

4

"Being-in-the-World": Embodied Interaction

Chapters 2 and 3 introduced tangible and social computing, two current research directions in Human-Computer Interaction. HCI, of course, encompasses much more than these two areas of research, but the goal was not to be comprehensive. The goal, instead, was to provide enough background to support an argument that, despite the fact that they are normally taken to be different research agendas, tangible and social computing are in fact two different aspects of the same program of investigation. This chapter sets out to show how.

Chapter 1 considered the development of HCI in terms of the human skills and abilities that interactive technologies draw upon. Understanding the relationship between tangible and social computing means finding the common skills and abilities they exploit.

One straightforward observation is that they both smooth interaction by exploiting a sense of "familiarity." Tangible and social computing both capitalize upon our familiarity with the everyday world, a world of social and physical interactions. As physical beings, we are unavoidably enmeshed in a world of physical facts. We cannot escape the world of physical objects that we lift, sit on, and push around, nor the consequences of physical phenomena such as gravity, inertia, mass, and friction. But our daily experience is social as well as physical. We interact daily with other people, and we live in a world that is socially constructed. Elements of our daily experience—family, technology, highway, invention, child, store, politician—gain their meaning from the network of social interactions in which they figure. So, the social and the physical are intertwined and inescapable aspects of our everyday experiences. Tangible and social computing are both attempts to capitalize on those experiences and our familiarity with them. They make interacting with the computer seem more like those arenas of everyday action with which we are more familiar and in which we are more skilled.

However, the idea of "familiarity" is a fairly shallow way to relate these concepts; I want to suggest deeper connection. In exploring the relationship between tangible and social computing, my argument is based on the hypothesis that they are not just exploiting similar approaches, but are actually founded on the same idea.

The idea that underlies each of them is what I will call *embodiment*. Embodiment is the common way in which we encounter physical and social reality in the everyday world. Embodied phenomena are ones we encounter directly rather than abstractly. For the proponents of tangible and social computing, the key to their effectiveness is the fact that we, and our actions, are embodied elements of the everyday world.

The goal of this chapter is to introduce, explain, and explore the idea of embodiment, and to present it as a unifying principle for tangible and social computing. Mainly, this will mean exploring the emergence of the concept of embodiment from earlier work. Embodiment is not a new idea. It is a common theme running through a great deal of the philosophy of the last hundred years, and in particular the area of phenomenology. My argument here is that by looking to the phenomenological tradition, we can develop a position that serves to explain, to relate, and to develop the tangible and social computing programs.

Embodiment

We have already encountered embodiment, indirectly, as a phenomenon underlying the ideas of tangible and social computing. The goal of this chapter is to focus on embodiment directly, refining it by exploring its antecedents in phenomenology and related areas. As a starting point, though, we need a working definition. A naive definition would be one that emphasized physical presence:

Embodiment 1. Embodiment means possessing and acting through a physical manifestation in the world.

However, physical presence is a more restrictive definition than I have in mind here. Certainly, embodiment retains this notion of immanent "presence," and of the fact that something occurs in the world; but it need not rest on a purely physical foundation. Embodiment extends to other phenomena that unfold directly in the world; conversations, mutually engaged actions, and so on. So we can start with a more elaborated definition:

Embodiment 2. Embodied phenomena are those that by their very nature occur in real time and real space.

This definition incorporates the sense of physical presence from the earlier one, but extends it to include a broader range of phenomena that may not be physical but are nonetheless occurrent in the world. Embodiment denotes a form of participative status.

This is much more than a concern with "making it like the real world." We are familiar with "real-world-ness" in user interfaces through the use of metaphors of all sorts, from windows to desktops, buttons, and virtual worlds. However, embodiment strikes more deeply than simply the use of familiar models and metaphors in an interface. Some might serve to make this distinction clearer.

Imagine a 3-D computer game. It exploits my familiarity with the structure of the three-dimensional world by using perspective geometry to create a convincing and compelling setting for the game. It might rely on the fact that I understand that objects can be hidden from view by walls or other intervening objects, that if I can see you then you can see me, and other features of the everyday world. This could be further exploited by a version of the game designed for immersive virtual reality. It might use a head-mounted display to match the movement of the scene to the movement of my head, and so give me a stronger sense of being surrounded by the computer-generated imagery. Both of these approaches take advantage of my deep familiarity with the nature and structure of the everyday world.

However, there is a considerable difference between using the real world as a *metaphor* for interaction and using it as a *medium* for interaction. As in this game, real-world metaphors can be used to suggest and guide action, and to help us understand information systems and how to use them. Even in an immersive virtual-reality environment, users are disconnected observers of a world they do not inhabit directly. They peer out at it, figure out what's going on, decide on some course of action, and enact it through the narrow interface of the keyboard or the dataglove, carefully monitoring the result to see if it turns out the way they expected. Our experience in the everyday world is not of that sort. There is no homunculus sitting inside our heads, staring out at the world through our eyes, enacting some plan of action by manipulating our hands, and checking carefully to make sure we don't overshoot when reaching for the coffee cup. We inhabit our bodies and they in turn inhabit the world, with seamless connections back and forth.

Similarly, "conversational" computational systems, which use natural language-processing techniques and attempt to incorporate the rules of conversational interaction, may well make it easier and more natural to interact with computer systems in as much as they can exploit familiar patterns of everyday human action. However, encoding conversational rules about turn-taking and anaphoric reference is a world away from responding to the way in which those conversational rules arise out of a world of human social action, conducted through the coordinated media of spoken language, gaze, and posture. We inhabit conversations as embodied phenomena in the everyday world.

Distinguishing between inhabited interaction in the world on one hand, and disconnected observation and control on the other, is at the heart of the embodied interaction proposal. First, though, we should ask: If we are all embodied, and our actions are all embodied, then isn't the term *embodied interaction* in danger of being meaningless? How, after all, could there be any sort of interaction that was *not* embodied? What I am claiming for "embodied interaction" is not simply that it is a form of interaction that is embodied, but rather that it is an approach to the design and analysis of interaction that takes embodiment to be central to, even constitutive of, the whole phenomenon. This is certainly a departure from traditional approaches to HCI design.

Tangible and social computing both reflect this central concern with embodiment. The tangible computing work attempts to capitalize on our physical skills and our familiarity with real world objects. It also tries to make computation manifest to us in the world in the same way as we encounter other phenomena, both as a way of making computation fit more naturally with the everyday world and as a way of enriching our experiences with the physical. It attempts to move computation and interaction out of the world of abstract cognitive processes and into the same phenomenal world as our other sorts of interactions. The trends in social computing are also built upon a notion of embodiment. The use of sociological approaches in the design of interactive technology has, however, been driven primarily by concerns with the interaction of computation and "the workaday world" (Moran and Anderson 1990). The paradigmatic perspective on social action motivating this approach is the "situated" perspective (e.g., Suchman 1987; Clancey 1997), which is grounded in the relationship between social action and the settings in which it unfolds, the relationship of embodiment.

The best way to see how the same form of embodiment underwrites both of these areas is to consider the origin of the concept as it has developed in the phenomenological tradition of the past hundred years or so.

The Phenomenological Backdrop

Although it is not generally incorporated into HCI design approaches, embodiment is not a new idea. It has been explored perhaps most extensively within phenomenology, a branch of philosophy that is principally concerned with the elements of human experience. In contrast to philosophical positions that look for a "truth" independent of our own experience, phenomenology holds that the phenomena of experience are central to questions of ontology (the study of the nature of being and categories of existence) and epistemology (the study of knowledge).

Originating in the latter part of the nineteenth century, phenomenology has gone through a number of transitions in the past hundred years and has separated into a number of distinct intellectual positions. However, the behavior of embodied actors going about their business in the world has been central to all of them. What follows briefly outlines aspects of the work of four phenomenological theorists—Edmund Husserl, Martin Heidegger, Alfred Schutz, and Maurice Merleau-Ponty—whose thought and writings have been particularly relevant to questions of embodiment and interaction.

Husserl's Transcendental Phenomenology

In this way, Hilbert discovered the solid foundation of mathematics in the consistency of its formal system: mathematics does not have to be "true" as long as it is "consistent" and as long as that is the case, there is no need for further foundation.
—Kojin Karatani, "Natural Numbers"

Edmund Husserl (1859–1938) was the founder of the phenomenological tradition. For Husserl, phenomenology was a method for exploring the nature of human experience and perception.

Husserl had originally trained as a mathematician. However, he was unhappy with the direction that mathematics and science were taking during his lifetime. This was a critical time for science, when foundational issues about the relationship of science to the world were in question. The advent of non-Euclidian geometries, and the explorations of formalists like Hilbert and Frege, had begun to question the idea of mathematics as an objective formalization of the world. Husserl was frustrated by the idea that science and mathematics were increasingly conducted on an abstract plane that was disconnected from human experience and human understanding, independently of questions of truth and applicability. He felt that the sciences increasingly dealt with idealized entities and internal abstractions a world apart from the concrete phenomena of daily life. In his later work, he pointed particularly to the work of Galileo[1] as a turning point in the development of this abstract, idealized reasoning:

For Platonism, the real had a more or less perfect methexis in the ideal. This afforded ancient geometry possibilities of a primitive application to reality. [But] through Galileo's mathematization of nature, nature itself is idealized under the new mathematics. Nature itself becomes—to express it a modern way—a mathematical manifold. (Husserl 1936:23)

Husserl's primary criticism of this idealized scientific conception of the world was that it had distanced science and mathematics from the everyday world and everyday practical concerns, and in doing so, had distanced it from the live experience of people acting in the world. Galileo was responsible for a

surreptitious substitution of the mathematically substructed world of idealities for the only real world, the one that is actually given through perception, that is ever experienced and experienceable—our everyday life-world. (Husserl 1936:48–49)

Husserl wanted to redress this balance and envisioned a science that was firmly grounded on the phenomena of experience, which in turn meant developing the philosophy of experience as a rigorous science. This had also been Decartes's intent; Husserl saw his program as a Cartesianism for the twentieth century.

Descartes had attempted to uncover how a subjective consciousness could know with any certainty about external reality. Franz Brentano, under whom Husserl studied, had further developed this into a theory of "intentionality," which described the way that mental states could refer to elements of external reality. Intentionality describes the relationship between the tree outside my window and my thinking about it; for Brentano, all mental states have this property of being *about* something. Husserl elaborated Brentano's ideas further, and proposed phenomenology as a method for examining the nature of intentionality.

Phenomenology aims to uncover the relationship between the objects of consciousness—the objects of intentionality, which Husserl terms *noema*—and our mental experiences of those objects, our consciousness of them, which he terms *noesis*. Making this separation allows the phenomenologist to begin to analyze how we perceive and experience the phenomena of the everyday world: how *noema* and *noesis* are related and how they feature as parts of our experience of the world. However, in order to examine these questions rigorously, the phenomenologist must suspend the "natural attitude" to the world that assumes the existence of the perceived objects on the basis of perception. Phenomenology's objective is to explore how the natural attitude comes about in the first place.

What Husserl posits is a parallelism between the objects of perception and the acts of perception. When I see a rabbit, I have not only to recognize that what I'm seeing is a rabbit, but also that what I'm doing is seeing it (as opposed to imagining or remembering it). There is a parallelism between these two domains, and mental acts can themselves become phenomena of experience as I recall or reflect upon them.

The separation that Husserl proposes between the objects of perception and the perceptions themselves is mirrored by a second separation between the elements of the world and their "essences" or essential characteristics. In recognizing that what I'm seeing is a rabbit, I move from the world of immediate everyday affairs—this particular set of sense-impressions—to the world of the formal, the essential. He argues that the objects of intentionality are always "essences."

These ideas and the phenomenological method were developed initially in *Logical Investigations* (1900) and *Ideas: General Introduction to a Pure Phenomenology* (1913). In his last major work, *The Crisis of European Sciences and Transcendental Phenomenology* (1936), Husserl further elaborated his principles (partly in response to criticisms from some such as Heidegger, below) and introduced the concept of the life-world, or *lebenswelt*. The life-world is the intersubjective, mundane world of background understandings and experiences of the world. It is the world of the natural attitude and of everyday experience. Although the life-world is the background from which any scientific understanding of the world emerges, Husserl argued, it had gone largely unexplored in earlier accounts of meaning, knowledge, and understanding. Incorporating the idea of the life-world into phenomenology served to direct its attention to the role of these unconscious, "sedimented" understandings in our dealings with everyday reality.

Phenomenology, then, was a significant departure from previous philosophical positions. Most importantly, it rejected abstract and formalized reasoning, looking instead at the pretheoretical, prerational world of everyday experience. Although (as we will see) many people later moved away from a pure Husserlian position, Husserl's work has had considerable influence in turning attention, first, to everyday experience rather than formalized knowledge, and second, to that experience as a phenomenon to be studied in its own right.

Heidegger's Hermeneutic Phenomenology

Although Husserl had first articulated the phenomenological position, it was one of his students who would most profoundly influence the development of phenomenological thought. That student was Martin Heidegger (1889–1976). Heidegger's magnum opus, *Being and Time* (1927 [tr. 1961]), took Husserl's work as a starting point but developed it in radically new ways by showing how mental life and everyday experience were fundamentally intertwined.

Heidegger followed Husserl in attempting to uncover the intentionality of experience. However, where Heidegger broke with Husserl was in rejecting the mentalistic attitude that Husserl had adopted. By "mentalistic," I mean a focus in Husserl's phenomenology on cognitive, mental phenomena separated from the physical phenomena of mundane existence.

This was a perspective that Husserl had inherited from Descartes. Descartes' famous dictum, "*cogito ergo sum*"—I think, therefore I am—had reflected a doctrine that we "occupy" two different and separate worlds, the world of physical reality and the world of mental experience.[2] This doctrine, called Cartesian dualism, holds that mind and body are quite different; thinking and being are two different sets of phenomena. In common with most philosophers, Husserl had adopted this dualism and had devoted his attention to mental life and cognition, to how we could know about the world "out there."

Heidegger argued that Husserl and others had focused on mental phenomena, on the *cogito*, at the expense of being, or the *sum*. However, he proposed, clearly one needed to *be* in order to *think*. Being comes first; thinking is derived from being. So, it would make no sense to explore intentionality independently of the nature of being that supports it. The nature of being—how we exist in the world—shapes the way that we understand the world, because our understanding of the world is essentially an understanding of how we *are* in it. So Heidegger rejected the dualism of mind and body altogether. He argued that thinking and being are fundamentally intertwined. Essentially, Heidegger transformed the problem of phenomenology from an epistemological question, a question about knowledge, to an ontological question, a question about forms and categories of existence. Instead of asking, "How can we know about the world?" Heidegger asked, "How does the world reveal itself to us through our encounters with it?"

This was a radical transformation of the traditional point of view. Most philosophers since Descartes had taken the position that the mind is the seat of reason and meaning. The mind observes the world, gives it meaning by relating it to abstract understandings of an idealized reality and, on the basis of that meaning, formulates a plan of action. Heidegger turned that around. From his perspective, the meaningfulness of everyday experience lies not in the head, but in the world. It is a consequence of our mode of being, of the way in which we exist in the world. Where traditional philosophical approaches argued that we proceed from perception to meaning to action, Heidegger stressed the way that we ordinarily act in a world that is *already organized* in terms of meaning. The world has meaning for us in the ways in which we encounter it and the ways that it makes itself available to us.

The most important aspect of the way in which we encounter the world is that we encounter it *practically*. We encounter the world as a place in which we act. It is the way in which we act—the practical tasks in which we are engaged, and how they are accommodated into the world—that makes the world meaningful for us. Heidegger rejected the very kinds of intentionality that Husserl and others had pursued—an abstract, disconnected intentionality, the intentionality of a Cartesian homunculus peering out at the world and seeing what's there. Instead, he argued for intentionality as an aspect of practical affairs:

The kind of dealing which is closest to us is as we have shown, not a bare perceptual cognition, but rather that kind of concern which manipulates things and puts them to use. (Heidegger 1927:95)

Meaning inheres in the world as we find it. The central element of our existence is to interpret that meaning through the ways in which we encounter the world. The interpretive nature of understanding is the basis for Heidegger's phenomenology, a hermeneutic phenomenology. [3]

At the center of Heidegger's work is the concept of *Dasein,* which is the essence of being human. Dasein is usually translated as "being-in-the-world," emphasizing the way in which being is inseparable from the world in which it occurs. It follows, then, that one of the central questions concerns how *Dasein* is oriented toward the world. As noted earlier, the orientation is a fundamentally practical one; it is purposeful and active. The world, however, is not simply the object of *Dasein's* action, but also, at times, the medium through which that action is accomplished. In other words, one of the ways that *Dasein* encounters the world is to be able to use what it finds in order to accomplish its goals. Heidegger uses the term *it* to refer to elements in the world turned into tools for our use. There are two important ideas captured by the term *equipment*. The first is that it refers not simply to the tool, but to the tool *as a tool* and *for some task*. "Equipment," Heidegger comments, "is essentially 'something in-order-to'" (1927:99). The second is that equipment does not stand alone. Equipment is linked to other equipment in the way that it relies upon, works with, suggests, is similar or dissimilar to, or is otherwise related to other equipment.

This aspect of Heidegger's phenomenology is already known in HCI. It was one of the elements on which Winograd and Flores (1986) based their analysis of computational theories of cognition. In particular, they were concerned with Heidegger's distinction between "ready-to-hand" (*zuhanden*) and "present-at-hand" (*vorhanden*). These are ways, Heidegger explains, that we encounter the world and act through it. As an example, consider the mouse connected to my computer. Much of the time, I act *through* the mouse; the mouse is an extension of my hand as I select objects, operate menus, and so forth. The mouse is, in Heidegger's terms, *ready-to-hand*. Sometimes, however, such as when I reach the edge of the mousepad and cannot move the mouse further, my orientation toward the mouse changes. Now, I become conscious of the mouse mediating my action, precisely because of the fact that it has been interrupted. The mouse becomes the object of my attention as I pick it up and move it back to the center of the mousepad. When I act on the mouse in this way, being mindful of it *as* an object of my activity, the mouse is *present-at-hand*.

Heidegger does more than point out that we have different ways of orienting toward objects; his observation is more radical. He argues that the mouse exists for us as an entity only *because* of the way in which it can become present-at-hand, and becomes equipment only through the way in which it can be ready-to-hand. And in being ready-to-hand, it disappears from view—or "withdraws"—as an independent entity:

The ready-to-hand is not grasped theoretically at all. . . . The peculiarity of what is proximally ready-to-hand is that, in its readiness-to-hand, it must, as it were, withdraw in order to be ready-to-hand quite authentically. That with which our everyday dealings proximally dwell is not the tools themselves. On the contrary, that with which we concern ourselves primarily is the work. (1927:99)

In other words, as we act through technology that has become ready-to-hand, the technology itself disappears from our immediate concerns. We are caught up in the performance of the work; our mode of being is one of "absorbed coping." The equipment fades into the background. This unspoken background against which our actions are played out is at the heart of Heidegger's view of being-in-the-world. So, in fact, although I suggested earlier that Heidegger had transformed the question of meaning from an epistemological question to an ontological question, the form of his answer is really "*pre*ontological." By preontological, I mean that it is outside of and prior to our focused attention. The way in which the world occurs as an unconscious but accessible background to our activity is essential to our mode of being.

We can see that although Heidegger had taken Husserl's work as his starting point, he soon departed from it radically. Our mundane experience of the world was central to his work, just as it had been to Husserl's; but for Heidegger, our engaged participation in the world came to play a central role in the questions of being and meaning. Where Husserl had turned his (and our) attention to the primacy of actual experience rather than abstract reasoning, Heidegger had moved the site of that experience into the world. *Dasein* is embodied being; it is not simply embedded in the world, but inseparable from it such that it makes no sense to talk of it having an existence independent of that world.

Although it has been extremely influential, Heidegger's was not the only elaboration of Husserl's work. Husserl's phenomenology was developed in different directions by others. One of these was Alfred Schutz, whose work is a key bridge from the concerns of Husserl and Heidegger to those of Harold Garfinkel and other sociologists.

Schutz's Phenomenology of the Social World

Husserl and Heidegger had developed phenomenology in different directions, but they had nonetheless both concentrated on the *individual* experience of the world. The critical contribution of Alfred Schutz (1899–1959) was to extend phenomenology beyond the individual to encompass the social world.

Schutz was Austrian, and lived for the first part of his life in Vienna. He published his first major work, *The Phenomenology of the Social World,* in 1932 [tr. 1967]. After working briefly with Husserl at Freiburg, he moved to the United States, where he spent the rest of his life, further developing his ideas about a phenomenological approach to the problems of sociology.

In particular, Schutz's program centered on the problem of intersubjectivity. At its most basic, the problem is this: given that our experiences of the world are fundamentally our own, how can we achieve, between different individuals, a common experience of the world, and a shared framework for meaning? If I don't know what you experience of the world, or what you experience when I talk to you, how can we ever understand each other or come to any understanding of the world around us? How can the relationship between two people's subjective experience be maintained?

The problem of intersubjectivity is a crucial one for sociology. Social order is mutually constituted by its members; it arises out of the collective action of us all. Collective action, however, depends on intersubjectivity. It depends absolutely on our intersubjective understandings of the world and of our actions in it. Unsurprisingly, then, the early sociologists had turned their attention to these foundational questions.

Schutz's starting point was the work of Max Weber. Weber was one of the founding figures of modern sociology. He held that the goal of sociology was the interpretive understanding of subjectively meaningful social acts. By interpretive understanding, Weber meant that sociology's goal was to study action in order to uncover the orderliness that lay behind it, an orderliness that could be expressed in terms of general rules. The objective reality of these laws and social facts was the unquestioned position of traditional sociology. Weber and other sociological theorists argued that society and the stability of social facts are a given, existing independently of their application or interpretation by social actors.

However, Schutz rejected this view. In particular, he was concerned with Weber's treatment of the problem of intersubjectivity. Schutz felt that Weber had passed over the issues of how those "subjectively meaningful social acts" that Weber wanted to explicate actually *became* meaningful to people, and could be recognized and understood by others as *being* meaningful. Clearly, the whole edifice of Weber's sociology turned on this issue. In contrast with the traditional approach, Schutz argued that the meaningfulness of social action had to emerge within the context of the actor's own experience of the world. Drawing on the phenomenological tradition and its concerns with everyday experience, he saw intersubjectivity not as some universal law, but rather as a mundane, practical problem, routinely solved by social actors in the course of their action and interaction.

In other words, Schutz identifies the source of intersubjectivity as Husserl's *lebenswelt*. This is the life-world that Husserl had introduced in his later writings, the "mundane world of lived experience already existing as a product of the unreflecting cognitions of ordinary actors" (Heritage 1984:44). For Schutz, this world of lived experience incorporates our social understandings, too—understandings of how our actions look to others and how others' look to us.

Essentially, Schutz argues that the actions of others seem to us to be the actions of reasonable social actors because we assume them, in the first instance, to be so. Intersubjectivity is achieved, as a practical concern, as a consequence of these assumptions; that we share a common reality, that we act rationally within that reality, and so forth. This assumption of rationality is part of the "natural attitude." We work under the assumption that others are rational as we are, and that others' experience is like our own:

A man in the natural attitude, then, understands the world by interpreting his own lived experiences of it, whether these experiences be of inanimate things, of animals, or of his fellow human beings. (Schutz 1932:108)

All genuine understanding of the other person must start out from acts of explication performed by the observer on his own lived experience. (Schutz 1932:13)

So, in Schutz's model, intersubjectivity is the outcome of these assumptions in the natural attitude. Intersubjectivity results only and entirely from the fact that people *do* it. It is a practical achievement of social actors, a response to the practical problems of engaging with each other in concerted social action.

Schutz recognized that this assumption of rationality could not be simply an instantaneous achievement. To interpret actions as rational requires that we can see them emerge within a pattern of goals, causes, requirements, and motivations. To this end, Schutz developed a model of the social world that reflected its orientation toward past events and future intentions as a feature of the practical achievement of intersubjective meaning.

The interpretive model of intersubjectivity that Schutz proposed applies not only to explicit acts of communication, but also to simple observable behavior. Following Weber, he used the example of watching a woodcutter chopping wood. One understands the woodcutter's actions by projecting oneself into the place of the woodcutter, imagining oneself to be carrying out his actions, and so interpreting the actions of the woodcutter from the point of view of one's own life-world and experience. This relies on the assumption that the woodcutter is, broadly, motived by the concerns that would motivate us in that situation, attentive to the same sort of issues that we would be, and so forth. Now, more or less other information—observable information related to lived experiences—may or may not be available to be able to tell more, such as whether the woodcutter is cutting wood to earn a living or for exercise. But, regardless, the assumption of rationality provides a starting point for the development of further understanding. This is one important aspect of the characterisation of the problem of intersubjectivity as a practical, mundane problem—that the solution need only be "good enough" for the matters at hand.

Schutz's approach brought phenomenological reasoning to the problems of sociology. In doing so, he opened up a new set of concerns for sociologist, by turning the life-world into a site of social scientific inquiry:

> For Schutz, the *lebenswelt* is a world of mundane events and institutions which the ordinary members of society constitute and reconstitute without even being aware of the fact. This mundane world is both the unnoticed ground on which social science is founded, and, in many cases, its unnoticed object of investigation. (Heritage 1984: 44).

Taking the life-world as a focus recasts the problems of sociology. It means turning away from the idea of general laws that operate outside the immediate purview of the actors whose behavior they regulate. Instead, it characterizes sociological problems as practical, mundane ones routinely encountered—and solved—by social actors in the course of their day-to-day activities. Social actors are, in effect, practical sociologists, solving the problems of sociology for themselves every day. This reorientation of sociology toward a new set of questions and a new method of inquiry was one of the critical motivations for Garfinkel's development of ethnomethodology, as introduced in the previous chapter and explored in more detail shortly. For the moment, however, I will address one further aspect of the development of phenomenology.

Merleau-Ponty and the Phenomenology of Perception

Of the various phenomenological thinkers presented here, the one for whom the notion of "embodiment" was most central was the French philosopher Maurice Merleau-Ponty (1908–1961). Like his contemporary and colleague Jean-Paul Sartre, Merleau-Ponty concerned himself broadly with questions of phenomenology and existentialism, and with the political implications of these positions. His major work, *The Phenomenology of Perception,* was first published in 1945 (with an English translation appearing in 1962), and deals directly with questions of embodiment.

Merleau-Ponty's objective was to reconcile Husserl's "philosophy of essences" with Heidegger's "philosophy of being." From Husserl, he inherited a concern with questions of perception. From Heidegger, he inherited an orientation toward being situated in the world. He resolved these two perspectives by focusing on the role of the body in perception.

The body, in Merleau-Ponty's phenomenology, plays a pivotal role in the mind/body, subject/object duality with which Husserl had struggled. For Merleau-Ponty, the body is neither subject nor object, but an ambiguous third party. Nonetheless, the body plays a critical role in any theory of perception. Perception of an external reality comes about through and in relation to a sense of the body. "A theory of the body," Merleau-Ponty argued, "is already a theory of perception" (Merleau-Ponty 1945:203). There are two important aspects to this proposal. One is the role that the body can play in mediating between Husserl's and Heidegger's positions. The other is a broadening of the role of body and bodily perception beyond the purely psychophysical.

The body can no longer be regarded as an entity to be examined in its own right but has to be placed in the context of a world. Moreover, being-in-the-world cannot itself be understood as a certain relation that obtains between a central body and a surrounding world, but has to be understood in terms of tasks, action to be accomplished, a free space which outlines in advance the possibilities available to the body at any time. (MacAnn 1993:174).

As should be clear, the embodied nature of action (and actors) was central to Merleau-Ponty's philosophy. Dreyfus (1996) points out three different meanings of embodiment in Merleau-Ponty's work. The first is the physical embodiment of a human subject, with legs and arms, and of a certain size and shape; the second is the set of bodily skills and situational responses that we have developed; and the third is the cultural "skills," abilities, and understandings that we responsively gain from the cultural world in which we are embedded. Each of these aspects, simultaneously, contributes to and conditions the actions of the individual, both in terms of how they understand their own embodiment (the "phenomenological body") and how it is understood by others (the "objective body").

Given the central place of "embodiment" in Merleau-Ponty's work, and his concern with the body and bodily experience, this may be an appropriate moment to say something more about the use I want to make here of the term *embodiment*. I am using the term largely to capture a sense of "phenomenological presence," the way that a variety of interactive phenomena arise from a direct and engaged participation in the world. As I outlined earlier, this includes both physically realized and socially situated phenomena, and the chapters that follow will explore both the dimensions and the consequences of this approach. However, in Merleau-Ponty's work, the idea of "embodiment" is used to draw particular attention to the role of the body. This concern with the body is echoed in much current work in Critical Theory, and particularly in explorations into the relationship between questions of self and technology, such as the "cyborg" work initiated by Donna Haraway (1991), Sandy Stone's (1991) comments on virtual presence, or (more distantly) Don Ihde's (1991) investigations of the mediating role of technology in science. I am sympathetic to their perspectives, but my concerns here are not those of Haraway and her colleagues, nor should my use of the term *embodied* be confused with the issues that they wish to identify. Indeed, the lessons I want to draw from the phenomenological perspective will be broader (and less specific) than those that primarily occupied Merleau-Ponty.

Although his influence in HCI has been much less significant than that of Heidegger or even Schutz, Merleau-Ponty has nonetheless made an appearance. Robertson (1997) uses Merleau-Ponty's work as the basis of a taxonomy of embodied actions for the analysis of group activity. For instance, Merleau-Ponty's emphasis on the "reversibility" of perception—how, in our bodily presence and through our bodily experience, we can apprehend aspects of the perceptions of ourselves that we engender in others—provides her with the tools to explore how groups manage their mutual orientations, both to each other and to external artifacts, in face-to-face and in virtual settings. Robertson's investigations show the relevance of embodied accounts of phenomenological perception in understanding how technology mediates interpersonal communication. While the communicative role of technology is quite clear in Robertson's work—she was, after all studying the use of video-communication technologies—I will argue that this same communicative role can be ascribed to a much broader range of technologies, and that phenomenological perspectives can be similarly enlightening.

Summary: Phenomenology and Being-in-the-World
It should be clear by this stage that embodiment is not a new idea—far from it. Instead, it has been central to a particular thread of philosophical thought since the late nineteenth century. However, for each of the phenomenological positions that have been outlined here, embodiment has played a different role. Husserl was concerned with how the life-world was based in everyday embodied experience rather than abstract reasoning; Schutz recognized that this conception of the life-world could be extended to address problems in social interaction. For Heidegger, embodied action was essential to our mode of being and to the ways in which we encountered the world, while Merleau-Ponty emphasized the critical role of the body in mediating between internal and external experience. Throughout these accounts, the idea of a world that we encounter directly rather than abstractly is of central concern.

What the phenomenologists have explored is the relationship between embodied action and meaning. For them, the source of meaning (and meaningfulness) is not a collection of abstract, idealized entities; instead, it is to be found in the world in which we act, and which acts upon us. This world is already filled with meaning. Its meaning is to be found in the way in which it reveals itself to us as being available for our actions. It is only through those actions, and the possibility for actions that the world affords us, that we can come to find the world, in both its physical and social manifestations, meaningful.

It should also be more clear, in light of this introduction, why embodiment and phenomenology are relevant to tangible and social computing. The relationship between tangible and social computing is not simply that they both exploit familiar metaphors for interaction. Instead, they both build on an account of the relationship between action and meaning that phenomenology has explored. They both place action and interaction prior to "theory" and abstract understanding. So, the phenomenological perspective offers a starting point for a foundational understanding of embodied interaction, one that the rest of the book will attempt to set out.

Before moving on, though, I want to spend some time discussing other approaches and show how they relate to the work discussed so far. Up to this point, I have primarily addressed the phenomenological tradition, but it is only one approach concerned with the relationship between cognition and action. In the rest of this chapter, I will introduce some other perspectives. These other approaches serve two roles here. First, they flesh out the picture of embodiment as an aspect of twentieth century thought; and second, they can provide us with further insights into the nature of being-in-the-world, both physical and social.

Being in the Physical World

A number of theorists, working in different domains and bringing different perspectives to bear, have recognized the importance of our physical embodiment in the world as a central aspect of how we act and react.

In HCI, the work of the psychologist J. J. Gibson is perhaps the most familiar, especially as explored in the writings of Donald Norman. Throughout his career, Gibson was principally concerned with visual perception; with how living creatures can see, can recognize what they see, and can act on it. Although psychologists had long studied the topic, Gibson became frustrated with conventional approaches. His frustration stemmed from the fact that they separated *seeing* from *acting,* while he regarded the two as being deeply connected.

Gibson's starting point was to consider visual perception not as a link between optics and neural activity, but as a point of contact between the creature and its environment, an environment in which the creature moves around and within which it acts:

One sees the environment not just with the eyes but with the eyes in the head on the shoulders of a body that gets about. We look at details with the eyes, but we also look around with the mobile head, and we go-and-look with the mobile body. (Gibson 1979:222)

Gibson placed visual perception within a frame of being and acting, and in doing so laid the foundations for what he and others came to call "ecological psychology." In contrast to approaches such as cognitive psychology, which tended to restrict their focus to mental processing and were defined by the boundaries of the head, ecological psychology was concerned with the organism living and acting in the world. From the ecological perspective, "cognition" was not purely a neural phenomenon, but was located within (and throughout) a complex involving the organism, action and the environment. Ecological psychology studies "knowledge in the world" rather than "knowledge in the head."

One central construct of Gibson's approach, which has had a particularly telling impact on the development of HCI, was the concept of "affordance." Technically, an affordance is a property of the environment that affords action to appropriately equipped organisms. For example, the glass of my window affords looking to me, because I have eyes that operate in that part of the electromagnetic spectrum to which the glass is transparent. The atmosphere at sea level affords comfortable breathing to me, for the oxygen content of the air provides my body with adequate sustenance; but at an altitude of 35,000 feet, the atmosphere no longer affords breathing to me, although it might afford it to some other creature with lower oxygen requirements. My office chair affords sitting to me, because its seat matches the length of my legs. My office chair does not afford sitting to a horse or a rabbit; they are not "appropriately equipped" individuals. Similarly, I am not appropriately equipped to be able to breathe underwater or see in pitch darkness, although other creatures are, and so those environments afford different kinds of actions to them than they do to me.

In other words, an affordance is a three-way relationship between the environment, the organism, and an activity. This three-way relationship is at the heart of ecological psychology, and the challenge of ecological psychology lies in just how it is centered on the notion of an organism acting in an environment: being in the world.

As noted, ideas from ecological psychology have made their way into the world of HCI. Donald Norman (1988, 1993) has made considerable use of Gibson's analytic framework, and particularly the concept of affordance, in his work on design and interaction in both the everyday physical world and the world of computer interfaces. Norman uses the concept of affordance to explore the relationship between form and function in design and to show how good design can make the appropriate use of a device clear and obvious to a user. Although Norman uses many examples drawn from the physical environment and physical product design, the same ideas also apply to the design of user interfaces, where the functionality (or the "opportunity for action") that a system offers can be made more or less obvious in its visual appearance.

Subsequently, William Gaver took affordances as a starting point for a model of interactive system design (Gaver 1991), as well as for the analysis of cooperative technologies (Gaver 1992). Gaver's goal was not simply to use the ecological approach to analyze interfaces, but also to build it into a systematic basis for interactive system design. For example, taking his cues from Gibson's discussion of the "eyes in the head on the shoulders of a body," Gaver argued that one failing of video-communication technologies was that they offer no means for visual exploration of the remote scene. Typical arrangements of cameras and monitors provide only a fixed view of the remote location, and that view is outside the control of the observer. By contrast, in the everyday world, our field of view is related to the way we are moving through the environment, and we have the opportunity to stop, look around, and so build up a better picture of what is around us by exploration. On this basis, Gaver and colleagues developed a prototype video-communication system (called the Virtual Window) that allowed users to explore a remote scene through head movements analogous to those by which we might look around us in the everyday world (Gaver, Smets, and Overbeeke 1995).

The idea of physical embodiment as an aspect of understanding the world was also one explored by Michael Polanyi. His book *The Tacit Dimension* (Polanyi 1966) explored the idea of "tacit knowledge": those things that we know, but unconsciously and inexpressibly. One source of examples of tacit knowledge is we might call "embodied skills," such as juggling or riding a bike. These are "tacit" skills in the sense that, while we might able to *describe* them, we cannot *explain* exactly what we do when we go about these tasks. We just do them. The understanding of "what" and the understanding of "how" are different kinds of knowledge:

Explicit integration cannot replace its tacit counterpart. The skill of a driver cannot be replaced by a thorough schooling in the theory of the motorcar; the knowledge I have of my own body differs altogether from the knowledge of its physiology; and the roles of rhyming and prosody do not tell me what a poem told me, without any knowledge of its rules. (Polanyi 1966:20)

Embodied skills depend on a tight coupling between perception and action. Polanyi distinguishes between what he calls *proximal* and *distal* phenomena. Loosely, proximal means "close by" or "at hand," while distal means "at a distance." He argues that, in cases of tacit skills, our focus is on the distal phenomena, while the proximal phenomena are those *through which* the distal is achieved. Take the example of using a stick to feel your way in the dark. You have the sense of exploring the ground in front of you (distal) while, in fact, what you are experiencing is a set of sensory impressions at the hand holding the stick (proximal). So, although your actual experience might be proximal, your attention is transferred to the distal phenomenon. Just as the environmental movement urged us to "think globally, act locally," so Polanyi observes that we think distally but act proximally. He notes that this transfer of attention, from proximal to distal, is associated with a semantic shift. The meaning we associate with proximal phenomena is actually that of their distal correlates. In the stick example, the pressure on our hands is interpreted to mean the presence of a barrier on the ground. Or again, on a boat, we interpret the subtle shifts in our balance in terms of the movement of the deck beneath our feet without even being aware that we are making the transition from proximal to distal phenomena. Polanyi sees this as a general phenomenon:

All meaning tends to be displaced away from ourselves, and that is in fact my justification for using the terms "proximal" and "distal" to describe the first and second terms of tacit knowing. (1966:13).

Even though bicycle riding and juggling seem to pop up as the quintessential examples of tacit knowledge, Polanyi's interests are broader than simply physical skills. His idea of tacit knowledge applies generally to situations in which we understand "what to do" without being able to express "how to do it." In *The Tacit Dimension,* what he actually has in his sights is not riding bicycles, but rather the question of how science is conducted and theory uncovered. A scientist before he turned to philosophy, Polanyi set out to address the observation that although science appears to progress through a thoroughly rational and regimented sequence of hypothesis, experimentation, observation, and analysis, it is equally dependent on such "irrational" phenomena as insights, hunches, and intuitions about results that do or do not "ring true." He makes the case that the relationship between proximal and distal phenomena is akin to that between a hidden reality and observable fact, and that it is through the scientist's relationship to this hidden reality that science progresses.[4]

The progress of science is not of immediate concern here (except in as much as we might be able to contribute to it). What is significant, though, is the way that Polanyi sees the relationship between proximal and distal in semantic terms, that is, in terms of the meaning they convey. This is strongly reminiscent of the concerns of the phenomenologists with the relationship between meaning and action, but we can see it, too, in the way that embodiment arises from these other perspectives.

Being in the Social World

The directness of embodiment is not only a phenomenon of the physical world. It is also crucial to a stance on the social world that has underpinned a good deal of the influence of sociological thinking on HCI in recent years.

We have already encountered one major trend in the role of embodiment in sociology, particularly with respect to issues of Human-Computer Interaction. That trend is the one represented by "situated" perspective, associated particularly with Suchman, but also with others such as Clancey (1997) or Lave (1988). And, as I have suggested earlier, Suchman's work can be related directly to the work of the phenomenologists, in that Suchman works in the ethnomethodological tradition established by Harold Garfinkel, who himself drew extensively on the work of Alfred Schutz.

We encountered these perspectives in the previous chapter, but let me briefly summarize in order to draw attention to the threads relating their positions. Suchman's critique of the prevailing cognitivist model in Artificial Intelligence and interaction design drew attention to the fact that the sequential organization of action is not formulaic outcome of abstract planning, but rather is an improvised, ad hoc accomplishment, a moment-by-moment response to immediate needs and the setting in which it takes place. The organization of action emerges within the frame of the action itself. Suchman demonstrated how a number of problems with interactive technology lay in the imbalance between the situated organization of practical action and the regimented models that systems embody. In coming to this conclusion, Suchman drew extensively on the ethnomethodological perspective that Garfinkel had pioneered. Whereas conventional sociological approaches take the position that we act in response to an objectively given social world, ethnomethodology claims that everyday social practice creates and sustains that social world by rendering it publicly available and intelligible. Members' methods for making action accountable are means through which the phenomenon of objective social reality is achieved.

As should be clear, Garfinkel's ethnomethodological approach is heavily influenced by Schutz and his work. Schutz had emphasized that intersubjectivity is the achievement of social actors in the course of their activity, and drew upon Husserl's formulation of the *lebenswelt,* the life-world of mundane experience, in claiming intersubjectivity as an achievement or outcome of the natural attitude. This approach is echoed in Garfinkel's concept of accountability, his concern with practical rationality and commonsense understandings, and his exploration of members' methods for rendering their actions meaningful to each other. Indeed, Garfinkel repeatedly observes that Schutz, almost alone among social scientists of his generation, had begun to uncover the ways in which social reality is the ongoing achievement of social actors. Subsequently, as discussed in chapter 3, Garfinkel elaborated Schutz's orientation toward the life-world and used it to initiate a radical reconsideration of the problems, topics, and methods of sociology.

So, the link that Suchman forged between HCI and sociology also connected it to a broader tradition that was, from the outside, oriented toward questions of embodiment. Ethnomethodology adopted a concern for these issues from Schutz's phenomenology. Garfinkel drew from other sources as well, however, and at least one other important basis for Garfinkel's work addressed questions of embodiment, albeit from a different angle. This was the ordinary language philosophy of Ludwig Wittgenstein.

Wittgenstein and the Meaning of Language
Like Elvis Presley, Ludwig Wittgenstein (1889–1951) had a professional career that fell into two distinct phases.

The first phase is his work up until his initial withdrawal from philosophy in 1919, and encompasses his investigations into the philosophy of logic and mathematics with Russell and Moore at Cambridge. The major work of this period was his dissertation, *Tractatus Logico-Philosophicus,* which he completed while a prisoner of war. Published in 1921, the *Tractatus* is organized as a series of terse, numbered propositions, arranged into seven sets and accompanied by some commentary. Proceeding from the first proposition, "The world is the totality of facts," to the last, "Whereof we cannot speak, thereof we must remain silent," the *Tractatus* attempts to explore the nature of facts and propositions. One of the best-known elements of this work is the "picture theory" of meaning, according to which language represents (or pictures) the relationships between entities in the world.

After 1919, Wittgenstein "retired" from philosophy and taught in an elementary school in rural Austria. Finding it hard to keep away, though, he returned to Cambridge in 1929 to take up his philosophical studies again. In this second phase of his career, though, he departed radically from the principles that guided his earlier work.

The major work of Wittgenstein's second career is the *Philosophical Investigations,* which appeared posthumously in 1953. Once again, the topic is meaning, but now Wittgenstein took a very different perspective. In this later work, Wittgenstein rejected the positivist view of language and meaning that had characterized the *Tractatus.* He no longer held the view that words simply signify states of the world. He now saw meaning as embedded not in language or linguistic expressions themselves, but rather in the practice or use of language.

Wittgenstein reoriented his view of language from a logical construction of facts and truth statements to a set of loosely connected "language games," socially shared linguistic practices "consisting of language and the actions into which it is woven." Language games reflect a common orientation toward action and experience that provides a context for determining meaning. Using language, he argued, is a human activity, and its effective meaning must be sought in the activity that it accomplishes, or in what Wittgenstein called the "form of life" that surrounds specific linguistic practice. It is on this basis that, in *Philosophical Investigations* (§43), he famously wrote, "the meaning of a word is its use in the language."

The "language games" perspective emphasizes that language is not simply an external expression of inner mental states, but rather is a form of action. It is something that people do. So, the utterance cannot be separated from the speaker, or from the systems of meaning in which speaker and hearer are enmeshed. From this perspective, the questions that he had struggled with in his early career were rendered meaningless. The "truth" of a statement was no longer a sensible topic; now, his attention was turned to the "appropriateness" of an utterance, that is, to what made it the right thing to say in such-and-such a circumstance, and what might make it meaningful to hearers. The question is how language is organized into systems of meaning or language games. Language games are the embodied practices of communities, and the context of the language game arises from the experience, needs, capacities, and so forth of those who are engaged in it. "To imagine a language," Wittgenstein observed, "is to imagine a form of life" (§19). In other words, the setting in which language is used contributes to the apprehension of its meaning, where "setting" is not just the local occasion of its use, but the very way in which the speakers of that language exist in the world.

So, embodiment is as central to Wittgenstein's approach to language as it is to Heidegger's view of Being. He argues that language and meaning are inseparable from the practices of language users. Meaning resides not in disembodied representations, but in practical occasions of language use. Although Wittgenstein was not working directly in the phenomenological tradition, his approach clearly resonates with much of that line of thought, and indeed, his exploration of meaning and rule-following figure as strongly as the influence of Schutz in Garfinkel's ethnomethodology.

Summary

This chapter has taken something of a whirlwind tour through the work of many people who have addressed the issue of embodiment in one way or another.

It began with the phenomenologists. I outlined Husserl's attempts to reorient the Cartesian program around the phenomena of experience; Heidegger's reconstruction of phenomenology around the primacy of being-in-the-world; Schutz's expansion of the phenomenological program to account for problems of social interaction; and Merleau-Ponty's elaboration of the role of the body in perception and understanding.

I also explored the work of others who, although outside the phenomenological tradition, followed similar paths. So, we saw how Gibson had initiated an approach to psychology that recognized the importance of the interaction between an organism and its environment, and how his work has subsequently come to be adopted in HCI. Similarly, I explored the ways that Suchman's program, introduced in chapter 3, traces its intellectual lineage to Schutz, through Garfinkel. Finally, I introduced Wittgenstein's work on ordinary language philosophy, another of the major influences on Garfinkel's work.

It has not been my goal to spin these all these threads into a uniform theoretical fabric; that would be a monumental and potentially misguided task. Instead, my goal is to take these related approaches and find some common patterns that might shed light on the relationship between tangible and social computing. There are three notable common elements to the approaches outlined in this chapter.

First, they all take embodiment as central. "Embodiment" does not simply mean "physical manifestation." Rather, it means being grounded in and emerging out of everyday, mundane experience. The claim of the approaches outlined here is that embodiment is a foundational property, out of which meaning, theory, and action arise. They all place the source of action and meaning in the world. Embodiment is a participative status, a way of being, rather than a physical property.

Second, the approaches focus on practice: everyday engagement with the world directed toward the accomplishment of practical tasks. They all take action in the world to be fundamental to our understandings of the world and our relationship with it. So, their perspective is not simply that we are embodied in the world, but also that the world is the site and setting of all activity. It shapes and is shaped by the activities of embodied agents.

Third, they point to embodied practical action as the source of meaning. We find the world meaningful primarily with respect to the ways in which we act within it. Whether this is through Gibson's affordances of the environment or Heidegger's concern with objects manifesting themselves through coming to be present-at-hand, the approaches outlined in this chapter see embodiment as a source for intentionality, rather than as the object of it.

Early in this chapter, I laid out some working definitions for embodiment and embodied interaction. After exploring how the idea has been used and developed by other schools of thought, we are, perhaps, now in a position to lay out some better ones.

The starting point was:

Embodied phenomena are those which by their very nature occur in real time and real space.

In light of the elements brought together in this chapter, we now have a better understanding of embodiment, and its consequences. We can now say:

Embodiment is the property of our engagement with the world that allows us to make it meaningful.

Similarly, then, we can say:

Embodied Interaction is the creation, manipulation, and sharing of meaning through engaged interaction with artifacts.

The major lesson that I draw from the phenomenological work is that embodiment is about the relationship between action and meaning. We have already spent some time, in considering social perspectives, talking about action. What we need to explore in more detail is just what is implied by "meaning."

5

Foundations

The backdrop is now complete. Chapters 2 and 3 detailed the emergence of tangible and social computing, presented examples of work in those areas, and discussed some of the issues they raise. Chapter 4 made a case for the idea of embodiment as a central aspect of both the tangible and social approaches, and showed how various theorists, particularly phenomenological philosophers, have addressed embodied action in their work. It is now time to develop a deeper understanding of the themes that have emerged so far, and to consider their consequences for the design of interactive software systems.

The major theme that arose in chapter 4 was the relationship between embodiment and meaning. In contrast with Cartesian approaches, phenomenology describes a much more intimate relationship between our inner experience and the mundane world that we occupy. Cartesians claim that meaning is an internal phenomenon, which we assign to sense-data. Phenomenologists point out that the world is already filled with meaning, arising from the way in which the world is organized relative to our needs and actions, not just physically, but also socially and historically. So from the phenomenological perspective, we encounter, interpret, and sustain meaning through our embodied interactions with the world and with each other.

Tangible and social computing each adopt aspects of this perspective. Tangible computing encourages users to explore, adopt, and adapt interactive technology, incorporating it into their world and into everyday practice. It allows users to create and communicate the meaning of the actions they perform, rather than struggle with rigid meanings encoded in the technology itself. Social computing similarly recognizes that meaning is something that users create through the ways in which they interact with technology and with each other, and it opens up the opportunity to explore and negotiate meaning in the course of interacting with and through software systems.

The questions to be answered are, first, how does embodied interaction come about, and, second, how do we go about designing systems for embodied interaction? Answering these questions will require a deeper understanding of the foundations of embodied interaction. That is the topic of this chapter.

This chapter has two goals. The first is to open up the notion of embodiment and explore the set of ideas that it brings together. In particular, the notion of "meaning" that featured so strongly in the last chapter needs to be examined more closely. Just what aspects of meaning are important, and how are they conveyed through embodied interaction?

The second goal is to begin to relate these topics to design. The chapters on tangible and social computing dealt with the design of specific systems, but only from a distance. Similarly, the last chapter dealt with embodiment simply as a feature of theoretical approaches to understanding human action. However, the motivation for exploring embodied interaction is to understand how to approach the design of technologies. We need to bring interactive software systems back into focus. So, this chapter will not only uncover the elements that comprise embodiment, but will also relate them to the design of software systems. We need to understand how current approaches to software and interactive system design constrain and enable aspects of embodied interaction.

Three Aspects of Meaning

The starting point for this exploration is the concept of meaning that played such a central role in the discussion of phenomenology. *Meaning*, though, is a vague term. Connecting it to design will require more precision. In the course of the discussion so far, we have encountered three different aspects of meaning: ontology, intersubjectivity, and intentionality. Each of these plays a different role in embodied interaction, and each raises a different set of issues for interactive system design.

Ontology

Ontology is the branch of metaphysics concerned with the existence of objects and entities. It deals with how the world can be separated into a collection of entities whose meanings can be established, separated, and identified, and how these entities can be related to each other; how, for example, my world can be populated with entities such as computers, deadlines, chairs, and political convictions that play no part in the world of grasshoppers. In particular, in attempting to talk about entities, ontology addresses the question of how we can *individuate* the world, or distinguish between one entity or another; how we can understand the relationships between different entities or classes of entity; and so forth.

Ontology deals with how we can describe the "furniture of the world." Critically, the furniture of the world differs depending on whose world it is. Here in the industrialized cultures of the early twenty-first century, we live in a world furnished with political scandals, Internet technologies, stock crashes, carpool lanes, and satellite broadcasts; but none of these featured in the worldview of the Australian aboriginal peoples in the time before European settlers arrived. Whether or not it is accurate, the oft-repeated assertion that Eskimo languages feature dozens of words for snow reflects an appreciation that our place in the world and what we do there determine how we understand the things around us.

Ontology is an aspect of meaning in the sense that it provides the structure from which meaning can be constructed. The previous chapter showed how Martin Heidegger had reformulated the problems that phenomenology addressed as ontological rather than epistemological ones. He proposed that our understanding of the world around us arises from the interactions in which we can engage with it; ontology arises from a state of awareness in which we can reassess our relationship to the objects in the world. We uncover meaning in the world through our interactions with it.

Ontological problems manifest themselves quite quickly in software design. From the very outset, designing a software system involves making decisions about entities, about their types and relationships, and determining how these will "line up" with the elements of the real world to which they refer.

In fact, the term *ontology* has some currency in computer system design, although not quite in the philosophical sense. System designers use it in a number of ways. On the technical side, it generally means the internal representational structure of a software system—what elements are present, how they are distinguished, and so on. This is the traditional stuff of object-oriented analysis, or data structure or database design. For example, when the designers of a hotel registration system debate whether a reservation should be recorded as a feature of a room or of a day or of a person, they are designing the "ontology" of their system. At the same time, "ontology" is also sometimes used to refer to the elements of a user's conceptual model—the model either of the user's own work or of the system's operation. Users' understandings are a matter of some significance to system designers, who needs to design a system model that will fit "the user's ontology."

Although it must seem quite alien to those with a philosophical background, I use the phrase "designing the ontology" deliberately.[1] It is a phrase that regularly crops up in technical talk, and it is a telling one, inasmuch as it hints at the sorts of user interaction problems that can result. Two particular questions arise—the first concerning the term *design,* and the second concerning the idea of a single ontological structure.

Consider the design question first. Outside this particular technical milieu, it seems odd to talk about ontologies being *designed.*[2] An ontological structure, in the philosophical sense, is an emergent phenomenon. It is something that arises out of participative practice, not one that springs fully formed from a design process. Just as practice is extended in time, so is any ontology subject to continual and ongoing revision, rather than being statically embedded in some artifact. A design may *reflect* a particular set of ontological commitments on the part of a designer, but it cannot *provide* an ontology for a user.

The second issue is that the idea of "designing the ontology" also reflects an expectation that there is only one "ontology" in play. Not only does this echo the notion that a user's ontological model is stable throughout his or her experience of an interactive system, but it also suggests that the user and the designer share a single ontological model of the domain, despite their very different experiences of it and ways of interacting with it. If ontology is a consequence of interaction, then the different modes of interaction and sets of practices that different groups of people share will result in different ways of understanding the domain.

Unsurprisingly, the idea of a single, static set of ontological commitments can lead to a variety of interaction problems, including some discussed in earlier chapters. First, for example, it results in mismatches between the assumptions encoded in systems and the expectations of the users of those systems, because the users and the designers do not, in fact, share the same model of the task domain. The print-shop workflow system discussed in chapter 3 showed this sort of problem. Second, this approach yields rigid procedures for accomplishing tasks even though different people go about their work in different ways, and in response to different requirements and circumstances. The drive to develop tailorable software systems is a response to this set of problems. Finally, the traditional model leads to brittleness in adapting systems to new purposes as practices develop and change, because the ontological assumptions are deeply embedded in the software itself. These problems are technological consequences of assuming that ontological structures are shared and static. Furthermore, when an ontology is presumed to be shared, the system's view of the world is rarely revealed directly, making it difficult to detect and address problems.

Approaches such as end-user programming (e.g., Nardi 1993; Cypher 1993) and tailorability (e.g., MacLean et al. 1990; Trigg and Bødker 1994; Malone, Lai, and Fry 1995) have attempted to tackle these sorts of problems. Others, such as Harris and Henderson (1999) have seen these interaction issues as symptomatic of deeper conceptual problems and argue for fluid, negotiated boundaries between users and systems rather than rigid, fixed ones. This is closer to the approach that I will take here, but first I want to explore two other dimensions of meaning.

Intersubjectivity

The second aspect of meaning is intersubjectivity, the topic at the heart of Schutz's work on the phenomenology of the social world. Where ontology was about a form of meaning, intersubjectivity is about how that meaning can be shared. The problem of intersubjectivity is how two people can come to share an understanding about the world and about each other despite the fact that they have no immediate access to each other's mental states. For physical phenomena, there may (at some level) be an objective fact-of-the-matter about which we can both agree; but there is nothing objective about a belief or an intention. Yet, you can learn about my beliefs and intentions in such a way that we can coordinate our behavior around them, despite the absence of an objective, observable reality.

We have already seen this problem in the context of Schutz and of Garfinkel, but others have also tackled it. For instance, Herbert Clark (1996) and his colleagues have explored the issue of how people develop common understandings in conversation. They have developed an approach based on the notion of "common ground," a set of commonly held and mutually established facts that provide the background necessary for interpreting and understanding utterances. On this basis, they analyze linguistic communication in terms of the mutual establishment and exploration of common ground. From a different perspective, we have encountered the "presumption of rationality" approach that, in different forms, underlies Schutz's phenomenological life-world or Dennett's "intentional stance" (of which more will be said shortly).

There are at least two ways that the problem of establishing intersubjective understandings surfaces in the design of interactive technologies. Both are cases where the user of a system needs to be able to understand the intentions and motivations of another party.

The first, related to the questions of ontology explored earlier, concerns communication between a designer and a user, and how it is conveyed through an interactive system. The designer must somehow communicate to a user a set of constraints and expectations about how the design should be used. The system can be thought of as the medium through which a designer and a user communicate.[3] The designer's intentions are communicated through the form of the interactive system itself, and through the ways in which its functionality is offered. "Making the system usable" means not simply making it appropriate to a particular form of use, but also making sure that the system adequately and appropriately reveals the purposes for which it was designed and the ways in which the designer intended it to be used. This information unfolds in the course of the interaction between the user and the system, so that the user develops an understanding of the consequences of objects and actions in the system. As with the issues of ontology discussed before, then, the successful achievement of this communication depends on those relevant aspects of the designer's model being made available to users in the course of their activity.

The second occasion of intersubjectivity in interactive systems is communication *between* users, *through* the system. Of course, some systems—such as electronic mail, video conferencing, or instant messaging—are explicitly designed for person-to-person communication, but that is not the sort of communication I have in mind here. Instead, I mean the way that people develop and communicate shared ways of using software systems and ways of doing their work with software systems. Systems come to be "appropriated" by their users and are put to work within particular patterns of practice.

For example, consider organizational information systems that are used in, and as part of, collaborative practices of information management. Examples might be shared document repositories or databases of organizational information. When we look at how these systems are actually used, we find that the "features" they offer—the official "functionality" of the system—tell only a small part of the story. What is important is not just what the system *can* do, but rather, *what it really does do* for people in the course of doing their work. That includes what decisions people make about when and how to use the system, what expectations they have of when the system is useful and what sort of information it contains, what they know about what other people do with the system, and so on. When we look at what goes on, we begin to see systems as embedded within the specific practices of filing, storing, categorizing, organizing, and retrieving information that surround it. So, we encounter such issues as the collective tailoring of information schemes; the central roles that certain documents or information sources play in coordinating a range of activities; the importance of questions of completeness; issues of accuracy, authenticity, and authorship; and so forth.

Studies of the organizational use of information systems present many examples. The investigations of "working document collections" carried out by Jeanette Blomberg, Lucy Suchman, and Randy Trigg (Blomberg et al. 1997; Trigg et al. 1999) show how these issues recur in a variety of settings. They use the term *working document collection* to draw attention to the fact that the document collection is not a static assemblage of paper documents, but rather is a site for the ongoing work of the group that owns it. The document collection plays a critical role in the work that is done, and conversely, the work that is done gives meaning to the contents of the collection and its organization. People communicate *through* the document collection and develop ways of using it as part of their work. In other words, they appropriate the technology in the creation of working practices, so that the two evolve around each other. Because interactive systems are often both the site at which this customization work is carried out and also the medium through which it is represented and communicated, they play a critical role in communicating and sharing meaning in communities of practice.

Other examples of the way that information systems are intimately bound into practices that make them meaningful for work include the study by Ackerman and Halverson (1998) of information hotline operators and their use of various information systems to do their work, or a comparative study of two information systems that I and my colleagues at Rank Xerox EuroPARC conducted (Dourish et al. 1993), exploring how features of the technology in practice affected how people interpreted the information they found there. These investigations into different uses of organizational information exhibit the common property that the information in the system makes sense only in the context of a set of common practices by which people can select, interpret, understand, and put the information to use in the course of their work.

Intentionality

The final aspect of meaning to explore here is intentionality. Again, this is an aspect of meaning that has already been encountered in the discussion of phenomenology. Now, however, I want to explore it in more detail and to begin to uncover its consequences for the design of embodied systems.

Intentionality is the term philosophers use to refer to the "directedness" of meaning. Intentionality proposes meaning as a relationship between some entity (perhaps a thought or utterance) and some other entity (its meaning). So, for instance, when I think about my editor at MIT Press, there is an intentional relation between my thought and a bearded man called Bob. When we say that the word *tree* means an example of that class of plants with woody bark, say, then we imply that there is an intentional reference, "directed" from the word to the concept. Thoughts, memories, and imaginings, then, are intentional acts.

Even just this simple definition throws up a host of complex problems. For instance, what does it mean to refer to a *concept* anyway? How does referring to the concept of a tree differ from referring to a particular tree (or to the set of all trees)? When I refer to the concept of tree, do I refer to the same one as you? What about when the concept is an imaginary one; do I do the same sort of thing when I refer to a tree as when I refer to a unicorn, or to Prospero, or to a square egg? Do I have to keep revising an intentional reference if the object of that reference is changing, like keeping a gun trained on a moving target?

Although I do not want to dwell on them here, the topic of intentionality has been the focus of many debates in the philosophy of mind and cognitive science, and especially to those concerned with the questions of machine intelligence. It centers on controversies around the physical reality of familiar mental phenomena such as thoughts, beliefs, and memories, as well as discussions of the relationship of meaning to action and language. Some, such as Jerry Fodor or Hilary Putnam, insist that psychological entities such as thoughts, beliefs, and memories must correspond with brain states that are their direct physiological analogs, while "eliminativists" such as Richard Rorty or Paul and Patricia Churchland claim that the familiar language of mental phenomena is a human invention or convenience that should be discarded, and that thoughts, beliefs, and memories will turn out to have no reality at a neurophysiological level. Daniel Dennett takes a less extreme stance. Although he joins the eliminativists in denying the literal neurophysiological reality of psychological events, he doesn't go so far as to advocate abandoning the language of mental phenomena, arguing that it remains a critical resource for our experience of the mental. Button et al. (1995) offer a critique of the concept of intentionality and its role in cognitive science from the perspective of Wittgenstein's ordinary language philosophy, arguing that the solution to arguments over the meaning and nature of thoughts, ideas, and so on must be rooted in the practical use of those words within everyday linguistic practice.

We owe our modern concept of intentionality to the nineteenth-century work of psychological philosopher Franz Brentano, and his explorations of the philosophical basis for understanding mental life. (Husserl studied under Brentano; hence, perhaps his interest in questions of intentionality.) For Brentano, intentionality was "the mark of the mental"; it distinguished conscious thought from the merely physical or mechanical operation of the world.

The simplistic interpretation of Brentano's position, though, is complicated by the social world in which we operate. If intentionality is a purely mental phenomenon, then how can things be invested with social meaning? Furthermore, does it mean that only mental phenomena can be intentional? Given that mental phenomena are irremediably private, how could there be any shared meaning?

One way of resolving these problems is to consider two sorts of intentionality, *original* intentionality and *derived* intentionality. Original intentionality refers to the phenomena that primarily concerned Brentano; intentional phenomena occurring in conscious creatures like ourselves who have the power to create intentional references—to mean things. Derived intentionality, on the other hand, is a form of intentionality that comes around only through the interpretations performed by others. So for example, when I think of a tree, my thought is an originally intentional phenomenon; but when I write the word "tree" on a piece of paper and hand it to you, the marks on the paper "refer" to a tree only because they can be interpreted by you and by me to refer to a tree. The intentionality of language is derived from the original intentionality of our mental lives.

An extreme form of this position is that taken by Dennett (1987). Dennett, essentially, argues that *all* intentionality is derived. Intentionality on the part of one entity comes about, he proposes, as a result of other entities taking an "intentional stance" toward the first. The intentional stance is, in effect, a presupposition of rationality and of the ability to make intentional references. In other words, Dennett's position is that intentionality is not solely the achievement of an individual, but rather that intentionality is a mutual achievement of both observer and observed. This position is not unrelated to that developed in Schutz's exploration of intersubjective meaning, discussed earlier.

How is it, then, that intentionality is relevant to the topics at hand here? Where does it feature in an embodied model of interaction?

Intentionality is central to any understanding of embodied interaction. The reason lies in an understanding of computation itself. Computation is fundamentally about representation. The elements from which we construct software systems are representational; they are abstractions over a world of continuous voltages and electronic phenomena that refer to a parallel world of cars, people, conversational topics, books, packages, and so forth. Each element in a software system has this dual nature; on the one hand, it is an abstraction created out of the electronic phenomena from which computers are built, and on the other, it represents some entity, be it physical, social, or conceptual, in the world which the software developer has chosen to model. In other words, computation is an intentional phenomenon; what matters about it is that it refers to things. At the end of the day, it is the things that matter.

So, if computational is intentional, then interaction with those computational elements also carries with it intentional connotations. If the key feature of the computational system is that it refers to elements in the world of human experience, then the key feature of interaction with computation is how we *act through* it to achieve effects in the world. When I click on the "Buy now" button on a bookstore Web page, what matters to me is not that a database record has been updated (though that is important, and the bits that get written—physically—onto the disk have some serious consequences) but rather that, in a day or two, someone will turn up at my door carrying a copy of the book for me. I act through the computer system.

In turn, this takes us to another element of the relationship between embodied interaction and intentionality. Embodied interaction places particular emphasis on interaction as activity in the world. Phenomenology argues that action and meaning are inherently inseparable. There is no way to talk about action independently of meaning—not simply how the action arises from conscious intent, but, more significantly, how intentionality arises from actions in the world.

Intentionality, ontology, and intersubjectivity each describe a different aspect of meaning, and so reveal different ways in which the representations that computer systems manipulate are related to the world and to each other. The way those relationships come about is our next topic of concern.

Coupling

So far, in exploring the elements that make up the embodied perspective, I have concentrated on three aspects of meaning—ontology, intersubjectivity, and intentionality—and focused in particular on intentionality as a central component. The relevance of intentionality is that it provides us with a route to understanding how the elements of an interactive system can take on meaning for users in the course of activity. However, it is only part of the story. Conceptually, intentionality sets up a relationship between embodied action and meaning. The other aspect to be considered is how this relationship is managed and maintained.

So to balance our exploration of intentionality, I want here to concentrate on a notion of coupling. Coupling is how an intentional reference is made *effective*. In the physical world, my local actions can have a remote effect, through a chain of couplings, from one thing to another to another—perhaps from my hand to a lever to a rock I want to move. I act on the rock by acting on the lever. As far as I am concerned, I am acting on the rock; from my point of view, the rock and the lever are coupled. This idea of coupling is not simply a physical phenomenon but an intentional one too. My actions are outwardly directed, through a chain of associations (including, as we will see, social and linguistic associations as well as physical ones). By coupling, I mean the way that we can build up and break down relationships between entities, putting them together or taking them apart for the purpose of incorporating them into our action.

To explore this, let's take the classic example of the hammer, which Heidegger uses to illustrate the concept of equipment. The essence of that example is in the way in which the hammer moves from being ready-to-hand to present-at-hand; that is, from being employed within the action of hammering as an almost "invisible" extension of my arm to become more immediately present and "visible" as an object of focus and attention. Significantly, this example highlights the different ways in which I can be oriented toward the hammer. When the hammer is present-at-hand, it is separate from me, while in the ready-to-hand case, my arm and the hammer feature as a single unit in my activity; they are coupled.

I want to do more than observe simply that these different modes exist. Instead, I want to make three points: first, that the existence of both modes is critical to effective use of technologies; second, that we need ways of being able to move between them; and third, that this is just as true for abstract representations as it is for physical objects like hammers.

The reason that variable coupling is so crucial is that it the effective use of tools inherently involves a continual process of engagement, separation, and reengagement. I need to realize that it's time to use the hammer; pick it up and orient it correctly; use it, probably adjusting it in my hand a couple of times as I do; and put it down again. Perhaps I'll even turn it around to use the claw on the reverse side, disengaging and reengaging as I do so. Inherently, a tool is something outside myself, something separate from me; but, equally inherently, the use of a tool requires that I be able to engage with it, and render it ready-to-hand in Heidegger's terminology. I can't use the hammer if I am continually, consciously, and attentively aware of how it sits in my hand; I need it to disappear (Heidegger uses the term *withdraw*) into the activity. But at other moments I need to be able to consider the tool as an entity in itself, when I need to reorient my relationship to it; when I wonder if the hammer is heavy enough to hold the door open, perhaps. Being able to disengage and reengage in different ways, that is, being able to control coupling, makes our use of equipment effective. It allows us to act with and to act through artifacts.

If there were simply these two states, and if we dealt with only one entity at a time, this would not, perhaps, be particularly interesting or challenging. However, the truth is more complex. As we have seen, the tools through which we operate when interacting with a computer system are not simply physical objects, but software abstractions, too. There are very many of these abstract entities in operation at any given moment, and programs link them together in a variety of ways. Abstractions can be layered on top of each other, embedded within each other, joined together in lists, made to operate on each other's behalf, and so forth. They operate at different levels, and my interactions affect them all.

The consequence, then, is that there are very many different levels of description that could be used to describe my activity at any given moment. Some, perhaps, are ready-to-hand and some present-at-hand at the same time; my orientation toward them each will change. For instance, sometimes as I move the mouse, the mouse itself is the focus of my attention; sometimes I am directed instead toward the cursor that it controls on the screen; at other times, I am directed toward the button I want to push, the e-mail message I want to send, or the lunch engagement I am trying to make.

As discussed earlier, the computational world distinguishes between abstractions and implementations. We work with abstractions, but rely on implementations to make them real. However, by focusing on abstraction, we often ignore the practical consequences of implementation. Running code has real consequences that belie the appearance of "abstraction." These seeming abstractions take up real memory, take finite amounts of time to operate, and so forth. If what Microsoft was selling were purely abstract, we would never have to upgrade the memory in our machines; but because the computer on my desk has 32,000 times as much memory in it as did the first one I ever used, it is a reasonable guess that something more than abstractness is afoot.

This dual nature, abstraction and implementation, gives computers their power. Computers are systems for manipulating abstract representations, but the fact that those representations can be backed by implementations means that they can be active. It may be abstraction that makes computer systems manageable and allows us to use them as complex simulation environments for both for abstract problems like logical proofs and real problems like weather prediction; but it is implementation makes them tools that actually get things done, from printing books to controlling air conditioning. Both aspects are critical. Similarly, the effectiveness of our interactions with computers rests upon the same dual nature. The structure that represents a keystroke is a pure description of an event that took place when I typed on the keyboard; but it is also an entity that can, in combination with others, affect the state of the system's memory, the record on the disk, the output that gets printed on the page and ultimately what is communicated to readers. Just as in the physical world I need to be able to coordinate my action with the hammer, so, too, when I approach a computational system, I need to find a level at which to address it that meets the particular task I need to get done. Finding the right level means finding a combination of abstraction and implementation that fit the moment.

So, at any given moment, my action may be directed toward one of any number of elements in the world and in the computer. I act *upon* some; I act *through* others. In this situation, coupling is not simply a question of whether the mouse is ready-to-hand or present-at-hand. Instead, the question is how to *assemble* the range of computational components available to me into a grouping through which I can achieve whatever effect I need. I use the term *assemble* here to draw attention to the wide range of potential configurations that are available. The traditional compositional model of computer systems design breaks a system down into multiple layers, each more abstract and each residing on top of a more concrete layer below it.

As an example, consider the traditional layered decomposition of an interactive system shown in figure 5.1. At the bottom, the most primitive layer, the system is organized in terms of input signals (such as key presses and mouse movements) and output signals such as pixel settings (the state of each individual dot on the screen). On top of these, we can successively

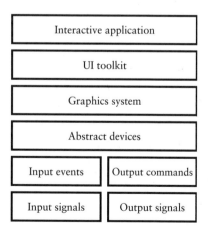

Figure 5.1
Layering of abstractions in interactive software systems.

layer more abstract notions. So we add input events and abstract devices that generalize across different sorts of hardware; then graphical objects such as lines and regions; then graphical widgets such as radio buttons and scroll bars; and finally the "high level" application operations such as creating objects, saving files, and printing documents. If we took this model at face value, then we might conclude that the question of coupling is simply to decide which layer you are focusing on at any moment—whether you are concerned with application features, graphical objects, or whatever. However, that would imply that the layered model is both a model of software *and* a model of the user's activity. But that is not the case. Layered models arose as useful tools for tackling the technical problem of developing interactive systems, and so to structure specific (software) solutions to that problem. They are not models of the intentions or concerns of the users of such a system. As a user, the terms in which I might interact with a system arise from my own activities, and not from the internal structure of the software, or even from the model that the software developer used to design it. So, for example, when I'm trying to click on "okay" to send an e-mail message on a system that is busily performing other background tasks, my attention can be directed toward an assemblage of components that includes both mouse-tracking ("why is it lagging behind?") and message-sending ("I need to get this message sent before people start to go home") without any conscious directedness toward the components in between (such as the application, the user interface toolkit, and the abstract event mechanism).

So, coupling in interactive systems is not simply a matter of mapping a user's immediate concerns onto the appropriate level of technical description. Coupling is a more complex phenomenon through which, first, users can select, from out of the variety of effective entities offered to them, the ones that are relevant to their immediate activity and, second, can put those together in order to effect action. Coupling allows us to revise and reconfigure our relationship toward the world in use, turning it into a set of tools to accomplish different tasks.

Coupling and Metaphor
One of the best developed uses of coupling in user interfaces does not concern the abstractions in terms of which interactive software is constructed,

but rather the abstractions in terms of which the user experience is design—user interface metaphors.

User interfaces are suffused with metaphors. The "desktop" metaphor and its relatives, including more recent metaphorical environments based on offices, streets, and shopping malls, are the ones that jump most immediately to mind; but even outside of these, we find that our interfaces are built out of "buttons," "pages," "dialogs," "files," "menus," "dragging" and "dropping," "cut" and "paste," and a host of other metaphorical models. Specific application domains feature their own common metaphorical models; multimedia applications, for example, frequently adopt the "VCR" metaphor (buttons for play, pause, stop, rewind, and fast forward, often with the same markings as they typically have on VCRs, CD players, and similar devices); calculator tools typically ape conventional calculators, note-taking tools adopt the conventions of Post-It notes or tabbed notebooks, and so forth.

I referred to Lakoff and Johnson's investigations of metaphor in chapter 3. Metaphor is such a rich model for conveying ideas that it is quite natural that it should be incorporated into the design of user interfaces. The use of metaphor essentially extends the intentional range of systems by providing new ways to conceive of one's actions in the system, and providing new entities for us to be directed toward. However—and following naturally from the discussion of coupling—the key to metaphors is the ability to manage the relationship between the metaphorical vehicle (the "file," "button," or whatever) and the referent (an actual set of bits or a function activation). The value of the metaphor is in suggesting some action, or simplifying how the action is carried out; but the action is to be carried out on the referent of the metaphor, not the vehicle. In addition, of course, the computational referent of the metaphor has a set of capabilities that the metaphorical object does not. Computer files can be indexed, copied, and transformed more easily than paper ones; user interface buttons can be moved around, renamed, or eliminated altogether more easily than those on my microwave oven; and when I empty the trashcan on my computer desktop, its contents really disappear rather than just being moved to somewhere else.

These may seem like trivial points, but in fact there is some subtlety here. Randall Smith (1987) has referred to interface metaphor as "the tension between literalism and magic." He points out that the design of a metaphor depends on the moment when the metaphorical vehicle is abandoned and "magic," or the extra power that the system adds, takes over. For example, the metaphor of a desktop is useful, but I want to be able to have the system tidy up the desktop automatically, make sure that things don't fall off it, and extend it infinitely in all directions; if there were none of this "magic," then I'd have a *simulation* of a desktop rather than a metaphor. In terms of our discussion here, then, metaphor hinges on the ability to decouple the metaphorical vehicle from its referent, while being able to maintain the coupling long enough and effectively enough to smooth the accomplishment of a task. Metaphor depends on coupling.

Coupling: Summary

While intentionality concerns the relationship between what is done and what is meant, coupling is concerned with how that relationship is maintained. It plays a critical role in any account of embodied interaction. It addresses how we assemble a set of abstract computational representations into a tool, and then act through that tool to achieve some end result. Doing this involves a continual process of separation and reengagement with a world of entities and artifacts, physical and virtual, each of which carries different meanings and plays different roles in the multiple, overlapping contexts in which it appears. Coupling allows us to sift through these multiple meanings and extract a particular registration of the world that is effective for whatever purposes are at hand. So, an account of embodied interaction purely in terms of meaning is not enough because it does not provide for how that meaning is made manifest from moment to moment and turned to use; that is where coupling comes in. How this works out in practice is the next topic to consider.

Embodiment and Technological Practice

So far, this chapter has been devoted to the basic elements from which we can develop an understanding of embodied interaction. My goal has been to lay these out and explain, first, how they are related to each other and, second, how they can be understood to contribute a more general foundational concern with embodiment as a basic element of interactive system use, particularly in domains such as tangible and social computing.

We can use the idea of embodied interaction in two ways. The first, which will be elaborated in much more detail in the next chapter, is as the basis for an approach to design, one that is oriented toward the way in which people interact with systems as a fundamentally embodied phenomenon. This aspect of embodied interaction is the primary one explored in this book, and it is the main motivation for looking at social and tangible computing, in that those are the current approaches that most directly incorporate the embodied approach. However, embodied interaction is not a specific form of technological design; it is a *stance* we can take on the design of interactive systems. As a consequence, the second way to use the idea of embodied interaction is as a way of uncovering issues in the design and use of existing technologies. Interaction is already embodied in current systems, and so we can find elements of the embodied interaction perspective in current practice.

So drawing on this second aspect, we will now explore some examples, presented in order to make the ideas discussed so far more concrete by showing how they figure as part of real cases. They also illustrate how we can use the ideas to understand settings of use—embodied analysis, if you will—and point to how we might use embodiment as an organizing principle to understand what is going on in interactive systems.

The first example we will look at is based in research in multimedia communication environments called media spaces; the second is MIT's "Illuminating Light," one of the prototype "tangible-luminous" applications introduced in chapter 2.

Embodiment in the Media Space

A "media space" is an audio, video, and computational network environment for communication and collaboration. The term was coined by a research group at Xerox PARC in the mid-1980s to describe a prototype system it had developed to explore new ways of supporting collaborative working (Stults 1989; Bly, Harrison, and Irwin 1993). They were not concerned with technological development per se, but rather with exploring the new working practices that technology might afford. So the Media

Space was built using off-the-shelf components such as everyday video cameras and monitors, along with professional analog video switches. Although this was expensive equipment at the time, it was relatively mundane and well understood technically. The group's intuition was that in years to come, the technology would be cheaper and more widely available, and so the idea of video-mediated communication would be more widely accepted. With the development of cheap digital cameras, streaming multimedia on the Internet and "webcasting," this has indeed come about.

The goal of media space research was to explore how audio and video technologies, in combination with computational tools for sharing work and controlling information, could create a medium for collaborative working across boundaries of space and time. From the initial site at PARC, media space technologies spread to other research labs that developed different technical approaches and explored different research questions arising from their development and deployment. One of these labs was EuroPARC, a systems research laboratory in Cambridge, England, where I and others worked on a media space called RAVE. As at PARC, a critical feature of RAVE was that it was not just an object of research investigation, but also a tool for everyday work. In fact, because the technology spread to every part of the building that housed the research lab, it would be more accurate to describe it as an environment in which we lived and worked than a tool that we used.[4]

One important issue in media space development is its basic adequacy as a communication environment. Although video-conferencing seems superficially similar to everyday face-to-face communication, experimental and observational accounts of video-mediated communication (e.g., Heath and Luff 1991) have documented the ways in which the technology interferes with natural models of conversational conduct. Natural interaction practices are undermined by things like the asymmetries of video connections, the narrowed acoustic spectrum, and the restricted field of view offered by a video camera. However, in RAVE, the long-term exposure and continual, day-to-day use that we experienced resulted in transformations of conversational conduct that were specifically adapted to the nature of the medium. What makes these transformations particularly interesting here is the way in which they reflect the embodied nature of the medium. The transformations are organized not simply around the characteristics of audio and video transmission, but around how those technologies are situated within physical environments, and in turn how those environments are the settings for finely turned social interactions.

A simple example, drawn from a particular connection that existed for a number of years between my office and that of a colleague, is the case of "pointing through" media space. My colleague wanted to visit a nearby store and asked if I knew where it was. I responded with directions on how to reach it, and my directions were accompanied by explanatory gestures and indications of direction. However, as illustrated in figure 5.2, the offices connected by our video connection had different orientations, and in particular, our video equipment was oriented asymmetrically. Consequently, the orientation of my virtual image on my colleague's monitor was not the same as my own *physical* orientation, so when I would point in one direction, my image would point in another. However, I was able to "point through" the connection; that is, to transform my original gestures in such a way that they would appear, on my colleague's monitor, to indicate the directions that made sense for her; so, for the arrangement shown in the figure, if P wanted to indicate the direction to point A, he would gesture *behind him* rather than to his right, so that his virtual image would appear to be pointing in the correct direction.

Pointing is, of course, a fundamentally embodied activity even in the most straightforward physical sense of the word. It involves a bodily orientation that occurs both with respect to the outside world and with

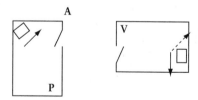

Figure 5.2
Pointing through the media space. P and V have asymmetric office layouts. When P points at A, as indicated by the arrow, the camera relays his image to V's monitor. In V's office, P's image appears to point in the direction shown by the solid arrow, rather than in the desired direction shown by the dotted arrow. P must point in a way that anticipates how his gesture will be transformed.

respect to an ongoing conversation. It is this second aspect that is important here; that is, the pointing gesture is only useful if it can be interpreted appropriately, which means that it is not simply the orientation of
the pointing finger that is important, but the mutual orientation of speaker
and listener. It is this mutual orientation that the media space interferes
with, of course.[5] This example highlights how the pointing gesture had
become reembodied in the new technological frame that the media space
presented. By separating and potentially differentiating the frames of orientation in which gestures are produced and received, the media space
technology had interfered with the relationship between action and
meaning; but over time, a new coupling had been established between
these two frames that could restore the participants' ability to produce
meaningful gestures.

A second example of the transformations in communicative conduct
that the media space introduced comes from this same long-term connection, but concerns not just the behavior of the individuals using the
connection, but that of others around them.

In each office, the camera was arranged so as to point roughly toward
the door. As it happens, this was not how our offices and video equipment had originally been arranged. Instead, it was an arrangement that
was worked out only after the connection had been in place for some
time. We rearranged our offices as we increasingly came to understand
that the video connection was not merely a technological artifact that
occupied some space in each office, but rather it was, itself, a warping of
the space of the building. The media space in general, and this long-lived
connection in particular, had created a new hybrid space that extended
across both the physical space of each office and the virtual space of the
audio and video link. The link was not simply between one person and
another, but between the spaces that we each occupied. Rearranging the
layout of the room and the equipment so that the cameras pointed
toward the door was a reflection of this idea of linked space. It enabled
each participant to be able to see toward, and sometimes outside of, the
door of the remote office. In doing so, it extended their ability to be
present and active in that space, by affording them a view of passers-by
and office visitors.

One particularly interesting thing about this blending of physical and virtual space was the way in which other people oriented toward it. It became accepted practice among our colleagues that, on arriving in one office, they should greet not only the local occupant, but also the remote "occupant," virtually present across the audio/video connection. At the same time, people understood that, to do this, they should ensure that they were standing in the area of the office that was "on-camera" for the remote participant; would engage in conversations with both participants at once whichever office they were in; and so on. Furthermore, they could come to either office to talk with either participant, whether local or remote. In other words, in the ways in which they organized their conduct, they oriented toward either physical office as one part of a larger, hybrid space that encompassed both the physical and the virtual. It was a single, hybrid, shared space.

Our experiences with the media space, and our attempts to explain them, led my PARC colleague Steve Harrison and me to articulate the difference between "space" and "place" that was discussed in chapter 3 (Harrison and Dourish 1996). As we saw there, the difference between space and place is an analytic one; *space* refers to the physical and mechanical elements of the environment, whereas *place* refers to the ways in which spaces become vested with social meaning through the emergence of mutually constituted practices and behavioral norms that develop when that space is populated.

This distinction, supported by the emergence of new practices in the media space, is enlightening when we look at other related technologies such as collaborative virtual reality environments. By arguing that the elements of place, not of space, are important when understanding group activity in a populated environment, we suggest that the three-dimensional, spatial nature of many collaborative environments is valuable not because it renders them intrinsically social environments, but only (and at best) as a shortcut to the establishment of shared social meaning. In fact, there are many examples of such social practices developing in environments or media that do not base themselves on "real-world" models, such as electronic mailing lists, online discussion groups, and chat rooms. These are places that succeed without an underlying model of space to build upon. "Space" is only a means to an end.

What makes hybrid environments like the media space particularly interesting, though, is that they force us to confront the embodiment of social action in a much more direct way. In a conventional immersive virtual reality system, a user is *projected* into a virtual space by means of datagloves and other sensor mechanisms. At the very same time as the VR system exploits a user's familiarity with three dimensions, gravity, and other features of reality that have been adapted to the virtual, it removes the user from the real physical world. The physical space and the virtual space exist in parallel, knowing nothing about each other.[6] In hybrid spaces, by contrast, there is no such projection; instead, the physical and the virtual are combined, each becoming aspects of the other. The unusual properties of the virtual medium highlight the ways in which commonly occurring behaviors in the everyday world, such as the use of eye contact to manage conversational turn-taking, or the reliance of gesture on mutual orientation and shared space, are embodied behaviors that depend for their meaning and effectiveness on the nature of the situation and circumstances in which they are produced.

This gives us an opportunity to see how embodiment, intentionality, and coupling are related in the real world of everyday face-to-face communication, and how new behaviors and new forms of interactional meaning can be developed around the specific features of novel technologies.

Embodiment and Tangible Applications

As a second example, let's explore in more detail one of the applications from the MIT Media Lab's Tangible Media group that we encountered in chapter 2. The one I want to focus on is "Illuminating Light" (Underkoffler and Ishii 1998). This was the first of a number of applications supporting specific forms of professional activity that are outside the normal computational domain. Because it was the first, it is more primitive than some of its successors; of course, this makes it even more appropriate as an example inasmuch as it is easier to explain and very direct in its demonstration of the basic principles we are trying to apply.

You will recall that Illuminating Light is a simulation environment for laser holography. Its developers describe it as presenting a "luminous-tangible" interface, by which they mean one that relies not only on the physical manipulation of artifacts for input, but also on the use of projected computer images for output. Like the Digital Desk, Illuminating Light creates an environment in which physical and virtual objects are combined to form a single, seamless working environment. In fact, Illuminating Light has a great deal in common with the Digital Desk; its primary differences are the benefits in technological improvements that six or seven years can bring, and an interface developed much more closely around a specific task and a specific set of needs. It is the nature of this interface that will concern us here.

The interface allows users to experiment with and explore configurations of equipment for laser holography. It is based on *phicons,* physical objects that act as icons for the task components. In particular, the phicons in this application represent task-specific objects such as beam-splitters, lenses, mirrors, and laser sources. By moving these objects around on a physical surface, users control the configuration of virtual task objects; a digital video camera connected to the application tracks the phicons' movements. At the same time, a video projector turns that surface into a display, providing a simulation of the state of the experimental apparatus in the configuration that the user provides. It does this by projecting images of the laser light beams. Projected from the laser source, the virtual "beams" are split by the beam-splitters, reflected by mirrors, focused by lenses, and so forth. This simulation of the effect of the objects on the optical configuration is maintained in real-time, and responds as users move "mirrors" and "lenses" around, and so forth.

Looking at Illuminating Light in terms of embodiment, we immediately encounter some interesting issues it raises about the multiple levels of meaning that can be associated with the objects and with manipulations over them. On the simplest level, a user might move the phicons around just as objects; to see what happens, to clear them out of the way, and so forth. On another level, they might choose to move the phicons *as mirrors and lenses,* that is, as the metaphorical objects that they represent in the simulation space. So, one object might be brought onto the table because a beam-splitter is needed in such-and-such a place, and so on.

On another level, we can see that, in fact, even these metaphorical objects are simply tools in another domain. The world of the simulation is laser holography, and what matters are the paths and alignment of beams of coherent light. So, rather than thinking of using the phicon as a tool to move a virtual mirror, we could take the next step and think of using the virtual mirror as a tool to redirect a virtual beam of light. Interestingly, the light paths are maintained and projected by the system itself, not by the users, so users must manipulate them indirectly by manipulating the objects that manage them in the simulation space. Both physical and virtual objects can be regarded as tools depending on the level of intentional coupling we choose for analysis.

There is one further intentional level at which we can think about actions over Illuminating Light's phicons. Illuminating Light actually provides for the manipulation of the simulation in two different worlds; the world of physical and continuous interaction and simulation, and the world of precise, mathematical abstraction. One goal of the Illuminating Light workbench is to give students of holography a direct experience of the physical reality of a set of phenomena that they would otherwise see largely through mathematical description and modeling. It is important, then, that if the application is to bridge between these two very different forms of description and experience, that it needs to find a way to relate them. So, part of the projected display of the application is *numerical* descriptions of the configuration that the user has set up physically. The distances between physical objects (that is, the distance that the light will travel between them) is given numerically, as are the incidence and reflection angles at mirrors and beamsplitters. These figures can be seen in figure 2.5. Like the projected light beams, these numerical values are updated in real time, making them responsive to the manipulation of the configuration. Interestingly, while some tasks involve achieving particular geometric arrangements of elements, others involve coming up with arrangements that are characterized numerically—particular angles or distances, for example. So, in fact, we can also see the *numbers* as the intentional objects of manipulation in this environment; through the rearrangement of the physical objects, specific *mathematical* arrangements of the simulation can be achieved.

Of course, these different kinds of manipulation are not alternatives to each other. They are all true simultaneously. Indeed, that is the whole point. What the tangible, embodied nature of the technology allows is for these different forms of interaction to be seamlessly combined, by layering them on top of each other rather than, in a more traditional interface, presenting them side-by-side or as alternative interaction modalities.

Summary: A Framework for Embodied Interaction

The earlier chapters showed the foundational role of embodiment in social and tangible computing and discussed how that idea had been explored in phenomenological philosophy. In contrast, this chapter has begun a more analytic exploration by taking the theme of embodiment from earlier discussions and beginning to tease it apart. The goal throughout has not been to propose a theory per se of embodied interaction, but rather to build a foundation for analysis and design. The first stage of this process is to understand the elements that contribute to the embodied perspective.

As we saw in chapter 4, the primary focus of the embodied perspective is on interaction with "the things themselves"; we take activity and interaction with the real phenomena of experience to be central, rather than focus on internal or purely cognitive interpretations. Embodied interaction is not what Wittgenstein called a "non-spatial, non-temporal phantasm"; it is something that happens directly in the world.

This chapter has put forward an view of embodiment that focuses primarily on meaning and coupling. Meaning involves a set of related but distinct phenomena, including intentionality, ontology, and intersubjectivity. Each of these plays a role in understanding embodied interaction. Intentionality concerns the directedness of our actions, and the effects that our actions are designed to cause. Ontology concerns the ways in which, through our interaction with technological systems, we come to understand the computational world in which and through which we operate. Intersubjectivity reflects the fact that this world is one we share with other individuals; the understandings we develop of technological artifacts and social action are ones that emerge in concert with other people. Coupling shows not just how we can understand and interpret interactive systems, but how we can operate through them. Effective action involves being able to reorient ourselves towards the technology, turning it from an object of enquiry and examination, into a tool that can be used. Technological artifacts have to be incorporated as part of a pattern of action.

The primary characteristic of technologies supporting embodied interaction is that they variously make manifest how they are coupled to the world, and so afford us the opportunity to orient to them in a variety of ways. We see, again and again, the ways in which embodied interactive technologies allow us to easily engage with them on multiple levels. The examples presented here display this characteristic. The media space reveals aspects of the interaction between communicative achievements (such as the regulation of turn-taking) and the features of the everyday medium on which they rest, and so provides us with ways to transform communicative conduct to match the transformations that the technology itself introduces. The Illuminating Light system provides multiple levels of information handling overlapped within a single frame of action, allowing us to move back and forth smoothly and easily between the different forms of interaction and the different forms of activity in which we need to engage. The embodied interaction perspective begins to illuminate not just how we act *on* technology, but how we act *through* it.

These understandings inform not just the analysis of existing technologies, but also the development of future ones. In the space remaining, I will begin to explore the implications of the embodied-interaction approach for the design of interactive technologies.

6

Moving Toward Design

The original motivation for exploring embodied interaction was to help design new systems. The discussion began by trying to understand the foundation on which tangible and social computing were built, hoping that this might reveal important lessons for designing and evaluating new systems. I started by looking at the emergence of novel approaches to interaction and how they have been realized in different generations of interactive systems. Although design was the eventual goal, the discussion took a step back and considered largely theoretical and foundational underpinnings. It is now time to try to make good on the original promise, and to cross from theory back to design.

This is a troublesome transition. It always is. The difficulty of articulating the relationship between theory and design has persistently dogged interdisciplinary work in HCI and CSCW for many years. This is not least because theory and design are fundamentally different sorts of activities, carried out by different people with different training and presented to different audiences. The goals and criteria for theoretical examinations are quite different from those for design exercises.

Consider the example of Computer-Supported Cooperative Work. As observed earlier, CSCW research has often tried to marry sociological investigations of working settings with technological design and interventions into the operation of those settings. What we have learned is that, despite our best intentions, field studies and design activities often sit uncomfortably together. Fieldwork and technological design require different sorts of sensibilities, and despite many attempts to cross "the great divide" (Bowker et al. 1997), combining the two remains problematic. Despite the premise that the field setting is an incomparably rich source of information—often, the only one that matters—it seems a rare occurrence for the design partners in these collaborative research projects actually to *visit* the field. Most often, they learn of the field through the reports of their fieldworker colleagues. In these cases, the success of the project often hinges on the fieldworkers' ability to communicate and translate their understandings in terms that are meaningful to the constructive activities of design. In many cases, though, even this level of communication is more than can be achieved, and instead communication takes place through the pages of journals and discussions at conferences. The different perspectives, concerns, orientation, and training of the participants result in each partner's feeling that the others fail to understand the complexity of their position. So, just as it has been a common critique of technological design for cooperative work that it fails to capture the subtlety and nuance of the setting (see, for example, Blomberg, Suchman, and Trigg's account [1997a] of a collaborative design project), so, too, have researchers on both sides of the "social/technical divide" bemoaned the bulleted lists that commonly appear under the title "Implications for Design" at the close of CSCW papers reporting on ethnographic fieldwork.[1] To the design community, these "implications" often seem obvious, insubstantial, or vague; to the sociologists, they deny the richness of the settings to which they refer.

This is not just a practical concern; it is a research issue. Plowman, Rogers, and Ramage (1995) analyzed those papers published over a few years' worth of CSCW conferences with a particular concentration on the role of workplace studies in the design process. They warn of the dangers of expecting or requiring workplace studies to address design concerns, and argue that the design implications of such studies should arise through an explicit dialogue between researchers from different disciplines (rather than require social scientists to be able to engage in design, or vice versa). Elsewhere, drawing on their experiences in a number of interdisciplinary CSCW projects, Hughes et al. (1995) present a framework that they use to communicate ethnographic results to audiences who are unfamiliar with the approach, and may be looking for ways to understand fieldwork findings as rubrics for design rather than as purely observational materials. The framework reflects the tension involved in "translating" the analytic materials of social science into specific proposals for design.

Of course, these problems are not unique to CSCW. The discussions of the relative roles of theory and design/practice in CSCW tend to echo similar discussions that have taken place elsewhere. For example, the latter half of the 1980s saw a similar struggle to find a workable relationship between theory and practice in HCI design (e.g., Long and Dowell 1989; Newell and Card 1985; Carroll and Campbell 1986; Carroll and Kellogg 1989; Carroll and Campbell 1989; Barnard 1991). On one hand, theoretical models of human cognitive processing offered complex, systematic accounts of the cognitive burdens associated with interface designs, while on the other, the pace of technological development and commercial interface design seemed to mitigate against the adoption of theory-based techniques in real-world settings.

Studying the practices of real-world interface designers, Bellotti (1989) noted two particular problems with using theoretical design models. First, the approaches were often laborious and time-consuming to apply, especially because they typically operated at a micro-level of analysis. Second, the models tended to be so "theory-laden" that, in fact, only their developers (who were well versed in the theories on which they were based) could apply them effectively, putting them beyond the reach of the practicing HCI designer. Attempts to produce lighter-weight versions of the theoretical evaluative techniques resulted in a move from "cognitive walk-throughs" to "cognitive jog-throughs" (Rowley and Rhodes 1992) and the emergence of "discount usability" techniques (Neilsen 1989). The debates over the theoretical and practical adequacy of these approaches were never satisfactorily resolved, although when the World Wide Web came along—not to mention the new business models and frenetic pace of development and deployment that came along with it—those who had argued in favor of speed won by default.

Despite the apparent difficulty of forging connections between theory and design practice, there is no question that such a connection is immensely valuable. Both theory and design gain value from being put together. Certainly, the argument is often made that theories become valuable only when they can generate practical results by being harnessed to design. Some—the religiously pragmatic—hold that theory is vague and abstract while design is "real." However, we could claim that this position is exactly backward; theory grounds design by providing a framework within which hypotheses can be constructed and tested, options explored and compared, and results analyzed, evaluated, and verified. From this perspective, design is simply speculative without an understanding of how and why it works; theory makes design real, because it places design in a context that explains it. Whichever position we hold, though, a working relationship between theoretical under-standing and design practice is crucial.

In this spirit, the theoretical explorations of the last few chapters are intended to ground design efforts in a variety of ways to be explored here. First, they should provide a common vocabulary and conceptual apparatus for thinking about design opportunities and design features. Second, they should help us understand how the different elements of embodied interaction are related to each other, to help cross-fertilization and to capitalize on the realization that this is a common framework. Third, they should provide a set of principles that shape and define the design of new artifacts.

The question of cross-fertilization will be addressed further in the next chapter. Here, I will concentrate on the design questions. First, I will explore the context for design that embodied interaction provides. Then, I will set out a set of design principles for embodied interaction that explore different concerns for designers of interactive systems based on the embodied approach.

A Common Framework

The core of my argument throughout this book is that social and tangible computing share a common foundation in embodied interaction. That is the theoretical perspective. However, social and tangible computing have both given rise to a variety of design principles and prototypes. It seems to make sense, then, to begin thinking about the design implications and consequences of the embodied approach by trying to understand what principles lie behind tangible and social computing, and what implica-tions they might have for each other. I will examine them separately.

At the heart of tangible computing is the relationship between activities and the space in which they are carried out. Tangible computing explores this in three related ways: through the configurability of space, through the relationship of body to task, and through physical constraints.

By "the configurability of space," I mean the ways in which tangible computing allows users to arrange the environment to meet their own particular needs. Tangible designs often associate particular sorts of functionality with different physical objects, whose distribution in a workspace is then under the control of the user (at least up to a point). The use of phicons in something like the metaDESK is an obvious example. By reconfiguring spatial arrangements, users can reconfigure system functionality; by tailoring the physical environment, they also tailor the computational environment to adapt it to their immediate needs.

Because the body's location and configuration in space is also adjustable, the idea of reconfigurable space leads naturally to the second issue, that of the relationship of the body to the task. Carrying out different aspects of an activity, we may need to be closer, farther away, or in different orientations to the objects of work at hand. We move around the action as the task requires. So the distribution in space introduced by tangible computing also supports a negotiable relationship between body configuration and the computation being employed in a task. Configuring the space and configuring the body are carried out relative to each other.

Of course, there are limits to reconfigurations of body and space that can be carried out in current tangible systems. Some limits are technical, imposed by the current state of the art in fundamental technologies such as sensing, tracking, or display systems. Others, however, are deliberate design features. Exploiting physical constraints is an important part of the tangible-computing design approach. Drawing on Gibson's notion of affordances, tangible-computing designers have sought to create artifacts whose form leads users naturally to the functionality that they embody while steering them away from inconsistent uses by exploiting physical constraints. As a simple example, two objects cannot be in the same place at the same time, so a "mutual exclusion" constraint can be embodied directly in the mapping of data objects onto physical ones; or objects can be designed so that they fit together only in certain ways, making it impossible for users to connect them in ways that might make sense physically, but not computationally.

Turning now to social computing, we see that, like its tangible counterpart, it centrally argues that interaction with software systems needs to be seen in a broader context than has been traditionally imagined, and that the influence this broader context has important consequences for the design of interactive technologies. The broader context on which it draws is the socially constructed setting within which the interaction takes place. Where traditional approaches formulate interaction in terms of two sets of capabilities—the raw functional capabilities of the software and the raw cognitive capabilities of the user—social computing introduces a new model. This model is based on alternative views of human social behavior, observing that the sequential organization of interaction does not simply result from the "execution" of a formal plan in the user's head, but instead arises from a process of continual response to the circumstances within which it was being produced—circumstances that include not only a set of prior expectations about likely actions, but also the outcome of earlier actions and the emergence of new concerns and opportunities. Users are not what Garfinkel (1967), in his critique of conventional sociological analysis, had dubbed "judgmental dopes," blindly following instructions whose sense is hidden from them; they are active participants, improvising action by creatively responding to the setting in which the find themselves.

What does this mean for design? The immediate response is to change interactive systems in two ways. The first is to support the improvised sequential organization action by giving users more direct control over how activity is managed, perhaps by organizing the interaction as informal assemblage of steps rather than a rote procedure driven by the system. The introduction of flexible workflow systems (e.g., Ellis, Keddara, and Rozenberg 1995; Dourish et al. 1996) demonstrate this sort of change. The second response is to help support the process of improvised, situated action by making the immediate circumstances of the work more visible. The insight here that the setting in which the work emerges *includes* the current state of the system; the system should make information available to the user to guide their activity moment by moment.

Just as before, we can see that although tangible and social computing share some concerns, there are differences of emphasis. The concern with the "setting-ed," contingent nature of action that social computing addresses has much in common with the relationship between activities and environment that is central to tangible computing. However, what social computing adds to this is the idea of action as *practice*. Practice implies not only the detail of what people actually do, but also that the action fits into a wider scheme of ongoing activity that makes it meaningful. Further, it implies that action is situated within a *community of practice,* which provides its members with a set of common orientations and expectations, fluid but persistent over time. The community of practice determines the shared systems of meaning and values; acquiring mastery of a practice involves the gradual movement of an individual into the community, and the ability to apply meaning and values in the way in ways appropriate to the community. This aspect of setting-ed behavior goes beyond the concerns that tangible computing introduces. It goes beyond the physical, of course, but it also goes beyond the immediate, here-and-now concern of a single user encountering tangible environments on a single occasion. It draws attention to the evolution of practice, and to the ways in which practices evolve *around* technologies, *over* time, and *within* a community. The idea that any given interaction between user and system is, in fact, just one point in a trajectory of interactions between that system and different users, or that user and different systems, is one that has generally been lacking from tangible computing analyses—even though, given its emphasis on familiarity and naturalness of interaction, it is clearly a central issue.

So, the broader idea of embodied interaction points out that action and meaning arise in specific settings—physical, social, organizational, cultural, and so forth. These are generally operative principles; the ways in which they work their way out in one case or another are matters for design.

Design Principles

So much for the background. Now it is time to focus on the question of design itself.

The way we will do this here is by setting out and exploring a set of principles. These are not design recommendations, rules, or guidelines. Rules would lay down a method for design; guidelines would suggest to a designer what to do. However, given the variety of settings in which the embodied interaction approach is applied, it would be inappropriate to give rules or guidelines here. Instead, these principles observe or comment upon general features of embodied interaction that occur across a range of settings. They take elements from the theoretical understanding developed so far, and show how they are particularly important for design. The principles will affect different designs in different ways; they overlap but reflect different aspects of the foundational position I have been developing. They point out a set of "things to pay attention to" when doing design and show how these concerns arise in specific design examples.

There are six principles that will be explored here: Computation is a medium; Meaning arises on multiple levels; Users, not designers, create and communicate meaning; Users, not designers, manage coupling; Embodied technologies participate in the world they represent; and Embodied interaction turns action into meaning.

Principle: Computation is a medium.

In the previous chapter, I presented a model of embodiment largely in terms of meaning. Embodied interaction concerns how meaning is created, established, and communicated through the incorporation of technologies into practice. Because meaning is being transferred and shared through interactive technologies, the first principle that can be drawn out from the model of embodied interaction is that *computation is a medium*.

The idea of computation as a medium has some history in the development of computer systems, and particularly interactive computer systems. Some aspects are straightforward and widely accepted—for example, the role of programming languages as media for the expression and communication of algorithms and models,[2] or the increasing range of communicative opportunities afforded by networked computers, including electronic mail, instant messaging, and video-conferencing. Certainly, these are examples of computers providing a medium for communication. They exploit the computer's ability to represent and convey information. However, they do not make computation the central element of the communicative act. In an audio or video conference, the role of the computer is largely incidental, or hidden; in fact, similar effects could be achieved using purely analog, rather than digital, technologies. What I want to do here is to consider the idea of *computation,* rather than *computers,* as a medium. Meaning is conveyed not simply through digital encodings, but through the way that computation enlivens those encodings with semantic and effective power.

This is an idea that has been particularly important to various proponents of computers in education. Pioneers such as Seymour Papert or Alan Kay have proposed the use of computers as a tool for learning, in contrast to the skills-based "computer literacy" approach that is often the spur to incorporating computers into the curriculum. Papert and his colleagues advocate computers as tools for constructive learning. Inspired by psychological theories of learning, they argue that by building active representations—programs—children learn how to explore abstract ideas and mathematical relationships, in much the same way that physical construction toys can provide children with an intuitive facility with mechanical ideas. This is a vision that has computation, rather than computers, at its heart. It is through computation that children's ideas will be expressed, and through computation that they will be shared, explored, communicated, and developed.[3]

Although the idea of computation as a medium is not new, it does shed some light on the design issues for embodied interaction through the questions it raises. What sort of communication is going on? And how is it taking place?

First, we can see communication taking place both across time and across space. Communication across space—from one place or individual to another—is manifested in the various uses of embodied technologies within groups, between people, or for collaborative tasks. Communication across time applies also to those cases in which the system maintains persistent information, such as records of activities. These forms apply both to direct and indirect channels of communication—the patient record card, for example, embodies both of these.

Naturally, these two modes of communication are often combined. One example encountered earlier is the communication between a designer and a user through the medium of the system itself. The structure of the system—its design and its functionality—communicates to the user some set of expectations that the designer held for its use—the uses to which it might be put, the circumstances in which it might be used, and so on.

Communication of this sort is an inherent feature of almost any technological design. What is particularly relevant here, exploring these questions from the perspective of embodied interaction, is the second question, How is this communication achieved?

The essence of a medium is that it can be *modulated*. Media are modulated when they are transformed in some way to carry information. Modulation is a very particular form of transformation—the medium's essential identity remains the same, but the transformation can be separated from it so that information can be both encoded and decoded. The modulation is the actual carrier of information—in terms of embodied interaction, the carrier of meaning. This implies that, in the case of embodied interaction, the modulation must encompass not only the technology, but also the practice in which the technology is embedded. So, meaning is communicated not simply in how the technology is transformed, but in how that transformation affects practice, by transforming it, restricting it, or extending it.

As an example of the way that meaning is transmitted not only through a system but also through the practices that surround it, consider the emergence of particular styles of information on the World Wide Web. At the simplest level, the Web is a medium for the transmission of information to end-users. But in terms of the broader perspective, we need to think of the Web not simply in terms of the information it carries, but in terms of, first, the expectations that people might have about the information they will find there, and second, the uses to which they will put the information they encounter. Bly et al. (1998) explored the emergence of personal Web pages in organizations and showed that the ways people represented themselves on their Web pages could be seen as a way of making their knowledge more available to coworkers. Elsewhere, Erickson (1996) explored the idea of the Web, and especially home pages, as a "social hypertext," concentrating in particular on the phenomenon of people whose pages link to those of their friends, who in turn have links to more friends, and so forth, so that the set of pages describes a social network. These sorts of observations point out patterns not just in the information that a Web page encodes, but also in the way in which people will use that information. Commonly held understandings like these—understandings of the *genres* of Web page that might be

encountered—create expectations and background knowledge that frames how people understand and interpret the information that they find. The meaning of the information is not simply what the system conveys, but how it fits into a wider pattern of practice. The medium is not simply the representation that is conveyed, but how that representation becomes active in practice.

Being able to encode a signal in a medium is of little value unless the signal can be decoded and the information content extracted. In interactive and collaborative systems, this typically arises as variety of issues around the topic of "visibility." First, there is the visibility of the activities of one person to another, across time and space; second, there is the visibility of the effect of the system in modulating that activity; and third, there is the visibility of the system's behavior in response to some user activity, whether that activity is being enacted or simply considered.

In the collaborative systems area, the problems of the visibility of the actions of one individual to another is known as "awareness," and has been recognized for some time as critical to the success of many collaborative technologies. Approaches to providing awareness information have included visualization mechanisms for real-time collaboration (e.g., Gutwin and Greenberg 1998; Dourish and Bellotti 1992), and information management and presentation mechanisms for asynchronous work (e.g., Hill et al. 1992).

The ability to "see" another's actions "through" the system can be provided explicitly by "awareness interfaces," but more often, it will be something that users must learn to do by observing activities that take place in the system or information space. However, only actions "within" the system tend to be visible, while frequently it is actions "without" that matter. Users must be able to understand how activities within the system are related to activities without; that is, how the system modulates the effects of a user's action. The most obvious way to learn this is through being able to see how our *own* activities are modulated when we interact with a system; developing an appreciation for how our own actions are reflected in the information space helps us to understand how a particular state of affairs might be the result of a sequence of activities by someone else. This is another area in which the embodied approach—and in particular, the emphasis that it places on direct engagement and feedback—is particularly related to the notion of computation as a medium. Embodiment offers opportunities for a much more direct apprehension of the modulating, mediating effect that computation plays in interaction.

Finally here, chapter 3 discussed the need for an interactive system to convey to users an account of how it operates, so they can have a more direct understanding of the potential and actual consequences of their own actions. At that point, we encountered this idea during an exploration of how sociological understandings could improve system design, exploring the nature of the "interaction" between user and system from the perspective of ethnomethodology. Here, we encounter the same idea in a different guise. Our reason to consider the visibility of a system's mechanism this time is for the "feedback loop" that it provides. By making a model of the system's action available, this feedback loop also presents a model of the outcome of user action—a communicative action conveyed through the medium of computation. Effective communication relies on the ability of the "sender" to be able to control the medium, and the feedback loop is an essential element of this control.

I do not want to present a *strict* account of embodied interaction as communication, or to draw analogies from formal understandings of communication such as Information Theory. Instead, I want to use the idea of computation as a medium to orient design toward certain perspectives and opportunities. It highlights the active nature of computer systems—the fact that they *do* things—in a different way; not as the actions of independent agents, but as augmentations and amplifications of our own activities. This encourages a focus not on the capabilities of the technology per se, but on how that technology is embedded into a set of practices. Practices modulate systems as signals modulate media. In turn, this orientation toward practice opens up a different set of design approaches and opportunities for embodied interaction.

Principle: Meaning arises on multiple levels.

The analytic exploration of embodied interaction has repeatedly uncovered the way that objects carry meaning on multiple levels: as entities in their own right, as signifiers of social meaning, as elements in systems of practice, and so on. Artifacts and representations carry different sorts of meanings simultaneously, and activities are caught up in many different tasks at the same time. This analytic perspective clearly has consequences for design, too. Systems or artifacts supporting embodied interaction need to be designed with an orientation toward the multiplicity of meanings that may be conveyed through them. As I will discuss shortly, creating and managing meaning cannot simply be the responsibility of the designer. However, the designer has a critical role to play in making systems open to multiple forms of use.

The different levels of meaning involve artifacts and representations in different ways. There is a variety of ways in which artifacts can convey meaning as a part of their patterns of use. Some of these can be separated out along two dimensions, iconic/symbolic and object/action. Although these dimensions do not support rigid classifications, they help unpack the issues by characterizing aspects of the representation and the entity to which it refers.

The iconic/symbolic dimension describes the relationship between the representation and whatever it represents. Symbolic representations are abstract ones, in which the form of the representation and the form of the represented entity are largely unrelated. So, the numeral "1" stands for the number one on a purely symbolic level. In contrast, an iconic representation attempts to *depict* the entity it represents, at some level of abstraction. For example, a map is a more iconic representation of a region of space due to the fact that it is a structural depiction of the space—its internal structure attempts to stand in some recognizable relationship to the space it represents. Of course, the distinction between iconic and symbolic representations is a rough-and-ready one; most representations have elements of both, and it can be hard to separate the features of the representation itself from the features of its cultural interpretation. For example, we are so familiar with graphical arrows that they seem to naturally, almost iconically, depict some kind of motion or directionality, even though, of course, they are purely abstract objects that we are used to interpreting in that way.[4]

The second dimension concerns the entity to which the representation refers. We distinguish between representations of objects—people and other entities—on one hand, and of actions—events, operations, and behaviors—on the other. Again, this is only an approximate classification. Direct representations of objects might well, of course, indirectly represent activities, by showing the movements or changes of those objects; and at the same time, representations of actions often convey something of the people who engaged in those actions or the objects to which those actions were applied. This blend of properties allows us to define a dimension between two extremes.

Figure 6.1 shows a number of features of embodied systems mapped according to these dimensions. The phicons on the Media Lab's metaDESK, for example, represent buildings on the MIT campus; they are iconic representations of objects. The lenses and beamsplitter phicons used in Illuminating Light are also iconic, but are more suggestive of actions, because users typically act *through* them to produce an effect upon the light beams. The lenses in the metaDESK are even more oriented toward actions, because they represent not objects in the target domain, but activities within the interface—magnifying objects or seeing other details. Similarly, Harrison et al. (1998) introduce a range of tangible interaction devices for information appliances, including a touch-sensitive strip that allows people to "turn the pages" of an electronic book, and a PDA augmented with accelerometers used to control a Rolodex application by tilting the PDA backward

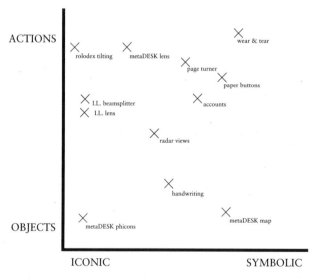

Figure 6.1
An abstract space of different forms of meaning-carrying.

and forward. The "page-turning" interface is again much closer to action than to object, but its stylized nature renders it less iconic than, say, the tilting mechanism embodied in the Rolodex application. Among the more symbolic representations, the wear and tear on the medical record cards is a symbolic indication of the activity that has been performed over them, while the handwriting is a less symbolic (more direct) indication of the person who wrote on them.

Representations of all these sorts are the stock-in-trade of user interface design, embodied or not. Interface metaphors are the conventional face of interaction—from sets of associations such as those classed as the traditional "desktop metaphor" to icons that represent files, progress bars that represent system action, and all the rest of the graphical conventions through which a system's activity and resources are conveyed. Interface designers draw on analogies and metaphors from the real world to convey the interactive opportunities a system offers to users. What embodied interaction adds to existing representational practice is the understanding that representations are also themselves artifacts. Not only do they allow users to "reach through" and act upon the entity being represented, but they can also themselves be acted upon—picked up, examined, manipulated, and rearranged.

The foundational exploration of embodied interaction forces us to revise our understandings of the relationship between representations, objects, and actions. Traditional approaches would insist on strong separations between representation and object, or between object and action, whereas the embodied perspective shows that these are simply different attitudes that we can take toward aspects of the world. Something can be simultaneously representation, object, and action, carrying different meanings, values, and consequences. From a design perspective, this draws attention to the way that artifacts may carry multiple meanings for users according to the different ways they are used, and any *or all* of these aspectual meanings may be in play at any given moment. Similarly, it also shows that, while system designers have control largely over just the representations encoded in the software, the meaning of the system extends beyond simply the software to the whole environment in which the software is used. Much of what will go on, then, is outside the system developer's direct control. It is important not to imagine that the application's boundaries contain everything that matters.

When there are multiple levels at which an entity can be manipulated, and when different degrees of representational effect are embodied in a single artifact, design needs to consider how those different levels of representation will be manipulated, and how users control whether they are acting "on" or "through" some artifact. The question is how to select and combine elements from different levels of meaning. This is a question of coupling, and it leads to another set of principles.

Principle: Users, not designers, create and communicate meaning.

Principle: Users, not designers, manage coupling.

Traditional interactive system design ascribes two sets of responsibilities to the designer. The first is responsibility for the artifact—for its form and function, and for how they are related. The second is responsibility for its use—for the sets of activities in which people will engage with that artifact.

The first of these, the artifact itself, is something for which designers have primary responsibility. It is not solely their responsibility, of course. Since the 1970s, new approaches such as User-Centered Design and Participatory Design[5] have reexamined the power balance between different "stakeholders" in the design process, and how their different needs and perspectives can be reflected in the design. At the same time, technological developments such as end-user programming provide a new basis for computational design that can remove the requirement for traditional programming training for designing software, making it more accessible to users and so encouraging their participation in the design process. Examples include the use of "macro" programming, which allows sequences of application action to be combined to create new specialized behaviors; "visual" programming, which uses graphical depictions of system behavior both to specify and explain system activity; and "programming by demonstration," in which the system can recognize repeated sequences of user action and make them available as new commands.[6] Despite these developments, though, end-user programming techniques have not made many inroads so far into common development practice, and so technical ability and qualification still stand as entrance requirements for participation in the design of technical systems. The "designer," formally designated, still has primary responsibility for the artifact.

However, the second responsibility ascribed to the designer—responsibility for the way the artifact is used—is open to considerably more debate. Obviously, artifacts must be designed with at least some expectation of their probable use. However, designers are continually surprised at the uses to which their artifacts are put, or the ways in which they are incorporated into the activities of users.[7] In some ways, this should not be a surprise in light of earlier discussions. Chapter 3 presented studies of working practice and situated action that describe the moment-to-moment organization of activity as an improvised affair, crafted in response to the immediate circumstances in which it arises. Improvisation draws on a variety of resources in the environment, including not only physical and social resources but also technological resources. So, how technology will feature as an aspect of working practice cannot be predetermined by the designer, but instead will emerge from the specific, situated activity in which the technology is incorporated.

Although it plays such a major role in successful technology adoption, the process of users adapting and incorporating systems into practice has rarely been studied explicitly. Some specific examinations of technology adoption, such as Orlikowski's explorations of the use of Lotus Notes (Orlikowski 1992, 1995), have shown this process of "appropriation" to be critically important, and one theoretical perspective—Adaptive Structuration Theory[8] (Poole and de Sanctis 1990)—directly incorporates this notion. However, a comprehensive understanding of how this process works has not yet been incorporated into the mainstream of interactive system development.

Nonetheless, the themes explored here such as the setting-ed nature of working practice, illustrate the importance of this process. Technological systems need to be adapted to the widely different nature of work process and practice in each setting in which they are used; they must be appropriated and incorporated *as a part of* a specific set of working practices. In designing software systems, then, we need to be alert to the ways in which systems offer, to their users, the resources that will allow them to adapt and appropriate it.

For embodied technologies, these issues manifest themselves in terms of these two principles. Embodied technologies are used to create and communicate meaning, managed at multiple levels through selective coupling; and because they can only have meaning through the way in which users incorporate them into working practices, then clearly the manipulation of meaning and coupling are primarily the responsibility of users, not of designers. This is partly a question of definition. *Coupling,* as I use the term here, is an intentional connection that arises in the course of interaction, so while designers might *suggest* a coupling, they cannot actually *make* one. Only the user can do that, because coupling only happens in use. By the same token, the forms of meaning that a tool might suggest will be incorporated into systems of meaning, categories, reference, and practice maintained by and shared within a community of practice; and this incorporation will, inevitably, transform them. So again, because meaning is an aspect of use, interaction, and practice, it is something that resides primarily in the hands of the user, and not of the designer.

These observations have an impact on designers in two ways. The first concerns the designer's *stance,* whereas the second concerns the designer's *activity.*

By the designer's stance, I mean the designer's conception of what he or she is doing, and in particular, of his or her role in an interaction between the user and the artifact. The traditional approach to interactive system design positions the designer as managing the interaction between the user and the artifact through control of the design parameters for the artifact. This stance is reflected in the tools available to interactive system designers—task-analytic methods to model the activities in which the user is engaged, user-modeling methods to understand the user's point of view in the course of interaction, cognitive-evaluative techniques to assess the cognitive impact of different design options, and so forth. The traditional approach offers these tools to designers so that they can explore the different possible interactive paths that a user might follow with an artifact and select from among them the path that best optimizes the different variables at work, such as suitability-for-task or ease-of-use.

This stance has to be transformed when we recognize that users play a much more active role in determining precisely how a technology will meet their needs—needs that are continually changing, and that will be satisfied using a variety of features of the setting, of which the technological artifact is only one. In other words, the precise *way* in which the artifact will be used to accomplish the work will be determined by the user, rather than by the designer. Instead of designing ways for the artifact to be used, the designer instead needs to focus on ways for the user to understand the tool and understand how to apply it to each situation. The designer's stance is revised as the designer is less directly "present" in the interaction between the user and the artifact.

So in turn, the revised stance will result in a different set of design activities and concerns. The designer's attention will be drawn to a different set of issues—a new set of problems and potential solutions. In particular, the designer's attention is now focused on the resources that a design should provide to users in order for them to appropriate the artifact and incorporate it into their practice.

The first resource is the ability to operate on entities at different levels—both acting *with* them and acting *through* them. This is one outcome of attempts to exploit "concreteness" in interfaces. For example, the user interface to the Self programming environment made concreteness a primary goal, reflecting the underlying philosophy of the language (Smith, Maloney, and Ungar 1995; Ungar and Smith 1987).[9] Their relevant feature here is that all actions can be carried out directly on the object to which they refer. By all actions, I mean not only the normal actions that one might expect to be able to perform (pressing buttons, selecting objects, etc.) but also "meta-operations" and configuration. So not only can users operate on a menu to select an operation, but they can also manipulate the menu itself—grab it; break it down into its individual components; pick up the menu items, move them around, and embed them in other objects; change the menus, colors, and feedback options; and so on.

In other words, a single locus of action supports both action on and action through the menu. In contrast, conventional approaches separate the use of an artifact from its manipulation and configuration. These "behind-the-scenes" operations are typically carried out through some other mechanism—often a separate configuration editor or control panel. The "concrete" approach offers both visibility (of which, more shortly) and direct end-user control. Coupling is a matter for users, not for developers. Separating forms of action in the interface typically prejudices one over another, as well as interfering with ways in which users can fluidly move back and forth between acting with and through;

between an orientation toward the system as an artifact or the system as equipment, in Heidegger's terms.

The second critical resource for embodied use that the designer must address is visibility. As mentioned earlier, in the CSCW community, visibility is generally addressed as the support for "awareness" in collaborative systems. Awareness is the informal, often tacit, understanding that collaborators have of each other's activities. Being aware of each other's activities helps collaborators organize their own activities to contribute to the progress of the group's work. For example, if I see that you're working on the text of a document we're writing together, then perhaps I'll realize that working on the text myself would interfere with what you're doing; instead, I'll work on getting all the citation information we need. The role of awareness as an element in the coordination of work emerged first from field studies of collaborative work, most markedly in co-present working settings such as the London Underground control room studied by Heath and Luff (1992). The idea also proved a useful analytic tool for laboratory studies of novel collaborative technologies (Dourish and Bellotti 1992) and in turn motivated the design of technologies explicitly oriented toward the promotion of an informal awareness among the members of a group (Borning and Travers 1991; Gutwin and Greenberg 1998). Awareness technologies provided group members with views or representations of each other and their work, to help them coordinate their actions smoothly. Awareness in collaborative systems may arise directly through the visibility of other people's action, or indirectly through the visibility of the effects of actions on the objects of work.

The "visibility of action" aspect is most obviously at work in systems like Portholes (Dourish and Bly 1992) in which low-resolution video images of offices and public spaces are provided to the members of a distributed work group in order to give them an at-a-glance view of group activity (see figure 6.2). The technology that supported Portholes is crude by today's standards, but high-quality moving images would have detracted from the system's goal of providing an awareness of "what's going on" that doesn't distract from the work at hand. Portholes, along with a number of other systems that have provided Portholes-like views (e.g., NYNEX Portholes [Lee et al. 1997]; Peepholes [Greenberg 1996];

Figure 6.2
The Portholes system helps distributed groups maintain an awareness of each other's activities by sharing slow-scan video images across a network. Reprinted by permission of Xerox Research Centre Europe.

Postcards [Narine et al. 1997]; ArgoHalls [Gajewska, Manasse, and Redell 1995]), provides participants with a direct view of the actions of others.

In contrast, systems that provide access to a common artifact can use a different approach, in which what is conveyed is not the activity of others but its *effects*. This is the "shared feedback" approach (Dourish and Bellotti 1992). This approach fit naturally with the synchronous shared editors that were, at that time, a common research tool. A shared text editor, for example, allows multiple participants, each working at a separate networked computer, to work simultaneously on the same document. Some systems maintain a single cursor in the document and allow the participants to negotiate for control over it; others provide multiple "edit points" in the document so that each participant can be entering and editing text simultaneously at different points in the same document. Though this sort of collaborative system occurs less often in more recent research, the ideas are now more common in commercial products—either groupware systems like GroupKit (Roseman and Greenberg 1996) or remote presentation systems like Microsoft's NetMeeting. The same shared feedback approach applies to all these systems. Shared feedback is a natural extension of the conventional feedback loop in any graphical interface. As I enter text in a normal, single-user text editor, the editor gives me feedback on my actions. I see the letters I type appear on the screen; I see the cursor move along, from left to right and wrap onto the next line; I see the scroll box move to reflect my current position in the document. Similarly, other sorts of applications—spreadsheets, Web browsers, file managers, and so forth—display the results of my action as I make them, giving me feedback on what I've done. There are two ways to think about this sort of feedback. One way is to think about it as part of the *interface;* it's a way in which the system displays information to me about how the application is responding to my actions. The second is to think about it as part of the *artifact* to which the application gives me access; my actions are transforming the artifact, and I can see that transformation take place. Thinking about feedback as a transformation of the artifact leads naturally to the shared feedback approach; in a multiuser application in which the artifact is shared, then naturally all users will see the results of an action because they all see the same artifact.

The shared feedback approach may seem obvious, but in fact it was put forward as an alternative to a number of other approaches that had been proposed to the problems of shared access and awareness. The prevailing opinion at the time was that being able to see other people's actions would be too distracting. In addition, shared feedback imposes some technical constraints. Some applications, for example, offer conceptual models involving independent action over *copies* of an artifact, which the system will later integrate. By separating the artifacts that different people work on, this approach interferes with shared feedback. Others applications choose not to use the artifact as a channel of communication, but instead present abstract representations of action as separate elements of the interface.

Awareness mechanisms in collaborative systems allow people to coordinate their activity as an ongoing feature of their work, rather than having the coordination provided rigidly by the system. They can adapt their work to the immediate needs of the moment. Similarly, chapter 3 introduced the "accounts" mechanism, which attempts to make the action of single-user software systems observable and intelligible to their users, so that people can coordinate their actions appropriately to the current state of the software system. Both of these techniques hinge on the importance of visibility in letting people manage their own actions.

The need to manage their own actions arises, in turn, from the fact that those actions take on meaning for the users, as a part of a system of meaning and practice arising around the work being done. Meaning, and its coupling to the features and representations the system offers, emerge from the actions of users, not designers. The principle that users are in control of these aspects of interaction leads to radically different approaches to design.

Principle: Embodied technologies participate in the world they represent.

One of the hallmarks of the embodied perspective is the relationship it puts forward between representation and action. Heidegger argued that meaning arises from engaged action in the world. Similarly, just as phenomenology rejects the Cartesian separation of mind and body, I have laid out a model of artifacts-in-use that rejects a traditional separation between representation and object. The embodied perspective is built on the unification of these dualities, on the fact that mind and body, or representation and object, are not entities that dwell in two different worlds, but are participants in a single coextensive reality. So, embodiment does not denote physical reality, but participative status. Similarly, the technologies of embodied action participate in the world they represent.

This is not just an analytic position, but also one with design consequences. It features in two ways—productively, in the process of design itself, and analytically, in how we might approach the environments into which we might want to introduce those designs.

From the design perspective, consider a "tangible" communication device developed at the MIT Media Lab called inTouch (Brave, Ishii, and Dahley 1998). inTouch consists of two units, each connected to computers linked by a network. As shown in figure 6.3, each unit consists of three rollers mounted side by side. The mechanism in which the rollers are mounted contains sensors and actuators; movement of the rollers is communicated to the host computer, which can also cause the rollers to rotate. The software on the computers uses the sensor information from each unit to control the movement of the rollers on the other, so that the actions from one unit are transmitted to the other.

Figure 6.3
inTouch, from The MIT Media Lab, supports a form of tactile communication by transmitting the movement of a set of rollers across a digital network. Reprinted by permission of The MIT Media Lab.

inTouch operates as an abstract communication device between two noncolocated individuals. They communicate by moving the rollers on their own unit, and by feeling the rotation in those rollers caused by the actions of the remote individual. Although there is no obvious language for formal communication through this system, the developers observed in trials that people soon found ways to engage each other through the system, playing games by, for example, attempting to oppose each other's action, or causing the system to engage in clearly "unnatural" movements such as regular periodic patterns of rotation, sudden starts and stops, and the like. People developed their own private communication mechanisms through inTouch.

The inTouch design directly capitalizes on the relation between representation and participation in embodied interaction design. Technically mediated communication involves the encoding of a communicative act into some representation (e.g., text, audio frequencies, or the position of semaphore flags) that can then be interpreted by the remote participant. In fact, there are two representations at work—a technological representation and a "human-readable" representation. So, when I talk to a friend on the phone, the electrical encodings of acoustic signals form a technical representation, while the spoken language we talk is another level of encoding. In the case of inTouch, the movement of the rollers is the basic technical representation; it is through their movement that information is conveyed from one unit to another. But the movement of the rollers is also the *topic* that the representation represents. The movement of the rollers isn't "about" human communication; it's "about" the movement of the rollers.

The idea of the technology participating in the world it represents emerges, here, in the way in which the rollers directly convey "information" about their own state. There is no further communication—no further meaning—encoded by the system. Users, of course, may develop signs, signals, and conventions that govern the ways in which they communicate through inTouch, but that is something that is familiar to us now—a "reaching through" the technology, a human-managed coupling of action to intentional meaning. The directness of the technological representation allows this flexibility in the management of communicative meaning by the participants.

The relationship between representation and participation can also arise in the analytic stages of system design, and in the exploration of design settings. Recall the discussion concerning medical record forms from chapter 1. In that example, system developers encountered problems when they attempted to create electronic replacements for the cards that were been used to record treatment histories. The reason was that the cards themselves, as physical artifacts, played an important role in coordinating the various activities that go on around a patient, including examination, medication, tests, and measurements. Not only did the words written on the card convey information, but the very writing did, too—tentative information written in pencil, for instance, or indications of corrections and erasures. In fact, the cards themselves carried important information. Old, worn, or dog-eared cards, for example, indicated that a great deal of activity had taken place over that card (and, by implication, over the patient). So, the card represented information not only about patient treatment, but also "about itself" and about the activities surrounding it.

Although the case of a physical artifact such as a record card is perhaps the most obvious example of this participative property, in other settings it can be encountered in nonphysical entities.

One example arose in an ethnographic study conducted by the Work Practice and Technology (WPT) group at Xerox PARC.[10] The site for the study was a local government organization responsible for the management and execution of large engineering projects. In this organization, which I will refer to here as The Department, a central coordinating artifact for engineering projects was a collection of documents known as the Project Files. Each project had its set of project files, which comprised a paper record of the accumulated history of the project, including all correspondence, internal documentation, plans, schematics, contracts, and so on, that surrounded and documented the activities of the project itself. Although the project files were maintained on paper, The Department was interested in the opportunities and challenges of moving some or all of them online; and it was this interest that provided the opportunity to study their document practices and engage in the cooperative design and deployment of early prototypes (Trigg, Blomberg, and Suchman 1999). The WPT group developed and deployed a set of innovative document-management solutions that were attuned to the specific document practices the group encountered at The Department, and it explored the issues and opportunities around the movement of the Project Files into electronic form.

Building on some of the other issues that arose from the ethnographic work, we developed a second prototype. This system, Macadam (Dourish, Lamping, and Rodden 1999), addressed the questions arising from the ways in which the engineers at The Department would customize the organization of the Project Files according to their own working requirements. The Department uses a common organizational scheme, called the Universal File System or UFS, which mandates how the Project Files are organized. The UFS is a hierarchical set of categories under which documents are filed. It assigns each of these topics a numerical identifier, which in turn defines the position of any given document in the set of binders that make up the Project Files for any given project. Documents are encoded according to their topic, or, by default, according to the source from which the document had been received. The UFS operates across all projects; it is a common code shared throughout the organization.

However, as Gerson and Star (1986) famously observed in their study of office procedures, "no representation of the world is ever complete or permanent." People working on projects invariably and inevitably find that the UFS was not entirely appropriate to their purposes. Categories prove to be too vague to make it clear where documents should be filed, fail to make distinctions important to the project, separate items that need to be considered together, and are poorly matched to the specific working practices of individuals and groups.[11] In order to get their work done, then, project members adopt a variety of strategies. One strategy, for example, is to file documents according to *expectations of later needs;* that is, coders try to anticipate when and why the document will be needed again, predict where someone might look for it in that context, and then file the document so that it will be found.

Another strategy is to adapt the UFS to each project's needs. The materials collected by the ethnographers included various "amended" UFS structures that people had created to suit their specific projects. In these revised UFS schemes, categories had been elaborated, expanded, and revised to suit the particulars of a project. This adapted use makes the UFS more expressive for a particular group, as well as reducing ambiguous filing by creating a shared "vocabulary" for the project. Although this might ease problems for the specific group using the amended UFS, it also introduces problems, especially for people outside the group. On occasion, other people need to browse the files or locate specific items, but variant forms of the UFS make this more challenging for them. This problem is compounded by the natural life cycle of the Project Files. As a project moves through different stages, carried out by different groups, some or all of the Project Files move with it; and when the project is over, a subset of the files are kept in storage for later reference. This life cycle has two consequences. First, the expectation is that documents will be filed by one person or one group but may be retrieved by another, so problems with the customization of the UFS are almost inevitable since the customizations are local to specific groups, not shared throughout the organization. Second, because the project moves through different groups, with different needs, there may in fact be a variety of customized UFS versions in operation for the same set of files. Customization interferes with mutual intelligibility; and the use of the project files seems to require mutual intelligibility as a criterion for success.

The problem we tackled was this imbalance between customization and mutual intelligibility, and what sort of technical provisions could be made to address it. The key observation was this: that the structure by which the documents were organized was not simply a means of carrying out the work but was, in fact, an object of collaboration in its own right. The adapted UFS schemes emerged from the concerted work of the group, and represented a collective response to the needs of the work in which they were engaged. As a common means through which their work was to be conducted, a revised UFS was also a common focus of attention and activity. The categorization structure that a group used was not merely a description of the shared information they managed, but an item of information in itself.

Building on this observation, we developed a prototype workspace for activities of The Department, which managed not only the activities over documents, but also the activities over the categorization schemes for those documents. User could transformed the filing scheme—by adding new categories, deleting others, or moving categories around in the schema to reflect different organizations of the work—within the same tool they used to work on documents. This allowed the tool to keep track of two associations. The first was the association between a particular document's category and the particular set of customizations in force at the time, for each individual and for the organizational groups of which they were a part. Essentially, that is the "context" in which the document was categorized. The second association was between the active customizations for one user and those for another—that is, the different ways in which different users had adapted used the UFS. These correspond to the different points of view of different people.

By keeping track of these two information structures, our system could essentially *translate* between one user's view and another. A document filed by one user, according to their version of the UFS, could be presented to a second user in terms of that second user's personal view of the UFS. The system could account for the differences between the perspective under which the document was filed, and the perspective under which it was viewed, and manage a translation that maintained the illusion of two different points of view. This was a step toward restoring the mutual intelligibility throughout The Department that had been disrupted by customizing the UFS.

So our system was inspired by observing that the categorization structures not only represented the work, but also participated in it. This relationship between representation and participation was fundamental to the group's work practice. Unlike medical records or inTouch, participation was not a question of physical manifestation, but one of the role that these conceptual structures played in the work. Nonetheless, the same principle applies to the analysis of work practice and provided the insight necessary to design a prototype that provided explicit support for The Department's requirements.

The relationship between representation and participation, then, can take many different forms, but the same principles apply. Representations work on multiple levels, and so interactive systems need to allow people to operate on them at multiple levels. In different contexts, the same entity may be an object of action or a means by which some action is achieved. The ways in which these transitions are manifested and managed, and the context in which they take place, are issues to which system designers need to pay particular attention.

Principle: Embodied interaction turns action into meaning.

The relationship between action and meaning is central to the idea of embodiment. The core idea of an embodied interface is the ability to turn action into meaning.

This does not happen in isolation from the rest of the world. Embodied interaction turns action into meaning as part of a larger system. Meaning, after all, does not reside in the system itself, but in the ways in which it is used. So, the idea of turning action into meaning does not imply that the system somehow *represents* meaning, in the ways that have been explored by researchers in areas such as Artificial Intelligence or Knowledge Management. However, even though we are not taking a representational stance, we must still take the relationship between action and meaning as a central concern when designing systems around embodied forms of interaction.

We saw that the relationship of action and meaning was central to the philosophies of Heidegger and Wittgenstein. They emphasize that meaning is embodied in practice, in action in the world. In thinking about the design of interactive systems, this turns our attention away from the artifacts themselves and toward the ways in which people engage with them in different settings. Instead of "technology," Heidegger talks about "equipment"—technology used *as* or *for* something: to achieve a goal, to serve a purpose, to amplify an action, and so on. This distinction applies as much to information artifacts as to physical ones.

Chapter 5 distinguished between three different aspects of meaning—intentionality, ontology, and intersubjectivity. Each has different consequences for technology and design.

One of the central questions of intentionality, and one that I have touched on briefly, is whether intentionality is an inherent feature of phenomena like words and actions, or whether they can have meaning only through their interpretation by other intentional actors ("derived" intentionality). So when we look at embodied interaction in a design context, our attention is naturally drawn to the question of interpretation. How can someone interpret and understand the meaning that may be conveyed through an action? What sort of representations might a system provide of the context in which an action arose? Will the user of a system be able to see an action or simply see its consequences? In which cases might the consequences, the action itself, and the context in which the action was carried out each play a part in understanding the meaning that is being conveyed?

These are questions that arise in designing awareness mechanisms for CSCW, for example, as discussed earlier. They also arise in Knowledge Management, a currently popular approach being adopted by a wide range of organizations. Proponents of Knowledge Management try to help organizations to capitalize on the skills embodied in their employees, by creating organizational knowledge bases that encourage people to share and distribute the information around which the organization's activities are arranged. The rhetoric of the Knowledge Management community frequently suggests some kind of commodification of knowledge. Knowledge is pictured as an almost physical phenomenon, something that can be extracted, transferred, exchanged, stored, indexed, retrieved, and managed. Various systems and products are available to assist in these different tasks. However, although the Knowledge Management literature concentrates on the repositories in which knowledge is stored and the networks across which it is transmitted, practical investigations show that the real cornerstone of organizational knowing is people. Knowledge Management consultants know this too. Successful efforts often involve appointing "knowledge managers"—people whose role is to understand how the information stored in the repositories can be applied to real problems. So, again, we see a distinction between, on one hand, the idea that knowledge, or meaning, can be represented and stored, and, on the other, the view that it has to be contextualized and made relevant to the settings in which it is to be applied. Meaning is not inherent to information; information is *made meaningful*. Intentionality is a matter of context, and of doing.

The second aspect of meaning, ontology, concerns how we understand the structure of the domain, and the ways in which people can separate one entity from another (or one kind of entity from another) and understand something of the relationships between them. Again, ways of understanding the structure of the world arise from the ways in which we interact with the world. As a perspective on design, this can perhaps be thought of as an extension of the role of affordances in interface design, as explored by Norman (1988) or Gaver (1991), and as discussed in chapter 3. Traditionally, affordances are features of the artifact (or, more generally, the environment) that afford particular sorts of action to appropriately equipped individuals, in the ways in which the keys on my laptop afford pressing to someone with the right sized fingers, and a doorway affords passage to someone of the appropriate general shape. However, features of the design also afford particular ways of understanding it, and particular ways of conceptualizing the relationship between the artifact and the environment or between the different conceptual structures that one might encounter in the use of the artifact. In the example of document filing in

The Department, for instance, the incorporation of different contexts for coding documents transforms the idea of the UFS from being something that is imposed from outside to actually being a variety of artifacts that can be called into play, singly and collectively, as needed.

The third and final aspect of meaning, intersubjectivity, concerns the way in which meaning arises as a collective phenomenon. Its relevance here is that meaning exists not for a single individual but for a community of practice. The concept of community of practice has featured particularly in the work on social theories of learning conducted by Jean Lave and Etienne Wenger (Lave and Wenger 1991; Wenger 1998). Communities of practice share histories, identity, and meaning through their common orientation toward and participation in practical activities. In Lave and Wenger's analysis, learning—and particularly the apprenticeship model—is reconceptualized as the "legitimate peripheral participation" in a community of practice and the gradual movement from peripheral to central participation in the community. In becoming a member of the community, one learns not only to exercise the skills of that community, but also to exercise them *as* a member of that community—with the same set of understandings, expectations, significances, and meanings that are characteristic of that community and how it sees itself. In technical terms, the issue here is that the technology does not simply afford certain sorts of actions, but that it also reflects particular sets of assumptions, conventions, and practices within a community. This has a number of implications. First, novel designs need to be sensitive to the way in which the artifact is not simply a tool for a job, but reflects these kinds of background assumptions. Second, they need to be designed around the different levels of participation that can be found within a community. And third, because community values change and are continually reproduced and transformed through ongoing practice, the designer needs to consider how the community can *express* its values through the tool, transforming them over time.

One interesting technical example that we have encountered already is the set of linguistic practices that Cherny reports in her study of an online community in a text-based virtual reality environment (Cherny 1999). Cherny's examples illustrate the ways in which distinctive patterns of interaction emerged within the community, and serve, essentially, as markers of membership. What is particularly significant about this example, from the perspective of the design of embodied technologies, is the relationship between technology and practice that it highlights. A number of the linguistic practices that Cherny documents were ones that had arisen, originally, around the peculiarities of the technology as a medium (that is, that the information is presented textually, that utterances are marked with the speaker's name at the start of the line, etc.) but without any specific support from the technology—that is, the verbal and graphical effects were achieved using the generic facilities that the system offered for virtual interaction. A number of them, though, were eventually coded into the system itself, reified and represented within the structure of the system. There are two effects at work here. One is that the members of the community are provided with shortcut tools (specialized commands) to engage in these behaviors; but the other is that the system itself acts as a malleable record of the practices of the community. These commands, and these practices, take on a special significance because of their history and because of the path they have followed. So, although we take a nonrepresentational perspective on the meaning that may arise from action in an embodied system, we recognize nonetheless that there are design opportunities surrounding the ways in which the technology might adapt to different patterns of activity, and that those adaptations might be, themselves, ways in which a community of practice might establish and convey meaning.

Beyond the Principles

By laying out a set of principles that describe aspects of how embodied interaction relates to the artifacts around which it happens, this chapter has attempted to turn from foundational issues to design opportunities. My concern here has been the issues that arise in attempting to create information artifacts that draw on the idea of embodied interaction, and how to evaluate or understand their use in specific settings.

It has been said that talking about music is like dancing about architecture. The same could probably be said of reading about design—especially in the abstract. A set of principles will take you only so far, especially when, as in this case, they really are general principles as opposed to design guidelines, rubrics, or rules of thumb. There are no recipes for successful technology design to be found among the principles. Instead, they are intended as stepping-stones, taking us from the more theoretical concerns that have occupied the last few chapters to real artifacts put to real use in real settings. Without specific design problems in front of us, the best way to judge the effectiveness of the principles is to see what kind of analytic purchase they give us in looking at examples of embodied interaction in current systems. Embodiment is a feature of interaction, not of technology. It does not distinguish one sort of interface from another—embodied from nonembodied. Certainly, some systems may lend themselves more to an embodied form of interaction than others, but in general, embodiment is a question of how the technology is used. So we can bring the embodied perspective to bear on a variety of interactional settings, as I have tried to do here.

Presenting the design implications as principles as I have done here is certainly problematic. For one thing, the principles overlap and interact in a variety of ways; they are certainly not distinct. For another, they suggest directions but do not provide hard-and-fast recipes.

However one reason to explore general principles rather than specific design recommendations is in the hope that they will be a little more robust to the rapid pace of technical development. Technological opportunities continue to evolve, and the sets of options available to designers is continually evolving. Principles should be more stable than design practice. A second reason is one that has also been a matter of research investigation here—the importance of context. I have deliberately discussed design implications at a level that will require designers and others interested in exploring embodied interaction to pick and choose how they apply the principles to the different settings, technologies, and needs that characterize each design encounter.

The principles are a starting point, then. They serve to orient us to a set of issues that any specific design may need to explore in more detail. They are the start of a much longer story.

7

Conclusions and Directions

This exploration is drawing to a close. It is time now to consider what
has been laid out, and to think about its broader implications.

My goal has been to uncover an underlying trend in recent HCI
research. By drawing together elements from different places and showing how they relate to ongoing research into interactive systems, I have
attempted to outline a new model for HCI design.

The foundation of this model is the notion of embodiment. Embodiment
is not a property of systems, technologies, or artifacts; it is a property of
interaction. It is rooted in the ways in which people (and technologies) participate in the world. In contrast to Cartesian approaches that separate
mind from body and thought from action, embodied interaction emphasizes their duality. We act in a world that is suffused with social meaning,
which both makes our activities meaningful and is itself transformed by
them. Our actions cannot be separated from the meanings that we and
others ascribe to them. Embodiment is about engaged action rather than
disembodied cognition; it is about the particular rather than the abstract,
practice rather than theory, directness rather than disconnection.

This notion of embodiment underwrites two areas of interactive system
research that have emerged in recent years. One of these is what I have
dubbed "tangible computing," although it goes under many related names.
Tangible computing is an attempt to move computation out of the "box on
the desk" and into the environment; to create "smart" environments and
specialized devices that are organized to work the way we do, in the world
and on the move. It attempts to exploit our physical and spatial skills and
to extend interaction into arenas where these skills can be brought to bear
for smoother and more natural forms of interaction and expression. By

capitalizing on the contextual factors of presence, location, and activity, it sets out to unify computational experience and physical experience, and to apply the experiences and skills of those who understand our relationship with the physical environment—architects, designers, artists, and others—to the design of computation and interaction. It attempts to unify the physical and electronic worlds to create a blend which is more closely matched to our daily experience and abilities.

The other is one that I have dubbed "social computing." Social computing draws on an increasing number of studies that have attempted to apply sociological methods and analytic perspectives to computer use, system interaction, and the contexts in which computation is put to use. These studies cover a wide range, from social psychological investigations of the use of computers and communication networks, to Suchman's use of ethnomethodological analysis in uncovering interactional problems with digital devices, and her exploration of the conceptualization of human action at the heart of plan-based interaction models. Social computing is an attempt to use these sorts of analytic techniques as a basis not just for analysis and critique but also for design. As with tangible computing, my aim is not to propose a new area of research, but rather to identify a particular attitude and program among ongoing research efforts.

I have argued that embodiment is central to both of these programs. Tangible computing draws on embodiment by recognizing the physical embedding of action in the world, while social computing draws upon embodiment by recognizing its social embedding in systems of meaning. These two forms of embedding are both forms of embodiment. They both reflect the participative status that is constitutive of the embodied approach. They are both founded on the same preontological apprehension of the world, one that identifies the physical, social world—and most particularly, the interface at which we encounter it—as the site of meaning.

Embodiment is important because it is not a new idea. The embodied perspective is a central theme of philosophical thought for more than one hundred years. Recognizing that tangible and social computing are both based on embodiment means not just that we have drawn a relationship between them, but that we have related them to a large body of thought which offers the opportunity to formulate some kind of foundational understanding. By turning to the phenomenological tradition in which embodiment has played a critical role, we can draw out a model of how and why embodied interaction works, a model that can support both analysis and design.

I have outlined the basic elements of the embodied perspective as they were developed by a number of twentieth century philosophers. I started with Husserl, whose work on the psychology of experience laid out the phenomenological position for the first time. Subsequently, Martin Heidegger rejected the Cartesian basis of Husserl's philosophy and developed an "existential phenomenology," which articulated a new position on the relation of mind and body and exploration of the issues of technology and "equipment." Alfred Schutz, who like Heidegger had studied with Husserl, took the phenomenological approach in a different direction, applying it to the social world and the sociology of Max Weber.

Schutz's exploration of the phenomenology of the social world—and in particular his elaboration of Husserl's concept of the *lebenswelt* or life-world—was one of sources on which Harold Garfinkel drew in framing his ethnomethodological critique of theoretical sociology. The other major philosophical inspiration for Garfinkel's work was Wittgenstein's ordinary language philosophy and his perspective on the relationship between language and social action. Although Wittgenstein's work is not directly in the phenomenological tradition, much of his later work mirrors the phenomenological themes.

Garfinkel's critique is particularly relevant to this argument because of the dominance of the ethnomethodological position in social computing. It provides one critical bridge to current work in HCI. Another bridge is provided by Hubert Dreyfus, whose critiques of Artificial Intelligence first brought phenomenology, and particularly the work of Heidegger, to the attention of the technical community (Dreyfus 1992); and another by Winograd and Flores, who, in their seminal *Understanding Computers and Cognition* (1986), first showed the consequences of this position for technological design.

In developing the argument and explaining the embodied interaction perspective, I have attempted to show how we can draw lessons from these foundational and philosophical explorations and apply them to the analysis and design of interactive systems in both the social computing and tangible computing traditions. I have outlined a framework organized around meaning and coupling that attempts, first, to uncover how embodied interaction works and, second, how we can develop systems that harness it effectively. This second concern led to the set of design principles that were outlined in chapter six.

Embodied interaction is not a technology or a set of rules. It is a perspective on the relationship between people and systems. The questions of how it should be developed, explored, and instantiated remain open research problems. My goal here has been to articulate it, to show how it draws together elements from a variety of currently active research areas, and to begin to explore what it might mean.

Broader Concerns

At this point, then, we can take a step back and see where this leaves us. In particular, it is interesting to consider how the approach that has been set out here provides us with a fresh perspective on current debates surrounding the future of personal computing.

Although it was once merely a nicety or an afterthought, HCI design is, these days, at the center of those debates. Since the introduction of the Macintosh, user interface design and user experience have taken an ever more prominent role in any discussion of the role that computing will play in our everyday lives. When, in 1984, Apple introduced Macintosh as "the computer for the rest of us," the implication was that the terms of reference were going to change; the "rest of us," after all, were people not interested in megabytes and megahertz, but in how those technical features could be harnessed. Fifteen years later, in 1999, Apple's introduction of the brightly colored and highly styled iMac signaled, again, that a sea change had taken place. This time, the observation was that Moore's Law[1] had given us machines with so much more power (at least a thousand times that of the original Mac) that further increases in memory density and processing capacity were, if not irrelevant, then at least no longer the primary or sole concern. Now, the concern for the market was to consider the environment in which the computer would be used, and so, in turn, ease its entry into new environments. Because almost any machine is vastly overprovisioned for traditional tasks, its color and shape join ease-of-use as the most salient terms of comparison. The user experience takes pride of place. By the same token, our considerations of the future of personal computing[2] reflect a similar concern. The question is not whether this or that technological facility will be available to us; the question is how we will be able to understand it, control it, interact with it, and incorporate it, into our lives.

My aim in outlining the embodied interaction perspective in this book has been to show a particular set of relationships at work between technology, social settings, and interaction. This perspective, though, also provides us with a view onto some current issues and debates about personal computing and interaction research. I will explore four here—the tension between "information appliances" and "digital convergence," the idea of invisible user interfaces, the relationship between social science and technological design, and the balance between physical and symbolic interaction in tangible computing.

Information Appliances and Convergence

One place to start is with a debate between two currently popular models for the future of networked personal computing. It is a debate about the cultural model of networked computing and everyday life rather than simply about technological development, and as such, it is carried on as much in newspapers and popular magazines as it is in technical journals and professional conferences. To me, the curious feature of this debate is that, most of the time, it is not framed as a "debate" at all. In fact, it often appears that the same people support both sides, despite their dichotomies.

One of the key terms in the Internet rhetoric of the mid to late 1990s was *convergence*. The idea behind convergence was that the Internet was about communicating with people. Although the original goals behind the ARPA-NET design were command-and-control and access to remote computational resources, the Internet revolution was really about putting people in touch with each other—electronic mail between friends and family members, instant messaging and chat rooms, discussion groups, publication on the Web, online magazines, and communication between consumers and corporations. The idea was to stop thinking about the Internet as a digital data network, and to start thinking about it as a communication medium. Obviously there are already many other organizations in the "delivery of information" business, of which the most obvious examples are the mass media—television, newspapers, radio, and the like. "Convergence" argues that these different media will come together, and that the Internet will provide a common media framework. All media will be delivered through a single communication channel. The particular vision of the convergence theorists is that the coming together of digital television and Internet access through something that would (probably) look more like a television set than a computer.

Although I associate the "convergence" argument with the mid to late 1990s, that is not to say that it is no longer relevant or even no longer appropriate. After all, I wrote the first draft of this chapter just a few days after one of the largest media companies—Time Warner—and the largest Internet service provider—America Online—announced their proposed merger into a single corporation. There could scarcely be a more telling example of convergence. Nonetheless, the technical convergence that has been predicted for many years now has been very slow in coming. Trials of interactive television, experimentally deployed in very limited markets, have been largely unsuccessful. Devices and services designed to provide Internet access through a television set rather than a traditional computer have sold sluggishly. Broadcasters have been slow to link their broadcast content to online information, and where those links exist, they rarely go more deeply than a website for the program, and perhaps some URLs appearing on the screen. The Internet revolution, it would appear, has not been televised.

Many still argue that convergence is our future. Sometimes, the notion of media convergence is extended to include computer applications and other digital goods as well as traditional media. However, after a few years, it is no longer the hot topic it once was. More recently, it has been largely supplanted on the pundit trail by a different idea—the idea of information appliances.

The basic idea behind appliances is simple, and perhaps better grounded than that behind convergence; at least, it draws upon both technical developments and experimental evidence. The evidence is the basic observation that computers are hard to use. In particular, they are hard to use for tasks that are, essentially, simple—or at least simpler than computers tend to make them. Writing a letter, looking up sports scores, keeping track of daily appointments, and sending an e-mail message are tasks that are, at their heart, fairly simple. However, they become inordinately complicated when we use a general-purpose computer to perform them, and are forced to deal with the complexities of operating systems, application incompatibilities, control panels, user profiles, and so forth. When computer use was largely limited to hobbyists and early adopters, few people questioned the complexity issue. It was taken for granted. But why should it? After all, we have many examples of devices in which computation has been harnessed much more effectively to our needs. The processor that controls my microwave oven, the one that monitors and adjusts the fuel intake on my car, the one that controls my fax machine, or even the one in my alarm clock that wakes me up every morning—these are all computational devices that I can use without the complications that PCs present. Why can't my PC be more like my microwave oven?

The key difference between the microwave oven and the PC is *specialization*. The microwave performs a much more restricted set of tasks than does the desktop PC. This specialization means that, first, the interface can be designed precisely around that limited set of activities, and, second, can incorporate special-purpose interactive components. A PC user interface has to be constructed using general-purpose components such as buttons and scroll bars; but for a microwave oven, there's no problem in making special-purpose designs such as a door handle that also halts the cooking process. This points to a second area where specialization helps—the integration of interaction and physical form. A microwave oven will always and only be a microwave oven; it won't be used to manage the household accounts later in the evening. So, its design can reflect a physical *commitment* to that use, and the software can similarly be designed with a commitment to a particular physical realization. The interrelationship between software design and product design also help smooth interaction with the microwave oven in a way that would be impossible for general purpose PCs, which are capable of all tasks but specialized for none.

This observation leads naturally to the idea of "information appliances." Suppose we abandoned the idea of the general-purpose PC, and instead employed a world of specialized computational devices—information appliances. Like the microwave oven, these devices could be designed for particular, limited tasks, with restricted functionality, marrying software design with product design to yield a device that is physically and interactionally specialized for the task at hand. By doing away with the overwhelming generality of the PC, and by incorporating the specific features of the particular task and setting, the appliance can be made much easier to use. In fact, just as we fill our houses with a variety of domestic appliances—appliances for cooking, appliances for washing clothes and dishes, appliances for playing music, and so on—we could imagine a range of information appliances specialized to different information tasks, such as e-mail, document tracking, personal information, management schedule maintenance, and so on. Indeed, a variety of such appliances have appeared, including specialized devices for online reading, devices for managing scanned documents, and of course devices like the Palm Pilot for managing personal information like schedules and telephone lists.

Individually, both convergence and information appliances seem to be reasonable models of the future of computation, but together they embody a contradiction. Convergence argues for the coming together of a variety of information streams, and so for the integration of them in a single device. The appliance argument, in contrast, takes the opposite position—it proposes a world filled with many devices, each specialized to their own tasks. The uniformity of the convergence vision and the diversity of the appliance vision are fundamentally at odds.

There are a couple of ways to resolve this paradox. One is to observe that both of these trends can be true at once *for a restricted domain.* Convergence—putting everything in one box—and appliances—the idea that boxes should do less—can both be true if we also adopt the model that people don't want to do very much with computers. That is, if all most people want to do with the computer is browse the Web, access multimedia content and send e-mail, then it is possible to imagine a single, specialized artifact that is a unified point of access to these different media streams. This satisfies the needs of the adherents of both the convergence argument and the appliance argument—but at the cost of the diversity of uses to which computers are put. We have resolved the paradox by eliminating games, spreadsheets, databases, desktop publishing, and a wealth of other application areas.

We gain a different view of the paradox, though, if we look at it from the perspective of embodied interaction. From this perspective, we can see that both the convergence argument and the appliance argument are technological arguments. The basis of convergence is the universal nature of digital representations. Convergence identifies a technological opportunity; the opportunity to encode a wide range of media signals in the same digital form. By the same token, information appliances are technological devices. Although advocates of appliances often argue on the basis of positions about human activities, their arguments nonetheless advocate a technical solution that will solve our problems. Convergence and appliances are both about technologies; they are not about interaction.

From the perspective of embodiment, the problem is one of interaction, and of the ways in which we, as users of technology, adopt those technologies, adapt them to our needs and incorporate them into our world and our activities. In particular, it highlights the fact that systems and their users do not partition the world in the same ways. Technological systems set up barriers between things—barriers between applications, barriers between files, barriers between activities, barriers between media, barriers between users, and so on. Applications on a PC exist in different worlds; even those that are integrated into "suites" still maintain barriers between different forms of content and different forms of interaction with that content. The technical infrastructures that deliver information into our homes and work environments create barriers that separate one stream of information from another and make coordination difficult. Humans respect barriers, too, but they are barriers of very different sorts; boundaries between public and private, between home and work, between personal time and the company's time, and so forth. These barriers are more or less flexible, subject to negotiation and adapted to the needs of the moment. However, they map poorly to the kinds of barriers that technological systems put in place. I might want to separate my personal activities from my working activities, but that is not the sort of boundary that technologies can recognize or respect. Instead, they set up barriers that make no sense in terms of the tasks I am engaged in—barriers that, for example, separate writing a message (with a word processor) from sending it to my family (with an e-mail client).

An interesting piece of evidence that supports this argument is a study of e-mail practices conducted by my colleagues Victoria Bellotti and Ian Smith (Bellotti and Smith 2000). They had originally set out to explore practices around personal information management (managing schedules, to-do lists, contact information and so forth). Many current tools take personal information management to be a specific sort of task that can be embodied in particular applications or devices (such as the Palm Pilot or other PDAs). What they found was that, as a practical task, personal information management was actually spread across a whole range of applications and a whole range of different situations. People put scheduling information on Post-it notes, they keep to-do lists in their inbox, they hoard e-mail messages so as not to lose contact information, and so on. Personal information management is seamlessly interwoven with the other things that people do, such as preparing documents, having conversations, working on artifacts, and so on.

The study showed, in particular, the important role that e-mail plays as a coordinating device. I mean "coordinating" in two senses. First, and most obviously, e-mail is a primary means to contact people, make arrangements, exchange information, set up appointments, and so forth. So e-mail is used to coordinate among people. Second, though, e-mail is also used to coordinate individual activities. The e-mail inbox becomes the primary site for all sorts of online activity, even activity that is not, directly, communication-related. So people keep attachments with their mail messages and use the mail system as a time-indexed storage system; or they retain e-mail messages for people to keep a note of their contact details, using the mail system as a contact manager; and so forth. E-mail is used to coordinate personal work.

Now, e-mail is one of the applications that is most frequently cited as a candidate for an information appliance. A number of companies have developed small e-mail-specific terminals that will connect to a phone line and manage Internet mail without the complexity of a full PC. But Bellotti and Smith's study shows the flaws in this approach, because the whole point of e-mail, for many people, is how it is integrated with other applications and other activities. An e-mail system is of little value to people if it doesn't allow them to send each other formatted documents or presentations, or if it cannot connect to a digital camera to download images of the children and send them to their grandparents. E-mail cannot be separated from other activities in that way. The application boundary doesn't make sense in terms of what people actually do.

What convergence and information appliances are about, then, and what they have in common, is the issue of barriers and boundaries. Convergence is a recognition of the boundaries that currently exist between information streams. Information appliances reflect a recognition of the boundaries that applications and infrastructures create, and represent an attempt to support more naturally the task and activity boundaries that make sense to us. Both approaches offer new forms of coupling by moving the traditional boundaries—coupling in the form of specialized devices for restricted functionality (appliances), or coupling in the form of otherwise unwieldy interoperation between media streams (convergence).

Of course, one of the design principles that we encountered in chapter 6 was that users, not designers, manage coupling. So, to the extent that convergence and information appliances both represent attempts to place the renegotiation of boundaries (and coupling) in the hands of designers, they both present problems. The evolution of new ways of using information and new communicative patterns on the Internet—such as, for example, the explosive rise of instant messaging—highlight the fact that people are continually moving these boundaries. Sending e-mail, as an activity, might well involve my digital camera; but my if the boundaries of my electronic mail appliance do not extend to encompass digital images, then the appliance won't help me. Even if it does support a digital camera, that doesn't help me with the digital video camera I might buy next year; its boundaries are fixed, but the boundaries of the *activity* are continually moving.

This suggests that convergence and information appliances both have roles to play, but they are not solutions for devices and designers. They are both means to an end in the hands of users; they are ways of achieving goals by negotiating the boundaries between components. They suggest an approach to infrastructure that allows convergence between media, between data, between system components, and between activities that can be put into the hands of users; devices that allow people to match system capabilities to everyday needs. Convergence and appliances, then, are the *outcomes* of embodied engagement with technology. When we see them in this way, the paradox disappears.

Invisible User Interfaces

The movement toward ubiquitous computing—under its various guises, including pervasive computing, augmented reality, and so on—initiated research programs in a number of different areas. Sensor technology, for example, has received considerable attention as a result of this initiative. Researchers have both investigated the opportunities for new sensing technologies (Smith et al. 1998) and appropriated existing technologies to serve new ends, such as the animal tags used by Want et al. (1999) or the television remote controls repurposed by Long et al. (1996). These explorations contribute to the vision of an environment suffused with computational power. Similarly, ubiquitous computing research fueled the development of wireless networking on a variety of scales—from the nationwide and metropolitan networks being deployed by telecommunications companies to the short-distance links of technologies such as Bluetooth. It also, of course, had a significant impact on user interface and interaction research.

In particular, the ubiquitous computing vision necessitated a reconsideration of the very idea of the interface. When computation had been spread throughout the environment—embedded in the very fabric of the environment—then the notion of "an interface" became problematic. Computation was no longer located in one place, so how could there be a single interface? Computation was everywhere—how could the interface be in one fixed location? Just like the computation it controls, the interface would also have to spread through the environment. Conventional models of interface—with screens, keyboards, windows, sliders, buttons, menus, and the rest—clearly do not apply to those sorts of environments, though, and for that matter, they would interfere so utterly with both the structure of the environment and the conduct of activity that they would defeat the point of the whole exercise. What was needed, then, was a form of interface which disappeared into the environment in the same way as computation had disappeared—an invisible interface (Weiser 1994; Cooperstock et al. 1995; Fishkin, Moran, and Harrison 1998).

The idea of the invisible interface resonated strongly with other approaches. In his book *When Things Start to Think*, MIT Media Lab researcher Neil Gershenfeld writes, "Invisibility is the missing goal in computing" (Gershenfeld 1999:7). The European Community is currently funding a research program entitled "The Disappearing Computer." Meantime, invisibility was a key feature of at least three other lines of argument. The first was the User-Centered Design approach (Norman and Draper 1986), which had long taken the rhetorical position that the greatest goal to which an interface could aspire was to disappear, to "get out of the way" between the user and the task. "I don't want to use a word processor," User-Centered Design advocates would argue. "I just want to *write*." The invisible interface—one that would not obscure the tasks and objects that lay underneath—was the holy grail of this style of design.

A second trend was the growing interest in information appliances, discussed above. Information appliance advocates argue that the complexity of traditional PCs rests not least in their general-purpose design. PCs and their operating systems are designed independently of the applications that run on them and the purposes to which they are put. This means that they cannot be specialized to individual tasks, and that each application somehow has to map its needs into a single, fixed interactive framework. The visibility, or even the obtrusiveness, of the interface is inevitable in that context. However, the emergence of specialized devices such as information appliances dedicated to tasks like audio communication, electronic mail, Web browsing, electronic imaging, and so forth, offers the opportunity to redress the balance and provides new opportunities for invisible interfaces. Donald Norman's book on information appliances is even titled *The Invisible Computer* (Norman, 1998).

The third trend, as we have seen, was tangible interaction. By focusing on direct physical interaction with computational devices designed as analogues of familiar real-world objects, some researchers such as Fishkin et al. (1998) argued that interfaces could become "invisible." They argued that because the interaction techniques that users would engage in were just those that they would use with everyday objects, there would be no interference from the interface; the mechanisms of the artifact would be directly available to the system's users.

So, invisibility has been held out as a laudable goal for interface design by researchers and interface design critics from a variety of backgrounds. There are various ways, though, in which it is a troublesome term.

One is that it appears to be at odds with another widely recognized feature of modern HCI practice, the influence of design. Where interfaces might once have been created by people whose backgrounds included engineering or psychology, they are most likely now to be created by people who come from backgrounds in areas such as graphic design or product design. The new discipline that has been formed at the intersection of these disciplines is generally called "interaction design" (Winograd 1996). The "design" perspective is one that differs in various important respects from the traditionally scientific or engineering perspective that it supplants. Its concern is not purely aesthetic, although that is certainly one component; but in addition to that, its concern is also *holistic* and *expressive*. By holistic, I mean that it sees interaction within a larger frame, often a cultural frame, and recognizes that an interactive artifact must be designed as a part of this larger system. By expressive, I mean that it recognizes the ways in which design and design motifs express systems of values. Design *communicates*. So a key component of interaction design involves considering the message that the design should communicate and how this relates both to the task at hand and to the details of the design.

The design perspective seeks to find a new level of engagement between system and user. It reflects an attempt to make interaction *engaging* and marks a transition from thinking about the user "interface" to thinking about the user "experience." But you cannot be engaged with something that essentially isn't there. Invisibility is not engaging; invisibility does not communicate. Invisibility and the design influence are somewhat at odds.

Another perspective on the problems of invisibility follows directly from the idea of embodiment. Looking at embodiment, intentionality, and coupling shows that the relationship between the user, the interface, and the entities that the interface controls or represents is continually shifting. The focus of attention and action is subject to continual and ongoing renegotiation. A system can take no single stance toward its subject matter; it must allow for this play. In the everyday physical environment, objects never disappear, even when we act through them; they are continually present in the ways in which they mediate activity. In Heidegger's "hammer" example, the hammer does not become invisible when it is in use. Certainly, it withdraws into a larger frame of activity; but it is, critically, present in the way in which I can act through it and feel through it. Invisibility would be a curse in a situation like that; an invisible artifact, one that does not impinge on my world at all, is not a tool I can use effectively for anything.

So the idea of the invisible interface is too simplistic. It frames interface interaction as an all-or-nothing issue. In arguing against the tyranny of complex interfaces that interfere with the job of getting things done, it misidentifies the problem, demonizes the interface, and abandons altogether the idea that the interface might *mediate* user action. In fact, this mediation is critical, but we need the resources to control it.

One could argue that it's all just a matter of terminology. Perhaps "invisible" is just the wrong term; proponents of invisible interfaces don't really *mean* "invisible," they just need to find a better term. But I believe that the confusion goes deeper than that. Even if the origin of the confusion was simply in adopting an inappropriate term, the idea of "invisible" interfaces is still conceptually misleading. The way it sets up the argument closes off various important avenues of investigation. The notion of the invisible interface correctly identifies the *inflexible obtrusiveness* of conventional interfaces as problematic—particularly as computation moves off the desktop and into the everyday environment, or even just into settings where it may not be the center of attention (out of the office and into the living room). However, we need richer models than "invisibility" to follow through on the consequences of that problem. Embodied interaction provides some conceptual tools for understanding how the interface might move into the background without disappearing altogether.

Social and Technical

Just as the discipline of Human-Computer Interaction arose from a fusion of interests in system design and psychology, so the discipline of Computer-Supported Cooperative Work is centrally concerned with a relationship between system design and the social sciences (including sociology, social psychology, organizational theory, and more). As we have seen, though, these two areas sometimes sit together uncomfortably. Certainly, the ways in which sociological ideas are picked up and used by computer scientists, and the way that technical concepts are understood and appropriated by sociologists, are the cause of many tense debates and discussions at CSCW conferences; and a persistent theme of workshop discussions is the thorny problem of quite how to bring social and design sciences together. Just as it is difficult to bridge the gap between theory to design, it is also hard to bridge from social analysis to technical engineering.

Embodied interaction gives us a new way of approaching this problem, because it provides a new way of conceptualizing the relationship between technology and social settings. This reconceptualization focuses on the concepts of *practice* and *appropriation*.

Practice is more than simply "what people do." In *Communities of Practice* (1998:51), Etienne Wenger comments, "Practice is, first and foremost, a process by which we can experience the world and our engagement with it as meaningful." In other words, the idea of practice is concerned not just with what people do, but with what they *mean* by what they do, and with how what they do is meaningful to them. Wenger uses the central idea of meaning to elaborate the concept of communities of practice, the social groupings within which this meaning is formed, negotiated, developed, and communicated. He also explores the ways in which communities of practice develop and employ various sorts of conceptual structures and artifacts—such as forms, procedures, manuals, and checklists—that reify aspects of practice. The representations embodied by software systems serve a similar role. The ways in which software reifies and represents aspects of practice can be a troublesome issue, as signified by debates over the politics of representations of work (Suchman 1994; Winograd 1994). What is at issue here, though, is the way in which software, as a representational phenomenon, relates to practice.

The embodied interaction perspective highlights the role of meaning in action; in Wenger's terms, it sets out a relationship between representation, action, and the production and reproduction of meaning within communities of practice. Embodied Interaction claims that technology and practice cannot be separated from each other; they are coextensive and will coevolve. Practices develop around technologies, and technologies are adapted and incorporated into practices. Similarly, we cannot talk about practices without talking about the technologies that are incorporated into them, and we cannot talk about technologies without talking about the ways in which they are used in practice.

The relationship between technology and practice—particularly as it develops over time—is one that, in chapter 6, I termed "appropriation." Appropriation concerns the way in which practices and technologies evolve around each other.

The idea of appropriation offers a new point for the coming together of technical and social concerns in CSCW and in HCI more broadly. Appropriation is, itself, a practice, as well as being fundamentally about the emergence, establishment, and evolution of working practices, and their relation to the settings—technical, organizational, physical, etc.— in which they emerge and are worked out. At the same time, appropriation is not purely a feature of the social setting; it relies on a variety of technological opportunities and design features. Studies of the coevolution of technologies and practice (e.g., Mackay 1990) show how specific features of technical design support or interfere with appropriation in a variety of settings.

The dual nature of appropriation offers a new opportunity to combine social and technical concerns. In fact, the means that it offers to bring the two research interests together is, in many ways, more satisfactory than the more traditional form of bespoke systems designed around ethnographic studies. Looking at how appropriation happens is, at the same time, more firmly grounded in the analytic concerns of ethnography (rather than specific field observations) and also more deeply related to principles around which software systems are developed (rather than specific system requirements).

Physical and Symbolic

The final area to be considered here is the relationship between physical and symbolic representations and how the embodied interaction perspective contributes to our understanding of that relationship.

A concern with physical representations has been one of the major contributions of the area of research I have called "tangible computing" here. Tangible computing expands the ubiquitous computing vision by concentrating on the physical environment as the primary site of interaction with computation. Tangible computing gives physical form to digital information.

Physicality arises in two ways. First, we can manipulate digital information and functionality through the manipulation of physical objects. In this model, we are presented with an environment in which digital entities—either data objects or actions that can be performed over them—have been mapped onto physical objects and the physical manipulations can be applied to them. Second, we can use the physical environment as a medium for the expression of digital information. In this model, various aspects of the physical environment can become "output channels" from the computer—so information can be "displayed" as changes in light patterns, audio signals, movement of physical objects, and so forth.

Why do this? The intuition behind tangible computing is that, because we have highly developed skills for physical interaction with objects in the world—skills of exploring, sensing, assessing, manipulating, and navigating—we can make interaction easier by building interfaces that exploit these skills. Most systems built this way provide functionality that could be provided by other means. They allow people to browse through online maps, to communicate over digital networks, to create multimedia stories, to annotate video documents, or whatever—but use physical interaction to make the interface more natural.

More natural than what, though? More natural, presumably, than the abstract, symbolic styles of representation and interaction that characterize conventional interfaces. Symbolic representation is the traditional core of computational media, and it carries over into interface design, which also relies on symbolic representations. This symbolic heritage results in abstract onscreen entities like interface widgets, the "indirect" manipulation implied by a mouse whose movements are mapped onto a symbolic cursor, not to mention such conceptual entities as records, files, URLs, mailboxes, and login names. With tangible computing, such symbolism can be displaced by more natural, physical interaction. So, tangible interaction does not simply argue in favor of physical representations; it argues for a transition from symbolic representations to physical ones.

Embodiment, though, provides a different perspective on this question of physical and symbolic. Rather than advocating a transition of one to the other, it encourages us to think about the relationship between the two.

Embodied Interaction is about the relationship between action and meaning, and the concept of practice that unites the two. Action and meaning are not opposites. From the perspective of embodiment, they form a duality. Action both produces and draws upon meaning; meaning both gives rise to and arises from action. The mutual constitution of embodied action and meaning is at the center of the argument that I have been developing here. This relationship between action and meaning implies a similar relationship between the physical and the symbolic.

An artifact itself may be physical, but as it is incorporated into a practice, it takes on a symbolic value too. The artifact, and the actions that people might engage in with that artifact, have meaning, both for the people engaged in those actions and for members of the community of practice. Interaction with physical artifacts, as has been explored, often also implies a reaching *through* those artifacts to a symbolic realm beyond. After all, if physical interaction was *purely* physical—if by moving an object from one place to another I was doing no more than making a minor change in the arrangement of the world—then there would be little point. In such a state of affairs, tangible computing would cease to be of much interest. But this is not the case. Tangible computing is of interest precisely *because* it is not purely physical. It is a physical realization of a symbolic reality, and the symbolic reality is, often, the world being manipulated. The Media Lab's "Triangles" system uses physical artifacts to tell a multimedia story (Gorbet, Orth, and Ishii 1998). By physically rearranging the triangular units, I operate on a multimedia story. If my goal is to entertain my niece, then it is not the physical objects but the story that I care about.

When we take this perspective, we gain a different view of the roles of the physical and the symbolic in tangible computing. Far from eliminating the symbolic element of interaction, tangible computing relies upon that symbolic element. The principal concern for design, then, is not how to map symbolic representations onto physical counterparts, but how the relationship between the two can be managed—how physical interaction models can "hold on" to the symbolic. The embodied interaction approach, then, argues that the design and analysis of systems based on tangible interaction needs to encompass more than simply their "tangible" characteristics, and to understand how they are caught up in larger systems of meaning that connect the physical to the symbolic rather than separating them into two disconnected domains.

Radically Embodied Cognition

Throughout this book, I have embraced a nonrepresentationalist stance toward interaction and cognition. Although this approach is unconventional, it is by no means entirely novel. Related approaches have been adopted, in different arenas, by authors such as Agre (1997), Chalmers (1999), Smith (1996), Stein (1999), and others. Andy Clark has termed this the "Thesis of Radically Embodied Cognition":

> Structured, symbolic, representational, and computational views of cognition are mistaken. Embodied cognition is best studied by means of noncomputational and nonrepresentational ideas and explanatory schemes involving, e.g., the tools of Dynamical System theory. (A. Clark 1997:148)

Although I do not subscribe fully to this stance as Clark describes it (I might quibble about "cognition," and Clark has concerns other than interaction in focus), it certainly applies to some extent. However, my goal is not to obliterate or denounce representations. Instead, the goal is, first, to question the role that those representations play, and, second, to observe that, in essence, "representations are as representations do." What it takes to *be* a representation is to be *used as* a representation in the course of some activity. I want to focus on representations as they feature in systems of meaning and in systems of practice.

A representationalist stance toward cognition may be subject to a variety of critiques from a phenomenological or sociological perspective (e.g., Button et al., 1995), but there is simply no questioning the central role of representation in developing computer systems. Software is a representational medium, from the interface on the screen to the bits on the disk. What is called for, then, is a more nuanced understanding of the role that those representations play, how they are subject to a variety of interpretations and actions, and how they figure as part of a larger body of practice. The opportunity is to break the link between an inevitably representationalist stance toward software and a much more questionable representationalist stance toward action and interaction. The embodied approach to interaction, as an aspect of emerging HCI design practice, is beginning to do just this.

Closing Remarks

The purpose of this book has been threefold. First, I set out to identify and crystallize a set of issues that are at work in some major elements of current HCI research. Second, I wanted to explore where these ideas had come from, and how this background could be elaborated in such a way as to set out some basic foundations for current HCI practice. Third, I wanted to see how, in the light of these investigations, we could return to the questions of design and analysis with some new insights and a fresh perspective. In the course of all this, I have drawn (often loosely) on many different disciplines—anthropology, user interface design, ecological psychology, analytic philosophy, software engineering, ethnomethodology, and more.

One branch of ethnomethodology—conversation analysis—is particularly concerned with the organization of spoken language, such as the ways in which people negotiate entry and exit from conversations—what Conversation Analysts call "openings and closings." This book has presented more openings than closings. By drawing attention to the issues of embodied interaction, and by using them to tell a particular set of stories about HCI, CSCW, and interactive system design, I have attempted to initiate a set of conversations. What I have hoped to provide here is a starting point for conversations between technologists and social scientists, designers and users, theorists and practitioners about the roles of computation and experience that matter to each. Embodied interaction begins to build a framework that draws these together; the critical observation, though, is that each of us holds only a piece of the puzzle.

Notes

Preface

1. Some, but certainly not all. Contemporary philosophy is separated broadly into two camps, analytic philosophy (practiced largely in the English-speaking world) and continental philosophy, which includes the work of Heidegger and the later Wittgenstein. The two sides do not see eye to eye. Writing of Wittgenstein and his work on linguistic philosophy, Ernest Gellner commented, "Academic environments are generally characterized by the presence of people who claim to understand more than in fact they do. Linguistic Philosophy has produced a great revolution, generating people who claim not to understand when in fact they do. Some people achieve great virtuosity at it. Any beginner in philosophy can manage not to understand, say, Hegel, but I have heard people who were so advanced that they knew how not to understand writers of such limpid clarity as Bertrand Russell or A. J. Ayer" (Gellner 1979:83–84).

Chapter 1

1. Readers who are not programmers will probably find the symbolic form just as impenetrable than the numeric form. Basically, the instruction says "load the value of the word stored in register number 2 into the memory location whose address is stored in register number 1, and increment the value of register number 1 to point to the next memory address." The details are largely irrelevant; what matters is, first, use of symbolic mnemonics to denote particular sorts of instructions, and, second, the emergence of particular instruction idioms such as indirection through a register, auto-increment, and so forth. Programs consist entirely of sequences of instructions like these, although programmers generally work at a higher level of abstraction.

2. Well, with some exceptions. John Dvorak commented at the time, "The Macintosh uses an experimental pointing device called a 'mouse.' There is no evidence that people want to use these things" (*San Francisco Examiner,* Feb. 19, 1984).

3. Other terms include *tangible bits, ubiquitous computing,* and *augmented reality.*

4. In this and other discussions, I use the term *work* as a generic description for a variety of activities. I mean this very broadly, to encompass not just wage labor, but pretty much any set of delineable activities carried out at the computer—not just order processing and report writing, but playing games, surfing the Web, and sending e-mail to friends.

5. In fact, it was precisely this lack of a foundational basis for design and evaluation, particularly in the area of tangible interaction, that motivated much of the work described here.

Chapter 2

1. Revising this chapter, I realize the danger of using statistics like these. In the six months since I first wrote this paragraph, things have changed again—my new laptop is twice as fast, half as heavy, and cost about half as much. Doubtless, by the time you read this, things will have evolved further.

Chapter 3

1. The volume edited by Kling (1996) is an excellent introduction to those issues for interested readers.

2. The French sociologist Bruno Latour has written on the sociology of door-closers (Latour 1988), so perhaps a sociology of screwdrivers isn't such a strange idea after all.

3. Frazier's classic *The Golden Bough* (Frazier 1922) is a quintessential example.

4. Although it is not an immediately relevant topic, it would be inappropriate to pass over this discussion of Malinowski without observing that his work is also the source of another aspect of ethnographic fieldwork that is still with us today—the vexed questions of representation, the ethnographer's role in the ethnography, and so forth. In particular, following the publication of Malinowski's diary (Malinowski 1967), it became clear that, while his ethnography might be intended to capture "the member's point of view," this did not originate in a common or sympathetic feeling for their lives and culture.

5. The use of ethnographic field methods was not the only, or even the primary, distinctive characteristic of the Chicago School, which was also a primary center for the development of the Symbolic Interaction approach and a variety of distinctive analytic tools for looking at social worlds. See Barley (1993) for an overview.

6. I say "work" here because that was, at the time, the primary use of computer systems. It should also be noted that many of those who came to engage in these sorts of studies, particularly in the Participatory Design community, did so from within a very specific agenda of workplace democratization. So workplaces were very much the primary focus of these activities when they emerged.

7. In their analysis of the disciplinary rhetoric of HCI, Cooper and Bowers (1995) use Bannon's paper as emblematic of a turning point in HCI discourse.

8. To say that this work was conducted "in the domain of CSCW" is to gloss over a much more complex set of historical antecedents. Both of the examples explored here also follow in the tradition of ethnomethodological studies of work, of which more will be said shortly.

9. As you might intuit from this quotation, the relationship between ethnomethodology and conventional sociology is, at times, rather strained.

10. For an account of the background to Garfinkel's work, see Heritage (1984).

11. Brian Cantwell Smith (1994) explores the messy underpinnings of discreteness in computer systems.

Chapter 4

1. It seems rather unfair to have laid all this at Galileo's door. The idea of a purely theoretical inquiry into the workings of the universe, independent of purpose or practicality, goes back to ancient Greece.

2. In fact, Descartes was quite specific about the relationship between the two worlds; he believed that the point of connection between them was at the pineal gland.

3. Hermeneutics is the interpretation of texts. The term was originally used to refer to the interpretation of religious texts. More broadly these days, it refers to the interpretive character of this sort of philosophical position.

4. More accurately, it is not through a single scientist's understanding, but the understandings of science as a whole. Polanyi discusses science as a social phenomenon marshaling diverse resources for authority, legitimation, and so on. In this, he anticipates a number of later writers on the sociology of science, such as Latour (1986).

Chapter 5

1. As an aside, one unusual feature of this phrase is what it means by "ontology" at all. "Ontology" is a branch of metaphysics; the word can also be used to describe a particular theory about the nature and kinds of being. By extension, it is used in technical talk to refer to a structure that reflects that theory, akin to a taxonomy. The extension of a term from an area of knowledge to the products of that knowledge seems to be a common feature of technical talk; in much the same way, "methodology" is often used to refer to methods.

2. Or even to hear about it being "engineered." Technical publications carry notices of openings for "ontological engineers," as if ontology were a pursuit akin to aeronautics.

3. The idea that users will read the manual is something of a quaint anachronism these days.

4. Longer accounts are given elsewhere; see Dourish et al. (1996) or Bellotti and Dourish (1997).

5. Similarly, Heath and Luff's observations point to the way in which, more generally, gestures are problematic in media space environments because, in everyday conversation, gesture is something that happens in the shared space defined by the bodies of the conversational participants, not on the two-dimensional plane defined by the video screen.

6. Recently, some VR researchers have begun to explore uses of VR technology to create more media-spacelike hybrid spaces; see Benford et al. (1998).

Chapter 6

1. There is an extent to which, of course, the "social/technical" divide is more of a rhetorical device than a practical problem; for many of the contributors to the collection edited by Bowker et al. (1997), the divide is as much of a foil as a topic. However, it has the property of being a commonly experienced rhetorical device, and so useful in framing a discussion. It may turn out to be one of the few things that all the disciplines involved in CSCW share in common.

2. In their classic introductory text, Abelson and Sussman (1985:xv) note, "Programs must be written for people to read, and only incidentally for machines to execute."

3. Seymour Papert at MIT was a student of the educational psychologist Jean Piaget, and has been a major player in developing Piaget's ideas in the context of computation and constructivist learning. This has been an important part of the Media Lab's research program since the lab was founded.

4. One particularly interesting exploration of the use of symbolic forms and cultural interpretations is the narrative and graphical conventions employed in comics, as explored by Scott McCloud (1993).

5. Although these approaches are often put together (as here), they are quite distinct perspectives on the design process. The User-Centered approach is one that has come to dominate HCI design, arguing that the usability and usefulness of an artifact are more important than its technological accomplishment, and that the needs and abilities of users should play a central role in determining the design of an interactive system. Participatory Design also argues the importance of users as stakeholders in design, but for different reasons and in different ways. Emerging from Scandinavian approaches to Information Technology design and deployment, Participatory Design recognizes that technical systems embody models of institutional and working relationships, and questions whose ends these models serve. In turn, then, it recognizes that technological design can be a powerful element in workplace democracy, and it encourages open and participative design processes

that give workers access to and control over the conduct of their work and the place of that work in organizations (Ehn 1989; Dahlbom and Mathiassen 1993).

6. See Cypher (1993) for an overview of the technical issues in this style of system, and Nardi (1993) for an exploration of how end-user programming features as part of users' practice.

7. The history of technology is rife with examples of unexpected uses that come to dominate the uses that designers or technology adopters anticipated. See Fisher (1992) for examples from the history of the telephone, Sproull and Kiesler (1991) for examples from the introduction of e-mail, or Yates (1989) on the unimaginable ramifications of the filing cabinet.

8. Adaptive Structuration Theory is derived from Structuration Theory, developed by Anthony Giddens (1984). Structuration Theory describes the emergence and continual transformation of structures of social practice under which actions are both constrained and enabled. Adaptive Structuration Theory augments Structuration Theory by incorporating the role of technology in the emergence of social structures, and specifically addressing the differences between the designer's intentions (the "spirit" of the technology) and the way it is incorporated into practice ("appropriation").

9. Some features had appeared, in different forms, in earlier Self interfaces, including Bay-Wei Chang's work on Seity (Chang and Ungar 1993).

10. The ethnographic and initial prototype work was conducted by Jeanette Blomberg, David Levy, Cathy Marshall, Lucy Suchman, and Randy Trigg. The system described here is a second prototype John Lamping, Tom Rodden, and I developed in collaboration with the WPT group.

11. These problems are by no means unique to The Department, or to the UFS. Any categorization or formalization of work carries with it larger implications that affect the way it is used. Garfinkel (1967) uses medical coding forms to point out the inevitably contingent nature of categorization tasks; and Bowker and Star (1999) explore the social roles and consequences of classifications as infrastructures for work and communication.

Chapter 7

1. Moore's Law is named after Intel cofounder Gordon Moore, based on his observation that the number of transistors that we can fit onto a given area of silicon doubles, through technological advances, roughly every eighteen to twenty-four months. By corollary, computers of the same power get smaller and/or cheaper at the same pace. Although Moore made his observation in 1965, it has remained largely accurate a description of the pace of technical development up until now.

2. I use "personal" in the most generic sense. Others have proposed models of "ubiquitous" computing, "interpersonal" computing, "intimate" computing, and other things that I take to be aspects of personal computing.

References

Abelson, H., and G. Sussman. 1985. *Structure and Interpretation of Computer Programs*. Cambridge, Mass.: MIT Press.

Ackerman, M., and C. Halverson. 1998. Considering an organization's memory. *Proc. ACM Conf. Computer-Supported Cooperative Work CSCW'98 (Seattle)*, 39–48. New York: ACM.

Agre, P. 1997. *Computation and Human Experience*. Cambridge: Cambridge University Press.

Bannon, L. 1991. From human factors to human actors: The role of psychology and human-computer interaction studies in systems design. In J. Greenbaum and M. Kyng (eds.), *Design at Work: Cooperative Design of Computer Systems*, 25–44. Hillsdale, N.J.: Erlbaum.

Barley, S. 1993. Careers, identities and institutions: The legacy of the Chicago School of Sociology. In M. Arthur, D. Hall, and B. Lawrence (eds.), *Handbook of Career Theory*, 41–65. Cambridge University Press.

Barnard, P. 1991. Building bridges between basic theories and the artifacts of human-computer interaction. In J. Carroll (ed.), *Designing Interaction: Psychology at the Human-Computer Interface*, 103–127. Cambridge: Cambridge University Press.

Becker, H. 1952. The career of the Chicago public school teacher. *American Journal of Sociology* 57:470–477.

Becker, H., B. Geer, E. Hughes, and A. Strauss. 1961. *Boys in White: Student Culture in Medical School*. Chicago: University of Chicago Press.

Bellotti, V. 1988. Implications of current design practice for the use of HCI techniques. In D. M. Jones and R. Winder (eds.), *People and Computers IV*, 13–34. Cambridge: Cambridge University Press.

Bellotti, V., and P. Dourish. 1997. Rant and RAVE: Experimental and experiential accounts of a media space. In K. E. Finn, A. J. Sellen, and S. B. Wilbur (eds.), *Video Mediated Communication*, 245–272. Mahwah, N.J.: Erlbaum.

Bellotti, V., and I. Smith. 2000. Informing the design of an information management system with iterative fieldwork. *Proc. ACM Conf. Designing Interactive Systems DIS 2000 (New York)*, 227–237. New York: ACM.

Benford, S., C. Greenhalgh, G. Reynard, C. Brown, and B. Koleva. 1998. Understanding and constructing shared spaces with mixed reality boundaries. *ACM Transactions on Computer-Human Interaction* 5(3):185–223.

Berndtsson, J., and M. Normark. 1999. The coordinative function of flight strips: Air traffic control work revisited. *Proc. ACM Conf. Supporting Group Work GROUP'99 (Phoenix)*, 101–110. New York: ACM.

Bier, E., M. Stone, K. Pier, W. Buxton, and T. DeRose. 1993. Toolglass and magic lenses: The see-through interface. *Proc. SIGGRAPH'93 (Anaheim)*, 73–80. New York: ACM.

Bittner, E. 1967. The police on Skid-Row: A study of peace-keeping. *American Sociological Review* 32:699–715.

Blomberg, J., L. Suchman, and R. Trigg. 1997a. Back to work: Renewing old agendas for cooperative design. In M. Kyng and L. Mathiassen (eds.), *Computers and Design in Context*, 267–287. Cambridge, Mass.: MIT Press.

Blomberg, J., L. Suchman, and R. Trigg. 1997b. Reflections on a work-oriented design project. In G. Bowker, S. Star, and W. Turner (eds.), *Social Science, Technical Systems, and Cooperative Work: Beyond the Great Divide*, 189–216. Mahwah, N.J.: Erlbaum.

Bly, S., S. Harrison, and S. Irwin. 1993. Media spaces: Bringing people together in a video, audio and computing environment. *Communications of the ACM* 36(1):28–46.

Bly, S., L. Cook, T. Bickmore, E. Churchill, and J. Sullivan. 1998. The rise of personal Web pages at work. Short paper presented at ACM Conf. Human Factors in Computing Systems CHI'98 (Los Angeles).

Boas, F. 1921. Ethnology of the Kwakiutl. *Thirty-fifth Annual Report of the Bureau of Ethnology*. Washington, D.C.: U.S. Government Printing Office.

Borning, A., and M. Travers. 1991. Two approaches to casual interaction over computer and video networks. *Proc. ACM Conf. Human Factors in Computing Systems CHI'91 (New Orleans)*, 13–19. New York: ACM.

Bowers, J., G. Button, and W. Sharrock. 1995. Workflow from within and without: Technology and cooperative work on the print industry shopfloor. *Proc. European Conf. Computer-Supported Cooperative Work ECSCW'95 (Stockholm)*, 51–66. Dordrecht: Kluwer.

Bowker, G., S. Star, and W. Turner (eds.). 1997. *Social Science, Technical Systems, and Cooperative Work: Beyond the Great Divide*. Mahwah, N.J.: Erlbaum.

Bowker, G., and S. Star. 1999. *Sorting Things Out: Classification and Its Consequences*. Cambridge, Mass.: MIT Press.

Brave, S., H. Ishii, and A. Dahley. 1998. Tangible interfaces for remote collaboration and communication. *Proc. ACM Conf. Computer-Supported Cooperative Work CSCW'98 (Seattle)*, 169–178. New York: ACM.

Brooks, R. 1999. *Cambrian Intelligence: The Early History of the New AI*. Cambridge, Mass.: MIT Press.

Button, G., J. Coulter, J. Lee, and W. Sharrock. 1995. *Computers, Minds and Conduct*. Cambridge: Polity Press.

Button, G., and W. Sharrock. 1997. The production of order and the order of production. *Proc. European Conf. Computer-Supported Cooperative Work ECSCW'97 (Lancaster)*, 1–16. Dordrecht: Kluwer.

Carroll, J., and R. Campbell. 1986. Softening up hard science: Reply to Newell and Card. *Human-Computer Interaction* 2(3):227–249.

Carroll, J., and R. Campbell. 1989. Artifacts as psychological theories: The case of Human-Computer Interaction. *Behaviour and Information Technology* 8(4):247–256.

Carroll, J., and W. Kellogg. 1989. Artifact as theory-nexus: Hermeneutics meets theory-based design. *Proc. ACM Conf. Human Factors in Computing Systems CHI'89 (Austin)*, 7–14. New York: ACM.

Chalmers, M. 1999. Structuralist informatics: Challenging positivism in information systems. *Proc. Conf. UK Academy for Information Systems*, 13–22. McGraw-Hill.

Chang, B.-W., and D. Ungar. 1993. Animation: From cartoons to the user interface. *Proc. ACM Symp. User Interface Software and Technology UIST'93 (Atlanta)*, 43–55. New York: ACM.

Cherny, L. 1999. *Conversation and Community: Chat in a Virtual World*. Stanford: CSLI Publications.

Clancey, W. 1997. *Situated Cognition: On Human Knowledge and Computer Representations*. Cambridge: Cambridge University Press.

Clark, A. 1997. *Being There: Putting Brain, Body and World Together Again*. Cambridge, Mass.: MIT Press.

Clark, H. 1996. *Using Language*. Cambridge: Cambridge University Press.

Cooper, G., and J. Bowers. 1995. Representing the user: Notes on the disciplinary rhetoric of human-computer interaction. In P. Thomas (ed.), *The Social and Interactional Dimensions of Human-Computer Interfaces*, 50–66. Cambridge: Cambridge University Press.

Cooperstock, J., K. Tanikoshi, G. Beirne, T. Narine, and W. Buxton. 1995. Evolution of a reactive environment. *Proc. ACM Conf. Human Factors in Computing Systems CHI'95 (Denver)*, 170–177. New York: ACM.

Crampton-Smith, G. 1995. The hand that rocks the cradle. *I.D.*, May/June: 60–65.

Curtis, P. 1992. Mudding: Social phenomena in text-based virtual realities. *Proc. Directions and Implications of Advanced Computing DIAC'92*. Palo Alto: CPSR.

Cypher, A. (ed.). 1993. *Watch What I Do: Programming by Demonstration*. Cambridge, Mass.: MIT Press.

Dahlbom, B., and Mathiassen, L. 1993. *Computers in Context: The Philosophy and Practice of Systems Design*. Cambridge, Mass.: Blackwell.

Davis, F. 1968. Professional socialization as subjective experience: The process of doctrinal conversion amongst student nurses. In H. Becker, B. Geer, D. Reisman, and R. Weiss (eds.), *Institutions and the Person*, 35–48. Chicago: Aldine.

Dennett, D. 1987. *The Intentional Stance*. Cambridge, Mass.: MIT Press.

des Rivières, J., and B. Smith. 1984. The implementation of procedurally reflective languages. *Proc. ACM Conf. LISP and Functional Programming (Austin)*, 331–347. New York: ACM.

Dourish, P. 1993. Culture and control in a media space. *Proc. Third European Conf. Computer-Supported Cooperative Work ECSCW'93 (Milan)*, 125–137. Dordrecht: Kluwer.

Dourish, P., and V. Bellotti. 1992. Awareness and coordination in shared workspaces. *Proc. ACM Conf. Computer-Supported Cooperative Work CSCW'92 (Toronto)*, 107–114. New York: ACM.

Dourish, P., V. Bellotti, A. Adler, and A. Henderson. 1996. Your place or mine? Lessons from the long-term use of audio-video communication. *Computer-Supported Cooperative Work* 5(1):33–62.

Dourish, P., V. Bellotti, W. Mackay, and C.-Y. Ma. 1993. Information and context: Lessons from a study of two shared information systems. *Proc. ACM Conf. Organizational Computing Systems COOCS'93 (Milpitas, Calif.)*, 42–51. New York: ACM.

Dourish, P., and S. Bly. 1992. Portholes: Supporting awareness in a distributed work group. *Proc. ACM Conf. Human Factors in Computing Systems CHI'92 (Monterey, Calif.)*, 541–548. New York: ACM.

Dourish, P., and G. Button. 1998. On technomethodology: Foundational relationships between ethnomethodology and system design. *Human-Computer Interaction* 13(4):395–432.

Dourish, P., J. Holmes, A. MacLean, P. Marqvardsen, and A. Zbyslaw. 1996. Freeflow: Mediating between representation and action in workflow systems. *Proc. ACM Conf. Computer-Supported Cooperative Work CSCW'96 (Boston)*, 190–198. New York: ACM.

Dourish, P., J. Lamping, and T. Rodden. 1999. Building bridges: Customisation and mutual intelligibility in shared category management. *Proc. ACM Conf. Supporting Group Work GROUP'99 (Phoenix)*, 11–20. New York: ACM.

Dreyfus, H. 1991. *Being-in-the-World: A Commentary on Heidegger's Being and Time, Division 1*. Cambridge, Mass.: MIT Press.

Dreyfus, H. 1992. *What Computers Still Can't Do: A Critique of Artificial Reason*. Cambridge, Mass.: MIT Press.

Dreyfus, H. 1996. The current relevance of Merleau-Ponty's phenomenology of embodiment. *Electronic Journal of Analytic Philosophy* 4.

Durkheim, E. 1938. *The Rules of Sociological Method*. New York: The Free Press.

Ehn, P. 1989. *Work-Oriented Design of Computer Artifacts*. Hillsdale, N.J.: Erlbaum.

Ellis, C., K. Keddara, and G. Rozenberg. (1995). Dynamic change within workflow systems. *Proc. ACM Conf. Organizational Computing Systems COOCS'95 (Milpitas, Calif.)*, 10–21. New York: ACM.

Erickson, T. 1996. The world wide web as social hypertext. *Communications of the ACM*, January.

Erickson, T. 1999. Rhyme and punishment: The creation and enforcement of conventions in an in-line participatory limerick genre. *Proc. Thirty-Second Hawaii International Conference on Systems Science*. Los Alamitos: IEEE Press.

Fisher, C. 1992. *America Calling: A Social History of the Telephone to 1940*. Berkeley: University of California Press.

Fishkin, K., T. Moran, and B. Harrison. 1998. Embodied user interfaces: Towards invisible user interfaces. *Proc. Conf. Engineering the Human-Computer Interface EHCI'98 (Heraklion, Crete)*, 1–18. Berlin: Springer.

Fitzpatrick, G. 1998. *The Locales Framework: Understanding and Designing for Cooperative Work*. Unpublished Ph.D. dissertation, University of Queensland.

Fitzpatrick, G., W. Tolone, and S. Kaplan. 1995. Work, locales and distributed social wOrlds. *Proc. European Conf. Computer-Supported Cooperative Work ECSCW'95 (Stockholm)*, 1–16. Dordrecht: Kluwer.

Frazier, J. 1922. *The Golden Bough*. London: MacMillan.

Frecon, E., and M. Stenius. 1998. DIVE: A scaleable network architecture for distributed virtual environments. *Distributed Systems Engineering Journal* 5:91–100.

Gajewska, H., M. Manasse, and D. Redell. 1995. Argohalls: Adding support for group awareness to the argo telecollaboration system. *Proc. ACM Conf. User Interface Software and Technology UIST'95 (Atlanta)*, 157–158. New York: ACM.

Garfinkel, H. 1967. *Studies in Ethnomethodology*. Cambridge: Polity Press.

Garfinkel, H., M. Lynch, and E. Livingston. 1981. The work of a discovering science construed with materials from the optically discovered pulsar. *Philosophy of the Social Sciences* 11:131–158.

Gaver, W. 1991. Technology Affordances. *Proc. ACM Conf. Human Factors in Computing Systems CHI'91 (New Orleans)*, 79–84. New York: ACM.

Gaver, W. 1992. The affordances of media spaces for collaboration. *Proc. ACM Conf. Computer-Supported Cooperative Work CSCW'92 (Toronto)*, 17–24. New York: ACM.

Gaver, W., G. Smets, and K. Overbeeke. 1995. A virtual window on media space. *Proc. ACM Conf. Human Factors in Computing Systems CHI'95 (Denver)*, 257–264. New York: ACM.

Geertz, C. 1973. *The Interpretation of Cultures*. New York: Basic Books.

Gellner, E. 1979. *Words and Things* (2d ed.). London: Routledge, Kegan and Paul.

Gershenfeld, N. 1999. *When Things Start to Think*. New York: Henry Holt.

Gerson, E., and S. Star. 1986. Analyzing due process in the workplace. *ACM Trans. Office Information Systems* 4(3):257–270.

Gibson, J. 1979. *The Ecological Approach to Visual Perception*. New York: Houghton-Mifflin.

Giddens, A. 1984. *The Constitution of Society: Outline of the Theory of Structuration*. Berkeley: University of California Press.

Goffman, E. 1959. *The Presentation of Self in Everyday Life*. Garden City, N.Y.: Doubleday.

Gold, R. 1964. In the basement: The apartment building janitor. In P. Berger (ed.), *The Human Shape of Work*, 1–50. South Bend, Ind.: Gateway.

Gorbet, M., M. Orth, and H. Ishii. 1998. Triangles: Tangible interface for manipulation and exploration of digital information topography. *Proc. ACM Conf. Human Factors in Computing Systems CHI'98 (Los Angeles)*, 49–56. New York: ACM.

Greenberg, S. 1996. Peepholes: Low cost awareness of one's community. Short paper presented at ACM Conf. Human Factors in Computing Systems CHI'96 (Vancouver).

Greenhalgh, C., and S. Benford. 1995. MASSIVE: A virtual reality system for tele-conferencing. *ACM Trans. Computer-Human Interaction* 2(3):239–261.

Grudin, J. 1990. The computer reaches out: The historical continuity of interface design. *Proc. ACM Conf. Human Factors in Computing Systems CHI'90 (Seattle)*, 261–268. New York: ACM.

Gutwin, C., and S. Greenberg. 1998. The effects of awareness support on groupware usability. *Proc. ACM Conf. Human Factors in Computing Systems CHI'98 (Los Angeles)*, 511–518. New York: ACM.

Haraway, D. 1991. A cyborg manifesto: Science, technology and socialist-feminism in the late twentieth century. In *Simians, Cyborgs and Women: The Reinvention of Nature*, 149–181. London: Free Association Books.

Harris, J., and A. Henderson. 1999. A better mythology for system design. *Proc. ACM Conf. Human Factors in Computing Systems CHI'99 (Pittsburgh)*, 88–95. New York: ACM.

Harrison, B., K. Fishkin, A. Gujar, C. Mochon, and R. Want. 1998. Squeeze me, hold me, tilt me! An exploration of manipulative user interfaces. *Proc. ACM Conf. Human Factors in Computing Systems CHI'98 (Los Angeles)*, 17–24. New York: ACM.

Harrison, S., and P. Dourish. 1996. Re-place-ing space: The roles of space and place in collaborative systems. *Proc. ACM Conf. Computer-Supported Cooperative Work CSCW'96 (Boston)*, 67–76. New York: ACM.

Heath, C., and P. Luff. 1991. Media space and communicative asymmetries: Preliminary observations of video-mediated interaction. *Human-Computer Interaction* 7(3):315–346.

Heath, C., and P. Luff. 1992 Collaboration and control: Crisis management and multimedia technology in London underground line control rooms. *Computer-Supported Cooperative Work* 1(1–2):69–94.

Hebenstein, R. 1954. *The Career of the Funeral Director*. Unpublished Ph.D. dissertation, University of Chicago.

Heidegger, M. 1927. *Being and Time*. English translation 1962. New York: Harper & Row.

Henderson, K. 1998. *On-Line and On Paper: Visual Representations, Visual Culture, and Computer Graphics in Design Engineering*. Cambridge, Mass.: MIT Press.

Heritage, J. 1984. *Garfinkel and Ethnomethodology*. Cambridge: Polity Press.

Hill, W., J. Hollan, D. Wroblewski, and T. McCandless. 1992. Edit wear and read wear. *Proc. ACM Conf. Human Factors in Computing Systems CHI'92 (Monterey, Calif.)*, 3–9. New York: ACM.

Hoare, C. 1985. *Communicating Sequential Processes*. Englewood Cliffs, N.J.: Prentice Hall.

Hughes, J., J. O'Brien, M. Rouncefield, I. Sommerville, and T. Rodden. 1995. Presenting ethnography in the requirements process. *Proc. IEEE Conference on Requirements Engineering RE'95 (York, England)*, 27–34. New York: IEEE Press.

Hughes, J., D. Randall, and D. Shapiro. 1992. Faltering from ethnography to designs. *Proc. ACM Conf. on Computer-Supported Cooperative Work CSCW'92 (Toronto)*, 115–122. New York: ACM.

Husserl, E. 1900. *Logische Untersuchungen*. Halle: Niemeyer. (Tr. J. Finlay. 1970. *Logical Investigations*. London: Routledge and Kegan Paul.)

Husserl, E. 1913. *Ideen zu euner reunin Phänomenologie und phänomenologischen Philosophie*. The Hague: Martinus Nijhoff. (Tr. F. Kersten. 1981. *Ideas: General Introduction to Pure Pheneomenology*. The Hague: Martinus Nijhoff.)

Husserl, E. 1936. *Die Krisis der europäischen Wissenschaften und die transzendentale Phänomenologie: Eine Einleitung in de phänomenologische Philosophie*. The Hague: Martinus Nijhoff. (Tr. D. Carr. 1970. *The Crisis of European Sciences and Transcendental Phenomenology*. Evanston, Ill.: Northwestern University Press.)

Ihde, D. 1991. *Instrumental Realism*. Bloomington: Indiana University Press.

Johnson, H. 1889. *Hints to Travellers*.

Karatani, K. 1995. *Architecture as Metaphor: Language, Number, Money*. Cambridge, Mass.: MIT Press.

Kay, A. 1993. The early history of Smalltalk. *Proc. Second ACM SIGPLAN Conf. History of Programming Languages HOPL-II*, 69–95. New York: ACM.

Kiczales, G., J. des Rivières, and D. Bobrow. 1991. *The Art of the Metaobject Protocol*. Cambridge, Mass.: MIT Press.

Kiesler, S., J. Siegel, and T. McGuire. 1984. Social psychological aspects of computer-mediated communication. *American Psychologist* 39(10):1123–1134.

Kling, R. (ed.). 1996. *Computerization and Controversy: Value Conflicts and Social Choices* (2d ed.). San Diego: Academic Press.

Lakoff, G., and M. Johnson. 1980. *Metaphors We Live By*. Chicago: University of Chicago Press.

Latour, B. 1986. *Science in Action: How to Follow Scientists and Engineers through Society.* Milton Keynes: Open University Press.

Latour, B. (as J. Johnson) 1988. Mixing humans and nonhumans together: The sociology of a door-closer. *Social Problems* 35:298–310.

Lave, J. 1988. *Cognition in Practice.* Cambridge: Cambridge University Press.

Lave, J., and E. Wenger. 1991. *Situated Learning: Legitimate Peripheral Participation.* Cambridge: Cambridge University Press.

Lee, A., A. Girgensohn, and K. Schlueter. 1997. NYNEX portholes: Initial user reactions and redesign implications. *Proc. ACM Conf. Supporting Group Work GROUP'97 (Phoenix)*, 385–394. New York: ACM.

Livingston, E. 1982. *An Ethnomethodological Investigation of the Foundations of Mathematics.* Unpublished Ph.D. dissertation, University of California at Los Angeles.

Long, J., and J. Dowell. 1989. Conceptions of the discipline of HCI: Craft, applied science and engineering. *Proc. HCI'89 (People and Computers V)*, 9–32, Cambridge: Cambridge University Press.

Long, S., D. Aust, G. Abowd, and C. Atkeson. 1996. Cyberguide: Prototyping context-aware mobile applications. Short paper presented at ACM Conf. Human Factors in Computing Systems CHI'96 (Vancouver).

Lynch, M. 1982. Technical work and critical inquiry: Investigations in a scientific laboratory. *Social Studies of Science* 12:499–534.

Lynch, M., E. Livingston, and H. Garfinkel. 1983. Temporal order in laboratory life. In K. Knorr-Cetina and M. Mulkay (eds.), *Science Observed: Perspectives on the Social Study of Science,* 205–238. London: Sage.

MacAnn, C. 1993. *Four Phenomenological Philosophers.* London: Routledge.

Mackay, W. 1990. *Users and Customizable Software: A Co-Adaptive Phenomenon.* Unpublished Ph.D. dissertation, Sloan School of Management, Massachusetts Institute of Technology.

Mackay, W., and A.-L. Fayard. 1999. Is paper safer? Augmenting paper flight strips to support air traffic control. *ACM Trans. Computer-Human Interaction* 6(4):311–340.

MacLean, A., K. Carter, L. Lövstrand, and T. Moran. 1990. User-tailorable systems: Pressing the issues with buttons. *Proc. ACM Conf. Human Factors in Computing Systems CHI'90 (Seattle)*, 175–182. New York: ACM.

Malinowski, B. 1922. *Argonauts of the Western Pacific.* London: Routledge.

Malinowski, B. 1929. *The Sexual Life of Savages in North-Western Melanesia.* London: Routledge and Kegan Paul.

Malinowski, B. 1935. *Coral Gardens and Their Magic.* New York: American Book Company.

Malinowski, B. 1967. *A Diary in the Strict Sense of the Term.* Tr. N. Guterman. London: Routledge and Kegan Paul.

Malone, T., K.-Y. Lai, and C. Fry. 1995. Experiments with Oval: A radically tailorable tool for cooperative work. *ACM Transactions on Information Systems* 13(2):177–205.

Mansfield, T., S. Kaplan, T. Phelps, G. Fitzpatrick, M. Fitzpatrick, and R. Taylor. 1997. Evolving Orbit: A progress report on building locales. *Proc. ACM Conf. Supporting Group Work GROUP'97 (Phoenix)*, 241–250. ACM: New York.

McCloud, S. 1993. *Understanding Comics*. Northampton, Mass.: Kitchen Sink Press.

Merleau-Ponty, M. 1945. *The Phenomenology of Perception*. English translation, 1962. London: Routledge.

Milner, R. 1995. *Communication and Concurrency*. Englewood Cliffs, N.J.: Prentice Hall.

Milner, R. 2000. *Communicating and Formal Systems: The Pi-Calculus*. Cambridge: Cambridge University Press.

Minsky, M. 1988. *The Society of Mind*. New York: Simon & Schuster.

Moran, T., and R. Anderson. 1990. The workaday world as a paradigm for CSCW. *Proc. ACM Conf. Computer-Supported Cooperative Work CSCW'90 (Los Angeles)*, 381–393. New York: ACM.

Nardi, B. 1993. *A Small Matter of Programming: Perspectives on End-User Computing*. Cambridge, Mass.: MIT Press.

Narine, T., A. Leganchuk, M. Mantei, and W. Buxton. 1997. Collaboration awareness and its use to consolidate a disperse group. *Proceedings of INTERACT'97 (Sydney, Australia)*, 397–404. Dordrecht: Kluwer.

Negroponte, N. 1995. *Being Digital*. New York: Vintage Books.

Neilsen, J. 1989. Usability engineering at a discount. In G. Salvendy and M. J. Smith (eds.), *Designing and Using Human-Computer Interfaces and Knowledge-Based Systems*, 394–401. Amsterdam: Elsevier.

Newell, A., and S. Card. 1985. The prospects for psychological science in human-computer interaction. *Human-Computer Interaction* 1(3):209–242.

Newman, W., and P. Wellner. 1992. A desk supporting computer-based interaction with paper documents. *Proc. ACM Conf. Human Factors in Computing Systems CHI'92 (Monterey, Calif.)*, 587–592. New York: ACM.

Norman, D. 1988. *The Psychology of Everyday Things*. New York: Basic Books.

Norman, D. 1993. *Things That Make Us Smart*. Reading, Mass.: Addison-Wesley.

Norman, D. 1998. *The Invisible Computer*. Cambridge, Mass.: MIT Press.

Norman, D., and S. Draper. 1986. *User Centered System Design*. Hillsdale, N.J.: Erlbaum.

Nygren, E., M. Johnson, and P. Henriksson. 1992. Reading the medical record I. Analysis of physicians' ways of reading the medical record. *Computer Methods and Programs in Biomedicine* 39:1–12.

Orlikowski, W. 1992. Learning from Notes: Organizational issues in groupware implementation. *Proc. ACM Conf. Computer-Supported Cooperative Work CSCW'92 (Toronto)*, 362–369. New York: ACM.

Orlikowski, W. 1995. Evolving with Notes: Organizational change around groupware technology. Working Paper 186, MIT Center for Coordination Science.

Parsons, T. 1937. *The Structure of Social Action*. New York: McGraw-Hill.

Plowman, L., Y. Rogers, and M. Ramage. 1995. What are workplace studies for? *Proc. Fourth European Conf. Computer-Supported Cooperative Work ECSCW'95 (Stockholm)*, 309–324. Dordrecht: Kluwer.

Polanyi, M. 1966. *The Tacit Dimension*. London: Routledge and Kegan Paul.

Poole, M., and G. de Sanctis. 1990. Understanding the use of group decision support systems: The theory of adaptive structuration. In J. Fulk (ed.), *Organizations and Communications Technology*, 173–193. Newbury Park, Calif.: Sage.

Rheingold, H. 1992. *Virtual Reality*. New York: Touchstone.

Robertson, T. 1997. Cooperative work and lived cognition: A taxonomy of embodied actions. *Proc. European Conf. Computer-Supported Cooperative Work ECSCW'97 (Lancaster)*, 205–220. Dordrecht: Kluwer.

Rognin, L., P. Salembier, and M. Zouinar. 1998. Cooperation, interactions and social-technical reliability: The case of air-traffic control, comparing French and Irish settings. *Proc. European Conf. Cognitive Ergonomics ECCE 9 (Limerick)*. Amsterdam: EACE.

Roseman, M., and S. Greenberg. 1996. Building real-time groupware with GroupKit, a groupware toolkit. *ACM Trans. Computer-Human Interaction* 3(1):66–106.

Rowley, D. E., and D. G. Rhodes. 1992. The cognitive jog-through: A fast-paced user interface evaluation procedure. *Proc. ACM Conf. Human Factors in Computing Systems CHI'92 (Monterey, Calif.)*, 389–395. New York: ACM.

Sacks, H. 1992. *Lectures on Conversation*. Oxford: Blackwell.

Schutz, A. 1932. *The Phenomenology of the Social World*. Evanston, Ill.: Northwestern University Press.

Sellen, A., and R. Harper. 1997. Paper as an analytic resource for the design of new technologies. *Proc. ACM Conf. Human Factors in Computing Systems CHI'97 (Atlanta)*, 319–326. New York: ACM.

Smith, B. 1984. Reflection and Semantics in LISP. *Proc. ACM Conf. Principles of Programming Languages POPL'84 (Salt Lake City)*, 23–35. New York: ACM.

Smith, B. 1994. Coming apart at the seams: The role of computation in a successor metaphysics. Presented at Biology, Computers and Society: At the Intersection of the "Real" and the "Virtual"—Cultural Perspectives on Coding Life and Vitalizing Code (Stanford University, Stanford, Calif.).

Smith, B. 1996. *On the Origin of Objects*. Cambridge, Mass.: MIT Press.

Smith, D., and R. Alexander. 1988. *Fumbling the Future: How Xerox Invented, Then Ignored, the First Personal Computer.* New York: Morrow.

Smith, J., T. White, C. Dodge, J. Paradiso, and N. Gershenfeld. 1998. Electric field sensing for graphical interfaces. *IEEE Computer Graphics and Applications* 18(3):54–60.

Smith, R. 1987. The alternate reality kit: An example of the tension between literalism and magic. *Proc. CHI+GI'87,* 61–67. New York: ACM.

Smith, R., J. Maloney, and D. Ungar. 1995. The Self-4.0 user interface: manifesting a system-wide vision of concreteness, uniformity and flexibility. *Proc. ACM Conf. Object-Oriented Programming Languages, Systems and Applications OOPSLA'95 (Austin),* 49–60. New York: ACM.

Sproull, L., and S. Kiesler. 1991. *Connections: New Ways of Working in the Networked Organization.* Cambridge, Mass.: MIT Press.

Stein, L. 1998. What we've swept under the rug: Radically rethinking CS101. *Computer Science Education* 8(2):119–129.

Stein, L. 1999. Challenging the computational metaphor: Implications for how we think. *Cybernetics and Systems* 39(6):473–507.

Stone, A. R. 1991. Will the real body please stand up? Boundary stories about virtual cultures. In M. Benedikt (ed.), *Cyberspace: First Steps,* 609–621. Cambridge, Mass.: MIT Press.

Strauss, A. 1993. *Continual Permutations of Action.* Hawthorne, N.Y.: Aldine de Gruyter.

Strong, R., and W. Gaver. 1996. Feather, scent and shaker: Supporting simple intimacy. *Proc. ACM Conf. Computer-Supported Cooperative Work CSCW'96 (Cambridge, Mass.),* 444–445. New York: ACM.

Stults, R. 1989. The experimental use of video to support design activity. Xerox PARC Technical Report SSL-89-19. Palo Alto, Calif.: Xerox Corp.

Suchman, L. 1987. *Plans and Situated Actions: The Problem of Human-Machine Communication.* Cambridge: Cambridge University Press.

Suchman, L. 1994. Do categories have politics? The language/action perspective reconsidered. *Computer-Supported Cooperative Work* 2(3):177–190.

Sutherland, I. 1963. Sketchpad: A man-machine graphical communication system. Technical Report 296, MIT Lincoln Laboratory.

Thacker, C., E. McCreight, B. Lampson, R. Sproull, and D. Boggs. 1982. Alto: A personal computer. In D. Sieworek, C. Bell, and A. Newell (eds.), *Computer Structures: Principles and Examples,* 549–580. McGraw-Hill.

Trigg, R., J. Blomberg, and L. Suchman. 1999. Moving document collections online: The evolution of a shared repository. *Proc. European Conf. Computer-Supported Cooperative Work ECSCW'99 (Copenhagen),* 331–350. Dordrecht: Kluwer.

Trigg, R., and S. Bødker. 1994. From implementation to design: Tailoring and the emergence of systematization in CSCW. *Proc. ACM Conf. Computer-Supported Cooperative Work (Chapel Hill)*, 45–54. New York: ACM.

Ullmer, B., and H. Ishii. 1997. The metaDESK: Models and prototypes for tangible user interfaces. *Proc. ACM Symp. User Interface Software and Technology UIST'97 (Banff, Alta.)*, 223–232. New York: ACM.

Underkoffler, J., and H. Ishii. 1998. Illuminating light: An optical design tool with a luminous-tangible interface. *Proc. ACM Conf. Human Factors in Computing Systems CHI'98 (Los Angeles)*, 542–549. New York: ACM.

Underkoffler, J., and H. Ishii. 1999. Urp: A luminous-tangible workbench for urban planning and design. *Proc. ACM Conf. Human Factors in Computing Systems CHI'99 (Pittsburgh)*, 386–393. New York: ACM.

Ungar, D., and R. Smith. 1987. Self: The power of simplicity. *Proc. ACM Conf. Object-Oriented Programming Languages, Systems and Applications OOPSLA'87 (Orlando)*, 227–241. New York: ACM.

Wager, L. 1959. *Career Patterns and Role Problems of Airline Pilots*. Unpublished Ph.D. dissertation, University of Chicago.

Want, R., K. Fishkin, A. Gujar, and B. Harrison. 1999. Briding physical and virtual worlds with electronic tags. *Proc. ACM Conf. Human Factors in Computing Systems CHI'99 (Pittsburgh)*, 370–377. New York: ACM.

Want, R., A. Hopper, V. Falcao, and J. Gibbons. 1992. The active badge location system. *ACM Trans. Information Systems* 10(1):91–102.

Wegner, P. 1997. Why interaction is more powerful than algorithms. *Communications of the ACM* 40(5):80–91.

Weiser, M. 1991. The computer for the twenty-first century. *Scientific American* 265(3):94–104.

Weiser, M. 1993. Some computer science issues in ubiquitous computing. *Communications of the ACM* 36(7):75–83.

Weiser, M. 1994. Creating the invisible interface. Keynote presentation at ACM Symp. User Interface Software and Technology UIST'94 (Marina Del Rey, Calif.).

Weiser, M., and J. Brown. 1996. Designing calm technology. *Power-grid Journal* 1(1).

Wellner, P. 1991. The DigitalDesk calculator: Tangible manipulation on a desk top display. *Proc. ACM Symp. User Interface Software and Technology UIST'91 (Hilton Head, S.C.)*, 27–33. New York: ACM.

Wellner, P. 1993. Interacting with paper on the digital desk. *Comm. ACM* 36(7):87–96.

Wenger, E. 1998. *Communities of Practice: Learning, Meaning and Identity*. Cambridge: Cambridge University Press.

Whalen, J. 1995. A technology of order production: Computer-aided dispatch in public safety communication. In P. ten Have and G. Psathas (eds.), *Situated Order: Studies in the Social Organization of Talk and Embodied Activities*, 187–230. Washington, D.C.: University Press of America.

Winograd, T. 1994. Categories, disciplines and social coordination. *Computer-Supported Cooperative Work* 2(3):191–197.

Winograd, T. 1996. *Bringing Design to Software*. New York: ACM Press.

Winograd, T., and F. Flores. 1986. *Understanding Computers and Cognition*. Norwood, N.J.: Ablex.

Wisneski, C., H. Ishii, A. Dahley, M. Gorbet, S. Brave, B. Ullmer, and P. Yarin. 1998. Ambient displays: Turning architectural space in an interface between people and digital information. *Proc. Intl. Workshop on Cooperative Buildings CoBuild'98 (Darmstadt)*, 23–32. Berlin: Springer.

Wittgenstein, L. 1921. *Tractatus Logico-Philosophicus*. London: Routledge.

Wittgenstein, L. 1953. *Philosophical Investigations*. Oxford: Blackwell.

Yates, J. 1989. *Control through Communication: The Rise of System in American Management*. Baltimore: Johns Hopkins University Press.

Index